UNLIMITED

This edition, 2023

ISBN: 978-0-6459890-0-7

UNLIMITED

THE ART OF BEING LIMITLESS

JASON DUNN

TABLE OF CONTENTS

Acclimating for "La Ultra - The High" at 15,000 ft above sea level in the Himalayas on Khardung La, Ladakh, India in 2014.

INTRODUCTION

"It's not the mountain we conquer, but ourselves"

— Sir Edmund Hillary

You have the power to transform your life. And when I say transform, I mean a real, profound change. It doesn't matter how old you are or what stage of life you're in right now – you can change it. Your best life is still ahead of you, but only if you make the choice to pursue it. Yes, you. You must decide to begin the journey toward your best life today. You are unlimited. Even though you may not realise or believe it yet. So, let's briefly discuss the problem and then dedicate the rest of our time to exploring solutions and creating change.

Sadly, a significant portion of humanity will never come to realise or accept their unlimited potential. Consequently, their most extraordinary capabilities will go untapped for eternity. Life often has a way of limiting our belief in what we can achieve, a belief often ingrained during early childhood. This belief then gains strength from a society entrenched in and constrained by societal and cultural norms that promote the idea of limitations. We end up thinking that we all have a designated place in life and that our existence should revolve around safety and comfort.

Many of us are conditioned to believe that failure is a sign of weakness, and as a result, it's safer to avoid risks and challenges altogether. Whatever the underlying reasons, these beliefs often lead people to choose the path of least resistance, avoiding hard work, effort, and sacrifice. Their reluctance to make short-term sacrifices or delay gratification in favour of future rewards demonstrates difficulty in making tough discretionary choices. You may be one of them, I know I was.

Most people are too weak to prioritise discipline or sacrifice, opting for immediate comfort or validation. This is not a judgment but rather an observation made over many decades – it's the state of the society and world we live in. I firmly believe that everyone has the right to choose their own path in pursuit of happiness. However, long ago, I recognised that my own path needed to change, and I will always be deeply grateful that it did. My reckoning with my own legacy occurred when I imagined how I would feel about my life a decade, two decades, and three decades ahead, based on what I had and hadn't done up until that point in my life. If someone had asked me two years before accomplishing my first impossible goal if I could have achieved such a feat, my response would have been, "You're joking, right? Never."

However, gradually, one by one, I unearthed 8 daily practices that empowered me to transcend limitations and realise my impossible aspirations and dreams. "Impossible" is primarily a

mental state that can be dismantled by making a single decision: one choice to forgo the path of least resistance. That one
decision can transform the impossible into the possible. And as
you persist in making the right choices, one decision at a time,
you will ultimately cultivate an unlimited state of mind.

Then, you achieve your impossible – whatever that may be. This
is the magical, life-altering transformation that I've been lucky to
witness in many individuals. Ordinary people, achieve extraordinary feats that they once thought impossible. By sharing my
own journey, my challenges, my setbacks, the lessons learned
from overcoming extreme adversity, and the 8 daily practices
I've employed to achieve more than I ever envisioned, my aim
is to inspire and empower you to pursue and accomplish your
own impossible.

Sometimes in life, we undertake seemingly crazy endeavours
that neither we nor those around us thought possible. People
often question why we do what we do because it doesn't seem
rational or even comprehensible. The responses from those who
have ventured into the realm of the extraordinary tend to be
similar: "Because I can" or "I wanted to see what I was capable
of." Regardless of the answer, it doesn't seem to change the
perplexity, often accompanied by furrowed brows, leading to
the typical response, "You are crazy!" Can you blame someone,
though, for their disbelief? Once upon a time, that would have
been my response, without a doubt. However, there is only one
response to such a question that has ever made genuine sense
to me. It encapsulates why those of us who are a little crazy drive
ourselves to achieve the impossible. John Collins, the founder
of the most iconic endurance race on the planet, the Hawaii
Ironman Triathlon World Championships, famously said, "The

difference between those who get, and those who don't, is those who get it, have, and those who don't, have not."

One of the most inspiring sights to witness is the growth and transformation that occurs when a person achieves something truly extraordinary. Now, when I use the term "extraordinary," I mean it within the context of their own life — something they once believed to be impossible. It doesn't have to entail solo climbing Mount Everest without oxygen support to be considered extraordinary. For example, it could be obtaining a higher education degree, mastering a musical instrument like the piano, completing your first 10k fun run, or even finishing your first Ironman triathlon. When someone achieves their first significant goal, a special transformation occurs. You can see it, feel it, and carry it with you for the rest of your life if you choose to do so. It becomes one of, if not the most defining moment of your life. It's a supercharged high that propels you onto an extraordinary journey of growth and self-discovery.

I'd like to take you on a personal journey of discovery, failure, tragedy, transformation, and the achievement of goals beyond the wildest dreams. As I recount my own deeply personal journey of transformation, I will introduce 8 daily practices that have greatly benefited me. I hope you will be inspired to consider incorporating them into your own life.

There was a time when I opted for the easier path and often boasted about my untapped potential, using "I could have" as a temporary ego boost. However, self-reflection made me realise I had grown to dislike this aspect of myself. It was time to become the person I had always aspired to be. Now, I am on the brink of turning sixty, a milestone I couldn't have fathomed when I was 35. Life has proven to be vastly different from my earlier expectations. During my journey of transformation, my primary focus has been on becoming the best version of myself. I've undergone profound changes and accumulated invaluable lessons about myself, others, the world, courage, humility, discipline, failure, vulnerability, and the relentless pursuit of seemingly impossible dreams. I've learned exponentially more in the past 25 years than I did in my first 34, reinforcing the idea that there are endless lessons to be learned, regardless of age, as long as you remain open-minded.

My pursuits have never been about extending my longevity because no matter what you do, you will grow old. Aging is an inevitable part of life - guaranteed! However, I am determined to live each day with strength and happiness for as long as I'm blessed with life.

My own transformation began with regular introspection, envisioning both the past and the future I desired. My inspiration has always revolved around helping others and reshaping my legacy. Sometimes, this involves imagining a short-term outcome, like envisioning the future you want later in the same day when you're faced with a challenging decision amidst excruciating pain. That inner voice may tempt you to quit, promising instant relief. "Just give up. You will instantly feel better." You must find the courage to persist because quitting, once you've grown comfortable with it, will hurt more than the pain urging you to give up. Making the right decision in the moment may also require subsequent correct choices in quick succession. Most importantly, empowering yourself to change your legacy involves projecting yourself far into the future and reflecting on your journey, a concept we'll explore shortly.

I've been fortunate to draw inspiration from many people, but I also feel privileged to have been a source of inspiration to others. Finding inspiration is often easier than people realise; you just need to choose to see the good in the world around you. For instance, this story has been 60 years in the making, and it took someone truly special entering my life to inspire me to share it. Inspiration is all around us if we make the choice to look for it.

My life, like everyone else's, is flawed, and I embrace those flaws. They are what make us beautifully human and provide opportunities for growth and self-improvement. This principle applies not only to ourselves but also to those we interact with. I've been working on one of my major flaws, which is common, especially in sales-related roles. For many years, I believed that being interesting and having something influential to say was key, but I've come to realise it's quite the opposite. When this flaw surfaces, I remind myself to "be interested, not interesting" and to remember that "we learn nothing when we are talking, only when we are listening." Therefore, it's an insatiable desire to learn and genuine curiosity that should drive our connections with others.

Throughout many decades, I've had the privilege of facilitating hundreds of conference and training sessions while also participating in many more. My professional journey has brought me into contact with exceptional athletes and individuals who have achieved remarkable feats, often starting from very humble beginnings.

Between the ages of twenty-five and thirty-five, I vividly remember attending conferences where I listened to speakers who left me in awe. I would momentarily imagine achieving their seemingly impossible accomplishments, and I'd eagerly discuss my thoughts with others in the audience. However, deep down, I knew that, like me, almost everyone in that audience would return to their regular lives and comfort zones, and very little would truly change. It rarely ever does.

A few years ago, a friend of mine, who works with individuals and teams to help them live their best lives, shared a story about a conference attended by the top 100 people in a particular industry. The number one person in that group was asked to reveal the secrets of her success during her presentation. Afterwards, someone asked her why she was so willing to share her winning strategies. Her response was revealing; she believed that at least 50% of the audience hadn't really been listening, and among the rest, only 3 to 4% possessed the inner strength and determination to change their behaviour significantly. She concluded by saying that she was confident she would still be number one by the end of the year. And she was.

A significant turning point in my life, one that propelled me into the 3 or 4% category of individuals with the strength of character to enact substantial change, stems from a story I heard at a Financial Planning Association national conference held in Cairns. This particular narrative remained in my mind for years, though I initially failed to grasp its full significance and, as a result, did not tap into its profound potential. The story was a deeply moving account of human experiences encompassing themes of greed, privilege, tragedy, and, ultimately, humility and a new perspective on life. When I first heard it, I was overwhelmed with emotions – I felt deeply moved, inspired, ashamed, fortunate, and a whirlwind of other sentiments. The closing words of this extraordinary individual, who had allowed themselves to become unconditionally vulnerable while sharing their life story, were:

"To be truly successful, you must first be prepared to do what you don't want to do, when you don't want to do it."

Many years later, I started living by this profoundly powerful mantra. I've applied these exact words countless times when my mind resists doing something because it's challenging or uncomfortable, urging me to choose the easier option. I push back by repeating these words, instantly recognising that the very thing I don't want to do, at that moment when I least desire to do it, is the action that will lead to true success.

For example, picture a scenario at 5 am in the middle of winter when I've just woken up, contemplating the day ahead, which may involve a run, a bike ride, or a swim. On this particular morning, it's a long swim, which means entering a dark, cold swimming pool first thing in the morning and swimming for an hour in the cool, chlorinated water. The thought of this is paralysing while I'm still comfortably nestled in my warm bed, tempting me to stay put until it's too late and the window of opportunity to complete the task before work has closed.

Consequently, overcoming this inertia demands technique and discipline, as it can easily become a habit if left unchallenged. Regardless of the specific choice, these are the discretionary decisions that offer a priceless chance to transform your life. So, I trained my mind to shut down that tempting inner voice within 4 seconds and simply get up. This time-bound technique, combined with the adoption of this potent mantra, could be the key component among the 8 daily practices that contributed most to my success. Although it might not be apparent to most people, these discretionary choices shape their day and, ultimately, their lives. Thus, you hold the reins of your day and your life. You are the only one capable of changing your life. The choice is yours.

In the upcoming chapters, I will delve into and share each of the 8 daily practices, drawing from my experiences in how I came to discover, refine, and incorporate them into my life. Each of these practices has individually enhanced my life, but when combined, they have brought about a profound transformation, making me a happier, healthier individual, both mentally and physically, and enabling me to embrace each day with gratitude. All you need to do is start with one of these practices today, just one, and I assure you that you'll begin to experience the same positive changes. The more you adopt and integrate into your life, the more you'll grow and realise your boundless potential.

OWN YOUR LEGACY

"To be truly successful, you must first do what you don't want to do, when you don't want to do it – until you do."

Transformation typically begins, in my view, when a strong impetus to change emerges, often prompting a sequence of decisions to take the more challenging road rather than the easier one. In my case, the driving force for change was the legacy I would leave behind. Without a doubt, your legacy is created, like it or not, by everything you undertake, and sometimes even more so, the opportunities you let slip by. Eventually, there comes a time when you must confront your legacy and live with it, often during a stage of life when you have the most time to think about it.

But when I say, "your legacy", I'm not referring to the one visible to others. I mean the one that you see, feel, and experience — which is the only one that truly matters. It is the one you can't

I had and hadn't done up until that point in my life.

Let's start this exercise with your own self-reflection. Imagine yourself looking back over your life at age 65 or 70. What you would want your legacy to be? If you haven't taken the time to complete this exercise before, I would strongly recommend that you dedicate time to ponder this question and write your answer down.

This introspective practice, which I've come to know as the "armchair test", generally and naturally occurs when people reach retirement. As they unwind in their armchairs, they consider the tapestry of their lives. I also suggest that you reflect on where you are now and evaluate how you are tracking progress towards the ideal legacy and future you would love to see. This exercise, though, comes with both a responsibility and an opportunity—to act purposefully and to command your destiny. You should also place your written legacy statement somewhere prominent as a persistent reminder. How does that prospect feel? At the conclusion of this chapter, you will find a more expansive exercise that forms the nucleus of this daily practice action.

Make no mistake about it. My purpose is absolutely clear: I aim to shock you, to jolt you, irrevocably, out of the snug cocoon of your comfort zone well before the window of opportunity shuts.

It's possible, though, that you're content with your current circumstances. If life were to continue without alteration, you might be content with your present achievements when looking back at 65 years of age. Should this be the case, I tip my hat to you. You are likely an immensely grateful person, and that would firmly place you amongst the minority of people. Should you not place yourself in this category right now, my genuine intention is to shake your world a little. Without change, deliberate planning, and personal sacrifices, the day could soon dawn when it's simply too late. It's highly likely that without decisive action today and without embracing the challenges over easier, more comfortable paths, you may eventually find yourself nestled in an armchair, besieged by regrets for the multitude of missed opportunities that you let pass by.

Drawing from my decades of interactions and working with retirees, I've seen that regret often serves as the seed of depression – which I have found to be the single greatest affliction of retirees in Australia. Among the most frequent and impactful regrets that have crossed my path is the saga of those who frittered away a significant chunk of their earnings without adequately saving from their most important asset. Naturally, the tougher road would have involved forgoing certain expenditures or abstaining from borrowing for items or assets that didn't contribute to their future. The judicious choice would have been to buy within their means and channel more toward their retirement nest egg—the largest financial challenge of their lives. Tragically, all too often, I have borne witness to individuals who spurned the chance to make sufficient sacrifices and, as a result, have fallen well short of amassing the means needed to live comfortably in retirement. The regret, for most people, by the way, is acutely palpable.

At the age of 34, I confronted my personal "armchair test," and the reflection wasn't kind. My go-to saying until then had been, "I could have". In truth, I truly could have. The realisation that

I could have achieved far more than I had, coupled with the persistent echo of "I could have," rendered both the mantra and, consequently, my impending legacy intolerable. And to this day, I am eternally grateful that I finally faced myself.

To context the significance of my midlife epiphany, the catalyst for a transformative journey during which I would reshape not only my life but also my legacy, it's fitting to start from the very beginning of my journey in Ware. "Ware?" I can hear you exclaim, a common reaction. Indeed, Ware in Hertfordshire, UK, is located roughly twenty-six miles North from the centre of London in the "green belt". For the most part, I remember my childhood very fondly. My parents raised me well, loved me generously and provided me with every opportunity to be happy. Both my mum and dad led active lives, playing sports regularly throughout their lives. My father was an accomplished cricketer, rugby, and hockey player, and I certainly inherited my dad's competitive nature. Ironically, the one pursuit he detested was running — his childhood antics to evade running at school are among his favourite stories. He would start a run at school with a pack of boys before hiding under a small bridge and lighting up a cigarette, then rejoin the pack again as they came back around to the point that he had abdicated. The irony of his aversion to running isn't lost on me as I recount this, and as you read on, I am sure it will not be lost on you. I often joke with my dad on this topic. Worth mentioning that at the time of my authoring this book, my dad is a spritely 87, lives in Melbourne, Australia, and still plays tennis twice a week, as well as 2 rounds of golf.

Growing up, I was a competitive athlete from an early age, and like most other young boys in the UK, my ultimate dream was to one day become a professional football player in the English topflight.

I am not sure what age I became an Arsenal fan, but I really was a fanatic. From the age of thirteen, I would travel on my own by train to watch my beloved Gunners play at Highbury, London. Come rain or shine, I would stand shoulder to shoulder with the thousands of devoted Gunners fans in Highbury's North Bank. Catching the train to and from the stadium was often a scary experience! I was quite an accomplished player from an early age, and by the time I turned thirteen, I found myself playing between 3 and 5 competitive games a week. These games were spread across my school side at Monks Walk, my Sunday league side at Welwyn Pegasus, and as County representative, firstly for schoolboys, then also for the Sunday League national association.

Playing as the number 9 centre forward, I absolutely loved playing football, and there was nothing in this world that I loved more than scoring goals. I dreamed of scoring goals – literally. Fortunately, it appeared that goal-scoring was destined to be my one true talent.

I could have... but I didn't

At the age of fourteen, my new team, Panshanger Yellows, made a significant announcement: our team was embarking on a tour in the USA. This was quite a big deal some 46 years ago when travel wasn't as accessible or affordable as it is today. The prospect of playing against teams in the US, especially during a time when soccer was rapidly gaining popularity and the fastest-growing sport in the US, filled me with excitement. To top things off, we were going to watch my hero, then as he is now the world's greatest player, Pelé, playing for the New York Cosmos.

15

By now, my parents had separated, and the decision was made that my mum would travel with me on the trip since a parent's presence was required. The adventure that followed turned out to be the greatest time of my life to that point. Our days were filled with matches, interspersed with trips to enormous shopping malls that were unlike anything we had in the UK. We fully immersed ourselves in American culture, relishing in burgers, mall trips, going out to the movies, and even managing to see "Grease" within a day of its world premiere. However, the pinnacle of the experience for me was watching my idol Pelé. What an unforgettable night that was.

When I returned, my passion for football and my desire to play in the top flight remained front and centre, and my love of the game was as strong as ever. But the time had come to knuckle down and focus on my studies, which I threw myself into, just as I did with everything that I set my sights on. Football wasn't my only sporting pursuit; I was also active in playing cricket, cross-country running, and athletics, representing my school and district teams. I even secured a commendable 7th place in the state championships for cross-country running. This is where my passion for running took root.

As I approached 15 years of age, distractions crept in, as they often do. Girls and nights out at local pubs became appealing pastimes, even during some school lunch breaks. Smoking entered the picture around this time as well, which, accompanied by the consumption of alcohol, didn't bode well for my sporting dreams. Nonetheless, destiny handed me my big chance at the age of fifteen.

During the school's state championship final, which I played in, and we won, a scout from Southend Football Club approached me. "Great game tonight, son," said the club scout as he shook my hand. "We'd be interested in discussing an apprenticeship at Southend if you're open to it."

The magnitude of the moment rendered me momentarily speechless for the first time in my life. Finally, everything I had dreamed of was materialising in front of me. "Of course I am," I blurted out, hardly able to contain my excitement. And as if this chance of a lifetime wasn't enough, he continued.

"I was watching you out there tonight, and I think that you have more potential than one of our other top apprentices, Danny Greaves."

"Is he who I think he is?" I exclaimed.

"Yes, indeed, he's Jimmy Greaves' son."

Wow, I thought. The legendary Jimmy Greaves was one of England's favourite sons and most celebrated footballers in English and world football.

"We will be in touch soon, and I will need to speak to your parents."

And that was that. Sleep eluded me that night as I replayed the game in my head in intimate detail, intertwining it with the prospect of a shot at my dreams. As days went by and Southend reached out again, the enormity of the challenge and sacrifices I faced came into sharper focus. To provide context, English professional clubs typically accepted 20 to 40 apprentices around my age, each year. Apprentices were expected to complete mundane tasks like cleaning the professional players' mud-encrusted boots, amongst other tasks, along with three weekly training sessions and playing games.

The risk was high and required complete dedication, which would almost certainly impact my school studies. To compound the risk, only a handful from each intake would likely be offered professional contracts, assuming you didn't suffer any significant injuries.

Adding to the complexity was the logistical hurdle of frequent travel to Southend, requiring two substantial train rides each way—nearly insurmountable given it would mean arriving home at close to midnight on the 3 training nights. Assuming that is, the trains were running on time, and the interchange went smoothly.

I felt a profound disappointment that I had to relinquish my dream—for now, and, perhaps, forever. It was a moment that would echo throughout my life, encapsulated by the words "I could have," a refrain I'd utter with profound regret until my awakening at the age of thirty-four. And that's how my mantra of "I could have" became the defining theme of my story for the next two decades.

With my dream disappearing in life's rearview mirror, I put my head down and studied hard as my O Levels approached. I continued to drink, smoke and chase girls. But my hard work and determination bore fruit, earning me a respectable pass mark for 9 O Levels—the second-highest score in my year of 200 students. Contemplating my trajectory from that point, I decided to follow my artistic talents and elected that two of my 3 A-Level subjects would be art-related, despite not really having thought about where that would lead me.

At seventeen and a little over a year into my A-level studies, life took an unexpected turn. My dad called me one day and said he had something important to talk over with me—setting up a meeting at a local pub called The Tin Pot—a conversation that would alter the course of my life. Of all the different topics that I pondered until we met, none came close to the intended topic of the conversation. The Tin Pot is a tiny historic pub situated on the edge of the local common. The day came to meet my dad. We ordered drinks, and so began that sliding door moment.

"Jas, I've decided that I am going to move to Australia, and I would like you to come with me."

Time seemed to stand still for what seemed like an eternity as I struggled to context what my dad had just revealed. It might have been mere seconds, but it felt like an eternity.

Finally, I said calmly, "OK, that sounds great. When do we go?"

After agreeing to pursue a new future on the other side of the world, the emigration process began in earnest. I underwent the mandatory medical examinations as part of this process. However, a shock awaited us. My father received the results, along with approval for our migration, but there was one significant caveat. The examination revealed scars on my lungs, which were highly likely to have been caused by tuberculosis, a potentially life-threatening condition.

The medical report concluded that the disease had gone, but it was recommended that I undergo further tests upon my arrival in Australia. This news was disturbing news and validated why I had experienced such prolonged illness, including severe bouts of chronic coughing, for approximately 18 months prior. While

I experienced a sense of relief that my application had been approved, there was also a looming feeling of uncertainty. The prospect of moving all the way to Australia and then potentially being sent back if any new activity was detected in my lungs cast a dark, foreboding cloud over me. Only time would provide answers, and I had no choice but to just get on with things.

May 1981 feels like a lifetime ago now. Well, in many ways, it truly was. In the blink of an eye, seventeen has transformed into nearly sixty, and here I am, sharing my story. From Heathrow, London, we set off bound for Africa, my dad and his partner, Julia. Our plans included stops in Kenya, Malawi, Swaziland, and Perth before alighting at our final destination, Sydney. Travelling around the world to live permanently in Australia, a country I knew extraordinarily little about, was a huge and daunting move for me, but exciting, nonetheless. As a boy growing up in semi-rural England, Africa's landscapes, sights, sounds, and experiences were both confronting and wonderful beyond my imagination.

My childhood had been comfortable, and I was fortunate in that I had travelled overseas a few times, but my experiences to that point had been relatively tame compared to Africa.

Landing in our first destination of Nairobi, Kenya, on the day of the grand start of the international Africa Car Rally (ARC), was chaos at its finest. The heart of the city was overrun by an additional 200,000 people who flocked to watch the spectacle, coinciding with our stay at the Hilton Hotel. Eager to absorb the culture, I ventured out to explore Nairobi's sights, sounds, and smells. Amidst the chaos and intoxicating atmosphere, I was confronted in ways that I could never have imagined. The sight of immense poverty and suffering made an indelible impression on me—particularly the countless homeless beggars surviving on tourist handouts. To this day, many of the images are indelibly etched into my mind. One vivid memory stands out: within minutes of heading out of the Hilton's comfortable surrounds, I was approached by a homeless man with no legs, perched on a wooden makeshift sled, dragging himself across the road by his bandaged knuckles. I looked into his eyes and fought to hold back the tears as I handed him a note, the value of which I had no comprehension. I just handed it to him.

In hindsight, that encounter reshaped my attitude towards people who face terrible hardship for the better. Regardless of whether they were self-inflicted, through unforeseen circumstances or tragic events, I made a conscious decision that day to be empathetic towards others, to try to walk a mile in their shoes, not to judge, and to offer help wherever I could. I like to think that I have always sought to better the lives of others, extending a helping hand without delay or seeking personal gain. Collaborating with charities to amplify awareness and raise essential funds for those truly in need has been a cornerstone of my commitment since.

Throughout my life, I've maintained a close partnership with the Salvation Army, engaging in activities such as speaking at fundraising events or raising money through my endeavours in sport. My involvement in the Vinnies CEO Sleepout stands out profoundly. This experience allowed me, albeit briefly, to immerse myself in the harsh realities of the everyday tragedies and struggles faced by many homeless individuals in our nation. Participating in the CEO Sleepout on 4 occasions left me feeling both humbled and deeply grateful. But gestures of compassion and kindness do not need to be planned or significant. Often, it's the seemingly trivial things, the small acts of random kindness, that we can do each day to help someone in need, which truly have the power to brighten their day, that really make a difference.

Our new life began to take shape in Sydney's northern hills suburb, Pennant Hills. Adjusting to the vibrant city life from my UK roots wasn't seamless, but I pressed on as I searched to find my place in such a large city. I sorely missed my friends and grappled with the separation from my mother, brother Nick, and the rest of my family. Amidst this, having given little thought to a career pathway in Sydney, I decided to follow my heart and my passion for drawing and painting flora and fauna. First, though, there was the daunting task of passing an immigration medical examination within 30 days of our arrival. Following the necessary imaging scans and a period of anxious waiting, I had to wait another few days before finally receiving a clearance to stay. What a huge relief that was. The following day, I purchased a range of art supplies and began to paint, without knowing where my endeavours might lead. With only basic art classes at school behind me and no formal art training to speak of, I turned my mind to exploring potential markets for my creative work.

With the internet still a few years away from either conception or creation and a long way away from proliferating our day-to-day lives, identifying opportunities was challenging, to say the least. In 1981, the only research option that was readily available was the voluminous editions of the Yellow Pages, which listed businesses that paid for advertising space.

Armed with my targets, I hit the telephone and began to call various publishers, periodicals, magazines, greeting card makers, and table place mat manufacturers. Good luck, persistence, or both eventually paid off, and I secured appointments with a range of companies. These resulted in fruitful outcomes, and I set to work on a range of commissions.

I secured my first exhibition in a St Ives gallery and was fortunate enough to sell a few paintings for between $500 and $1,000. Encouraged by my early success, I was further inspired a few weeks later by a wonderful lady, June, whom I had struck up a close relationship with at the picture framing gallery in Pennant Hills. June asked me if I would be interested in submitting some sample paintings to the global head of interior design for the Intercontinental Hotels worldwide chain. She explained that he had approached the gallery seeking a local Sydney artist to commission to paint classical botanical studies of Australian native flowers for the soon-to-be-completed Intercontinental Hotel. Somewhat awed by this immense and prestigious opportunity, I hurried home to gather a select range of samples that the gallery could submit.

A week passed before I received a call from June. "Hi Jason. I was wondering if you had some time to call in and see us this afternoon about the work that you submitted?"

My excitement was palpable as I contemplated the prospect of a major commission. By 4 pm that day, terms and project details were ironed out. At the tender age of eighteen, I became the youngest artist commissioned to create artworks for the global Intercontinental Hotel chain. Without delay, I plunged into researching native Australian wildflowers, unfamiliar terrain for a UK transplant like me. A series of ten botanical artworks began to take shape.

As I spent my days and nights bringing nature to life for the Intercontinental project, my dad and I met the local TV repair guy, John, at his Beecroft store, sparking a discussion about the emerging technology of video recorders in Australia. Fortunately, having recently left the UK, which was advanced in terms of technology at that time, we were already familiar with and had utilised a Betamax video recorder extensively. Discussions evolved over the next few weeks as we worked on a strategy to partner and stock the repair shop with video rental cassettes.

Before I departed the UK, my academic pursuits had been limited to the high school curriculum and my work experience was confined to part-time jobs in local supermarkets. This was hardly a strong platform for embarking on the creation of one of Australia's first video rental shops, but I was up to the challenge. Renting videotapes was a highly capex business, with each fragile tape costing between $75 and $85 all the way back in 1982. Consequently, the selection of appropriate titles and the fragile nature of the cassette tapes left little room for error in terms of making a profit. As the opening of our new video store approached, I completed the ten original artworks for the Intercontinental Hotel. To my great delight, all ten of my submissions were approved, destined for reproduction as eight hundred limited edition prints—all of which I would need to sign and number individually.

As the grand opening of the luxury hotel approached, an invitation to the grand gala opening found its way to my mailbox. This distinguished event would be attended by the then deputy Prime Minister, alongside countless celebrities and stars, such as Aussie Joe Bugner, the former World Boxing Champion. The transformation of the historic Treasury Building into the resplendent Intercontinental Hotel carried profound historical and cultural significance, sparking interest and coverage not only within Australia but also across international media outlets. The very first edition of the Sydney Morning Herald Good Weekend colour magazine featured the grand opening on its front cover and showcased some of my botanical prints in the article. A similar story, with corresponding pictures, ran in that month's edition of Belle and Vogue magazines, focusing on the talents of the interior designer, Bill Embrey. I felt an enormous sense of pride and accomplishment at what I had achieved, and I was completely overwhelmed attending the official Black Tie Gala evening.

Silver Screen Video had been up and running for a while. I was fully engaged in the venture, dedicating myself to its demands seven days a week, week after week, a consistent routine that persisted unrelenting for two whole years. Whilst I loved what I was doing, seventy-plus hours a week had started to take its toll. Simultaneously, I was pursuing another goal —moving out of home to go and live on my own before reaching nineteen.

Close to death...the first time

Time swept by in its unrelenting current, and before I knew it, my formidable Nan, Phyllis - at the age of eighty, flew over unaccompanied from the UK for a holiday. Remarkably, this would not be her last time making a long solo journey out to Australia. In fact, even more remarkably, her last trip to Australia came at the age of ninety! My Nan was tough, though, as typified by her refusal to go with her family down to the air raid shelter near their home in the UK as the Germans bombed London and its surroundings. You see, on principle, my Nan refused to let the Germans force her into defeat and out of her home, remaining in her home, alone, as the sirens sounded.

During my youthful years, I had the privilege of accompanying my Nan on her Co-op milk run on a few occasions while I stayed with her. It was a tough 16-mile run with a milk cart stacked high with crates carrying glass bottles filled with milk. On one particularly memorable day when it had been snowing heavily, leaving a three-inch blanket of snow that covered everything in sight, I watched on in awe as she hauled milk crates in a small sled across the treacherous stretches of snow. Oh, how cold that day was, and the world seemed to be draped in frost, yet undeterred, my Nan still woke me at 4 am and off we headed to load up her milk float and complete the entire round in the snow. Further exemplifying her indomitable character, my Nan was the sole female delivery driver at the local depot in Ware. She exhibited a tenacity that knew no bounds, insisting on loading her cart unaided each morning. As if her character and resilience needed further validation, the Co-op finally insisted that my Nan retire when she turned age 63, despite the female retirement age in the UK and at the Co-op being sixty for a female.

I consider myself extremely fortunate and privileged to have had endless experiences with my Nan during my childhood. These encounters spanned the spectrum from delightfully enjoyable to character-building, which are still so vivid almost over half a century later. Amongst them all, I would rate the endless summers spent at my grandparents' home in Norfolk as the highlight. My Nan taught me what honest, arduous work really was, along with the corresponding satisfaction that came from receiving a fair day's pay. The endless summer days in England, spent picking strawberries or various berries, while kneeling under the warm sun, were just as influential as any other experiences during my early life. I recall with fondness how I would keep a running tally of my earnings throughout the day, with the promise of eight pence at the end of the day for each large cardboard basket filled with the strawberries that I had picked.

And when the day ended, my pockets jingling from the coins I had accumulated, my hands and knees stained and stinging from my labour, I truly understood what my Nan had been trying to teach me. The message was simple but profound - work hard, and everything will look after itself. This understanding has been my guiding light throughout my life, a beacon steering me toward the rewards that await those who embrace the ethos of dedicated labour.

We also spent many hours playing cards together, each draw and shuffle creating a shared moment. I would watch my Nan cook the most amazing food while we talked about anything that she wanted to. Nan took over four hours to steam cook her famous steak and kidney puddings, which tasted better than anything else in the world, except for her tapioca pudding with the baked top! She was a prolific knitter, a creator of skilfully crocheted tablecloths and other garments and a master cake decorator who made every tiny, iced decoration for every cake, including elaborate wedding cakes. I miss her dearly to this day and often reflect on the sadness of the decline and potential extinction of the crafts that she had mastered and was so proud of.

Nan was such an adventurer at heart, and she revelled in the Australian sunshine and our newfound way of life. A few weeks later came that fateful day. Nan went to visit a friend she had made at the local bowling club, from whom I had arranged to pick her up. The traffic was quite heavy as I set off on the short drive before the Friday afternoon rush hour, and the rain drizzled on the windscreen. I rounded a bend on the busy Pennant Hills Road, careful not to exceed the speed limit on such a greasy road surface, and then, in an instant, daylight disappeared.

I partially awoke from my unconscious state, completely unaware of the time that had elapsed since I last saw the world, or even where I was. I woke up to the screaming noise of the ambulance's siren. I was completely disoriented as we sped towards the nearby Hornsby Hospital. Barely conscious, the only thing I can recall from that fateful day was the searing pain emanating from my face, mouth, and skull. Instinct got the better of me, raising my hand to my face to explore the source of such extreme pain. What I found turned my stomach and instantly caused tears to course down my face. In my head, I heard:

"What the f... have you done, Jason? What have you done?"

My fingers found and traced the front teeth that had splintered, snapped, and then pierced through the skin on my chin. At that moment, I was convinced that my life was over and could not bring myself, either mentally or physically, to explore anywhere else on my body. Things hurt so badly in so many separate places. Later, I learned that my poor Nan, who had been waiting for me to pick her up just a few hundred metres up the road, had surmised that because I had not shown up, I was in the ambulance that screamed past her as she waited for me to arrive. She said she felt sick to her stomach. She just knew.

The next couple of days are unclear as I drifted in and out of consciousness in the emergency room and then in the ICU. One thing I do recall was the doctor and the surgeon sitting by my bedside the next day to explain what had happened to me.

"How are you feeling, Jason?" asked the surgeon, but my ability to respond coherently was hampered by my jaw already being wired shut, exacerbated by substantial swelling that had enlarged my face size by at least 50%. The uninterrupted stream of morphine weaved its magic, reducing my pain but leaving me dazed and struggling to find clarity amidst my mental fog. He continued, recognising that I was unable to respond.

"Well, you are a very lucky boy."

"Lucky!?!? What the ****!!" exclaimed the voice in my head.

"From what I have been told, another driver skidded uncontrol-lably across Pennant Hills Road and into your path. Your seat belt partially stopped your momentum. However, your face and head collided with the steering wheel, and the force caused the bonnet of your car to crumple, effectively compacting your body virtually into a ball. Essentially, your face and skull took the brunt of the impact", explained the surgeon.

I swallowed hard as I processed the confronting information he was sharing, fully aware that the most unsettling part was yet to come.

"Would you like a drink?" he asked, to which I nodded. He picked up the glass beside my bed, fed the straw between my blood-ied, swollen lips, and carefully maneuvered it through one of the many gaps in my teeth. I sipped, coughed, and eased back.

"We operated on you for five hours yesterday evening into the small hours of the morning. Given you sustained sixteen fractures throughout your upper and lower jaw and your cheek, we've had to wire your jaw together. This wiring will remain for about six to seven weeks to facilitate proper healing. You've also experienced a considerable loss of teeth, with a substantial number requiring root removal. The tooth fragments embedded throughout your mouth will need to be surgically removed over the course of the next six months or thereabouts."

"Oh god," I thought.

He smiled empathetically, "We also had to insert two wire ties into your jaw to secure the most severe fractures. These ties will probably remain permanently in your face forever." He paused as my eyes glassed over.

"Are you ok?" he asked. I nodded again.

"In addition, you have sustained three fractures to your skull, which we cannot treat. You must exercise extreme caution while they heal. Aside from these injuries, you have incurred some deep lacerations. It's quite remarkable that your injuries are not more severe or that the accident did not kill you."

I imagine he sensed the depth of my emotions, and it's possible he intuited that I had something to convey. Tears welled up in my eyes and started to flow down my face. I made a movement with my hand, which he gently clasped, to offer reassurance. Amid the overwhelming turmoil caused by his diagnosis and the throbbing pain in my head, which lurked beneath the veneer of morphine's relief, there arose within me a sense of luck and a wave of appreciation. I wanted to convey this sentiment. He smiled in response, and his recognition of my unspoken message provided a sense of ease and connection in that moment.

Perhaps, lying there in the Hornsby ICU, a mere day earlier, a vigorous 18-year-old brimming with vitality, I faced my next profound trial of perspective. Now, I struggled for consciousness and was not yet brave enough to confront the potentially irreparable damage to my face and head in the mirror. All of this was inflicted in the blink of an eye. As I drifted in and out of awareness during the subsequent days, occasionally rousing to find my dad stationed by my bedside, I contemplated the injustice of the situation and attempted in vain to understand why this had happened to me or what I could have done differently to avoid this catastrophe. Yet, in truth, there was nothing I could have done differently. But it was just meant to be, destiny had woven its thread. There were moments of self-pity, I will admit, but I waged an internal battle, determined not to let these corrosive emotions consume me. For the first time in my life, I needed to find perspective and gratitude in chaos and disaster. And I did find it. Life is fragile, and I was alive. That comfort was enough.

After two weeks of discomfort, pain, and extreme boredom, I was at last granted release from the hospital's confines. I expressed my heartfelt thanks to the exceptional individuals who had devoted themselves to my care, shedding a few tears as I did so. Those two weeks had provided ample space for introspection, granting me the opportunity to mull over the trajectory that lay ahead as I tenaciously navigated my journey to recovery. At the time of the accident, I had already left home and taken up residence in a shared apartment. I needed to get back to my video store ASAP to pay the bills.

The very next day, I found myself standing on St Leonards station, propped up by crutches. I had a face full of stitches, along with others in my arms and knees. My jaw was still wired tightly shut, and there were huge gaps in my teeth. At least this provided some convenience in accommodating the straw that would supply my nutrition for the next six weeks. I was a messed-up, sorry sight, and I knew it. The routine of catching four trains a day continued to necessitate the commute between home and the video store until such time as I could drive again. This transitional phase was fraught with discomfort, bouts of excruciating pain, and spells of self-pity as I gradually reintegrated into the rhythm of everyday life. However, a nascent method of practising gratitude emerged from within me, a technique that would serve as a counterpoint

- 'just beginning
- developing
- few

to moments of self-pity. Although I hadn't yet mastered it - this technique would be honed over the ensuing decades - especially in the face of similarly challenging circumstances that I will delve into with deeper insight in the forthcoming chapter.

A couple of months elapsed before my Nan departed to return to England. In many ways, I sensed that she felt partially responsible for my accident, given that I had been en route to pick her up at the time. She confided in me about this after the accident, but I reassured her that, in my mind, this was never the case. I was sad to see her go, but I drew solace in the fact that I would see her again soon. During my fortnight-long stint in hospital, Dad engaged a lawyer to seek compensation for my case. However, it eventually transpired that the solicitor had neglected to initiate court proceedings in a timely manner. Consequently, for us to contest the relatively meagre settlement offer put forth by the insurer's solicitor, an additional four years of waiting would be required. Faced with ongoing bills and the potential to bolster my modest savings, I made the decision to allocate the offered sum toward supporting my financial endeavours, including a deposit for my first property purchase at the tender age of 19. And thus, with some compromise, we acquiesced to a somewhat diminished offer.

Work remained as hectic as ever, and I juggled the seemingly never-ending schedule of dental procedures to operate, extract, and restore my injured or absent teeth, all while fulfilling my business obligations over the next 12 months. In the short term, I endeavoured to sustain a semblance of normalcy in my daily routine, even venturing out to nightclubs a few times despite my wired jaw and the conspicuous gaps in my teeth. At least I could manage to sip the alcoholic spirits through my straw, but my inclination to smile was notably curtailed during these outings.

Approximately six weeks following my accident, I made a return visit to Hornsby Hospital for a minor surgical procedure. This operation entailed the removal of the wires that had meticulously held my fractured jaw together, accompanied by a series of X-rays to assess the progress of healing in my jaw, cheek, and skull. The x-ray results were encouraging, revealing substantial healing of the fractures. This positive outcome indicated that, aside from the wire removal procedure, no further operations would be necessary. Small mercies. Lying on the surgical table under the bright theatre light, infused with only a local anaesthetic, the surgeon carefully made incisions near my temples on both sides of my face. With utmost care, he began the task of undoing each of the wire connectors that had been intricately threaded through my facial tissues, linking them from inside my face to my jaw. The wires looped beneath my jaw and then ascended to be anchored in an identical fashion on the opposite side.

Whilst I felt no pain, my stomach turned from the sensation of the wire sliding through my flesh, down one side of my face, then under my jaw, and eventually up the other side until it slid free. Sweat poured from my skin as I struggled not to faint. Despite the prospect of enduring another year of dental interventions and reconstructions every fortnight, there was a glimmer of hope that at least the major injuries were showing signs of completely healing. In the days that ensued, as I sat in the hushed waiting room of the dentist's office, the thought that a period of respite might finally emerge crossed my mind. Little did I know that another significant accident was silently edging its way into view.

Through work, I met a new friend, Sean, who was from Scotland and would become one of my lifetime best friends. Sean, in turn, introduced me to Marty, Sylvia, Tom, and eventually, Carol, who would eventually become Sean's wife a few years down the line.

We were a tight bunch, along with a wider group of UK friends. Our collective energy was nothing short of exuberant, and we were all a little wild. We spent much of our time partying at night clubs, camping and kayaking down rivers or going on water skiing weekends on the Central Coast of New South Wales. By this juncture, I had achieved the acquisition of my second property in Sydney, a feat accomplished before the age of twenty. While I was doing okay for myself, it is important to highlight the degree of risk I had undertaken. The purchase of my initial apartment was facilitated with only a twenty per cent deposit. The second, which I owned concurrently, necessitated borrowing the full 100 % of the purchase price. Back in those days, such complex financial arrangements were attainable through the right connections. Fortunately, my solicitor at the time introduced me to a bank manager who would extend me the deposit loan, subsequently steering me toward a building society that facilitated the remaining 80% for the second mortgage.

Life was good but also challenging to manage. As the proprietor of a business, shouldering the responsibilities of a car loan, a personal loan for one of the houses, and overseeing two mortgages, every cent had to be accounted for and managed. In an era, devoid of spreadsheets or even the idea of them, I purchased a ledger made of graph paper. I drew up a 12-month calendar in which I accounted for rental income, loan payments and every conceivable expense that I could think of to plot out my cash flow and enable me to survive. It was tough, though, and the meal I ate most of the time during that period was sausages, mashed potatoes, and baked beans! This was all I could afford. But to achieve success in anything, you must be disciplined and prepared for great sacrifice. An adage that echoes resolutely is, "To be truly successful, you must first be prepared to do what you don't want to do, when you don't want to do it." Worn down by the relentless workload and the weight of working almost every day for two years solid, I was craving an escape, a respite from the daily toil. I arranged a getaway with Sean and the gang – to go motocross riding in the bush areas down past Menai for a few days. My friend and partner from the video shop, John, had a large 5 ft by 7ft box trailer at his house in Thornleigh, the suburb that had witnessed my life-altering car accident not too long ago. The trailer was a necessity to haul a couple of motocross bikes for our adventure.

Early on that beautiful morning, just before our scheduled departure, I pulled up at John's place. Perched atop a steep and significant hill in Thornleigh, his house offered a commanding view. The sun was casting its warm glow as I parked my car outside John's house in the leafy suburb. With limited experience in reversing a car with a trailer attached, I decided to park the car in the street, just below John's driveway. That way, I could wheel the box trailer by the front extension bars until I could sit the steel cup on the tow bar ball. As fate would have it, John wasn't home, but his wife Janet was. And so, I embarked on the task of moving the trailer down the driveway towards the road, where my car was waiting.

The trailer was extremely heavy, I thought, guessing that it probably weighed about half a tonne or thereabouts. I began to move the trailer with my hands wedged under the extension arms where that ball cup was fixed at the very end, with my body hunched over it, shuffling backwards down the hill. As I navigated the trailer over the curb and onto the road, it ground to a sudden halt, the wheels stubbornly caught in a small rut where the driveway met the concrete curb. Oh no, not now, I thought. I began to rock the trailer backwards and forwards, attempting to dislodge the wheels from the small rut that they had settled in. The momentum increased as I rocked harder until suddenly, the wheels relinquished their grip and bumped over the tapered driveway curb. My monetary joy and relief turned to paralysing fear in a split second.

"Oh Fuu......!" I blurted out aloud, my voice carrying disbelief as I experienced the unstoppable force of the half-ton trailer surge forward on the sloped bitumen road. With every ounce of strength that I possessed, I attempted to slow or halt its momentum, but I instantly acknowledged that neither objective was possible. The sheer force of the trailer propelled me backwards as I turned my head, my gaze fixed on the road below.

On one side of the road, a line of cars stretched down to the bottom, while the other side had a clear stretch of about thirty metres before another row of cars began. In that terrifying second, my mind was consumed by the certain and considerable damage that the hurtling trailer would inflict on the rows of parked cars. I knew I had to avert that catastrophe at any cost. Instinct took over as I summoned a final burst of herculean strength to change the trailer's trajectory, aiming to veer it sideways toward the opposite curb. My feet scampered urgently, my body twisted, and I strained to redirect the trailer while desperately keeping my balance. The consequences of failure were dire – the weighty trailer could easily run me over, dragging me mercilessly down the road. How I managed to maintain my footing while altering the path of that colossal projectile remains a mystery to me, even now. But somehow, against all odds, I succeeded. In a split second, I found myself stumbling backward toward the opposite curb, grappling with the question of how to escape the path of the hurtling projectile that I now clung to for dear life. From the very furthest corner of my eye, I caught a glimpse of the curb's edge and instinctively leapt over it, unaware of anything that could happen consequently. Suddenly, I was suspended in mid-air, hurtling toward the ground some five feet below. In that fleeting moment, I felt the frigid, unyielding steel of the trailer's cup extension connect with the upper left side of my back. Even in mid-flight, the steel traced a path down my back, jarring against my spine. With a resounding impact, I collided with the rocky ground, my body instinctively bracing for what might be the end for me. By a sheer miracle, a tree stump that had remained since the road's construction intervened, diverting the trajectory of the entire trailer. The collision resonated with a resounding clatter, and by some twist of fate, the trailer and I parted ways in separate directions. I was miraculously spared a disastrous fate.

Suffering immediate and extreme shock, I leapt up with an instinctive surge, a response I would replicate on several other occasions in my life and vaulted from the gulley to the road in a single motion. Agonising pain surged through me, swiftly replaced by a gripping sense of panic. I dared not cast a glance backward as I sprinted toward John's house, desperate for help. Within 30 seconds, Janet had heard the commotion and came bursting through the front door screen.

"What in the world have you done?" she shrieked, her voice laced with panic and fear.

I crumpled to my knees as she hurriedly circled around to survey the carnage.

"The trailer... it fell on me. God, it hurts. What have I done? What have I done?" the words escaping as I cried out breathlessly.

The pain was beginning to surge rapidly, yet I remained in a state of deep shock. If you've ever been through a severe impact, you'd recognise that unsettling feeling—the realisation that something violent and grave is about to unfold, followed by the sickening awareness that you're in a dire physical state. Regrettably, this was becoming an all too familiar experience—one that I would become intimately acquainted with as my life unfolded. Fortunately, Janet was a nurse and instantly recognised the gravity of what I was experiencing, as well as the potential consequences of my accident. She could also see that the 12-inch gash across my back intersected with my spine around the middle of my shoulder blades. Kneeling beside me, she gently removed the remnants of my torn t-shirt to examine my spine. The shirt was so shredded that with just a couple of slight tugs, it fell away from my body.

"Jason, try to stay still and take slow breaths," Janet advised in a soothing tone. I could feel my body drenched in sweat as the rush of adrenaline began to subside, leaving behind a wave of nausea and dizziness.

"Are you feeling dizzy?" she asked.

I nodded, "Yes, I feel very sick." My head was starting to spin.

Janet jumped up, grabbed the shredded remains of my t-shirt, hastened to the garden tap, and doused the t-shirt in chilly water. As she returned, she handed it to me, her voice composed yet urgent.

"Here you go, hold this against your forehead and the back of your neck. Concentrate on the cold sensation," she directed with a steady tone. "Take slow, deep breaths. Inhale, and then exhale. That's it. Let me know when the dizziness passes, and I'll call for an ambulance."

But her words became unnecessary, as the commotion had caught the attention of her neighbours. They rushed towards us in the front garden.

I could hear the voice in my head once again. "What on earth have you done to yourself this time, Jason? What the hell."

Though she didn't vocalise her worries, Janet's foremost concern was the potential for spinal damage, a distressing possibility. With lying down ruled out, a pair of neighbours carefully raised me and settled me into a chair that had been swiftly procured. Despite their efforts to maintain composure, an unspoken apprehension lingered in the air that you can read in bystanders when you find yourself confronted with such dire circumstances. It's a feeling you simply sense. As the agony surged, I concentrated on my breath, the discomfort growing more acute, and the distinct wail of approaching sirens now audible. The ambulance arrived with a sudden halt, its doors flung open, and the two compassionate paramedics leapt out. As I write this, another twist of irony dawns on me. Considering the recurring presence of ambulances in my life, one can't help but find it uncanny that my yet-to-be-born daughter, Emma, would eventually choose a path to become a paramedic herself. I am filled with immense pride for the unwavering courage and care that she demonstrates every day to help others in their desperate time of need.

"Right, Jason, is it?" The male paramedic asked as he surveyed my back. "Can you describe what happened?" he continued, more of a diversionary tactic as he carefully applied pressure around the area of impact on my spine.

I began to recount the events, but the pain was too great, now surging down my spine.

"Jesus!" I screamed as I jumped away.

"Green whistle", he directed his partner, a quick instruction that hinted at the relief soon to come.

Ah, the magic green whistle. We had already been acquainted, thanks, and would get to know each other intimately by the time I turned fifty-nine. I sucked down hard on the green whistle as though my life depended on it, but the paramedic gently pulled it away. A mild haze settled over my mind as the extreme pain began to abate slightly. By now, a small crowd of concerned neighbours had gathered, evoking a perverse thought as I reflected on how fortunate it was that the ill-fated trajectory of both me and the trailer hadn't wiped out any of their parked cars.

"OK folks, if we could just step back a bit and give us some space here," the paramedic calmly requested. "Ali, could you please move the ambulance up into the driveway?" the male paramedic instructed.

And just like that, I was on my way to Hornsby Hospital once more. "Gosh, how did this happen so soon?" I pondered, a sense of déjà vu washing over me. The ICU team ushered me into the emergency room, where they diligently checked my vitals and administered a dose of morphine to ease the pain. As I lay there, enveloped by the all-too-familiar hospital surroundings, a mix of emotions coursed through me. I couldn't help but wonder what series of events had led me back to this point, but I quickly pushed aside any inklings of dejection. Instead, I reminded myself of how fortunate I was to be alive, to have narrowly escaped another potential disaster. Yes, I had once again dodged a bullet, and for that, I felt a renewed sense of gratitude. As I reflected on the recent incident, I couldn't shake the feeling that there was something almost miraculous about the way things had unfolded. That split-second decision to redirect the careening trailer, the precise location I had chosen to jump—right where that tree had been felled years ago as if it had been perfectly orchestrated to deflect the trailer's path. Just as I was lost in these thoughts, the curtain was abruptly drawn aside, and my contemplation was interrupted.

"Hello, Jason. Fancy meeting you here again," the nurse quipped with a playful grin. "You must have really missed us to come back so soon." Her words were laced with a sense of familiarity and good-natured humour.

In my morphine daze, I couldn't recall the nurse's name, nor even read her name badge, but I did recognise this wonderful lady who had appeared like an angel in the emergency room on the day of my car accident. I smiled as best I could.

"Hi, yes, I missed you so much I had to come back again," I managed to roll my eyes and replied with a hint of humour.

Her name was Alice, and she was one of the wonderful nurses who had cared for me during my last desperate time of need. I've always believed that our nurses are the most underpaid people in our society, and no amount of money could adequately recognise the difference they make to so many lives, along with the many other carers in our medical and care system. We had a chat as Alice once again checked my chart and took some vital readings before they prepared to x-ray my spine. A couple of hours later, the x-rays were done, and they put in a request for them to be ready that evening. Around 11 pm, the attending doctor returned with the x-rays in his hand. Standing at the end of the bed, he carefully studied them, then informed me that I had fractured two vertebrae – to be exact, they were compression fractures. The prognosis was simple: rest and extreme caution for a few weeks. After having my gouge dressed and another shot of morphine, I settled in for an overnight stay as a precaution. The next morning, I got the green light to head home with a handful of potent painkillers and strict instructions to rest. I followed those instructions for a couple of days, but then boredom hit me like a ton of bricks, so I decided to return to my normal routine and waited for the fractures to heal.

In 1984, the itch to play football again emerged, and I decided to play in Sydney. A friend of mine introduced me to the coach of Sydney Olympic, a team with a strong history in the National League and a string of premiership victories under their belt. I was well aware that making a comeback at the top level after a six-year hiatus would be a daunting task, but I needed to test whether I still had what it took. I loved playing, and the thrill of being on the field again was invigorating. I worked hard to regain my fitness just in time for the round of preseason trial games, where I would compete for a coveted spot on the first team. The day of the first game approached swiftly, and soon enough, it was match day. We were due to play a local State League 1 side, and I had clinched a spot on the bench as a reserve player in the first team. To give me game time, the coach decided to play me for 30 to 35 minutes in the reserve game, which would also add a bit of pace to the reserve front line.

The game started well, and I managed to score a straightforward tap-in goal at the 10-minute mark. However, it seemed I was drawing more attention than I had anticipated. The towering sweeper, not as fleet-footed as I was, resorted to some less-than-sporting tactics – a bit of shirt tugging and a couple of trips – all to thwart my progress. Then came the pivotal moment at around the twenty-third minute when I swiftly pivoted on the halfway line to chase a well-placed through ball. The opposing number five was standing right behind me as I swivelled and took off past him in one smooth motion. I left him behind, surging forward up the pitch and recall fully expecting to secure my second of the game. Then, in an instant, I suddenly felt a bone-crushing impact on my shin, sending me crashing to the grass like a sack of potatoes. A few moments later, I summoned my strength and pushed myself up from the grass, determined to rise. However, as I attempted to put weight on my injured leg, an intense surge of pain shot through me, causing my leg to buckle beneath me, and I found myself once again collapsing onto the turf. The agonising sensation was relentless. After a brief interlude during which cold spray was applied to my throbbing shin, the coach made a decision. It was time for me to come off the field and wait to see if I'd be fit enough to participate in the first team game.

Sitting on the touchline, the throbbing in my leg seemed to intensify with each passing moment, and I couldn't ignore the swelling that was rapidly engulfing my leg below the knee. Being reliant on public transport, I had caught the train to get to the game, and I didn't have my own car at hand, nor would I have been able to drive in my condition. Fortunately, one of the parents of a fellow player came to my aid, kindly offering to drive me to a local medical centre. The name "Geoffrey Edelstein" was familiar, as these medical centres had been springing up all over Sydney, offering 24-hour medical care. Despite my unfamiliarity with the place, both of us were impressed by the plush reception area.

There was no Medicare system back then, and I was taken aback when they informed me that they wouldn't provide medical attention until I could pay for the appointment. Unfortunately, I hadn't brought much cash with me to the game, and I didn't own a credit card either. They did allow me to call my girlfriend, who told me that it would take about an hour to get there with money. I settled down on the expensive leather waiting lounge, still caked in mud, waiting for her arrival.

"What have you done?!" She exclaimed as she pushed through the doors and hurried across to the lounge where I sat.

"It doesn't look or feel good," I responded, wincing as I moved on the couch, trying to alleviate the discomfort.

We settled the payment at the counter, and after about ten minutes, the male doctor emerged through the door leading to the treatment area. It struck me as ironic that there had been no other patients during the entire hour I'd spent in agony on that couch. I couldn't help but find a small sense of satisfaction in the fact that their beige leather lounge was now caked with mud due to their refusal to provide immediate treatment. The doctor started asking me a series of questions as he carefully examined my leg and shin.

"Well, I don't think we need to x-ray your leg as it appears to be just severe bruising. I'll apply a pressure bandage to keep the swelling under control, and you can take some of these stronger painkillers. How does that sound?" he declared.

And that was that. As I hobbled out to the car and clumsily climbed into the passenger seat, I couldn't shake the feeling that something was off – that my leg was more than just bruised.

By Tuesday, my right lower leg was far from okay. It had turned various shades of black and blue, and the swelling hadn't let up. The pain was relentless, and I found it impossible to sleep or even put enough pressure on it to hobble around. So, I decided to make an appointment with another doctor. The following day, I visited the surgery and proclaimed that I thought I had broken my leg, revealing my now black and blue limb as the doctor knelt and began to softly press around the impacted area.

"Hmmm, I think we need to get you in for an x-ray straight away," he said.

"Do you think it is broken, doctor?" I asked.

"Well, let us see in a couple of days. Please book an appointment at the front desk for Thursday," he replied.

Two days later, I was back in the doctor's room, clutching my x-ray results.

"Yes, as I suspected, you have a complete fracture of your right fibula." he declared after examining the X-ray images.

"So that was pretty unprofessional of the clinic not to send me for an x-ray on Sunday?" I inquired with a hint of frustration.

"Most certainly! As it is now four days later, the bone will have already started to knit together again. There probably wasn't anything else that could have been done except possibly a full cast, which would have alleviated some pain and protected your leg over the last four days. I'm hoping that walking around on it during this critical period hasn't caused any displacement."

45

"Shit," I thought to myself.

"Let's get a partial cast on you then. I can't see much point in a full cast, given the delay."

The doctor picked up the phone, called reception, and asked his receptionist to push out his appointments for another hour. She came in and helped me hobble into the treatment room, where I waited for my leg to be plastered.

Life went back to normal once again, at least for the next few days, until the final icing on this cake was applied on Sunday of that week. I had been managing to get through showers so far with large plastic bags covering my foot and leg up to my knee, but on this Sunday, I must not have taped the top of the bag correctly. Within a few minutes of hopping in the shower, I felt dribbles of water running down my skin between the cast. An hour later, it began to soften and move. A few short hours after that, it was so unstable that there was little choice but to remove it completely. The entire leg ordeal had continued to unravel, evolving into an absolute disaster. For the following three weeks, I maintained my routine as best I could, exerting minimal pressure as I shuffled between places on my crutches just to carry out essential tasks. Despite the doctor's strict instructions to avoid walking on my leg for six weeks, I found myself increasingly restless due to the monotony, and a curiosity grew about the state of my healing leg. I wondered how it might influence my ability to resume running and exercise. One day, taking advantage of my girlfriend's absence for a shopping trip, I stealthily slipped out the front door wearing my running shoes. The experience was far from pleasant, yet it accomplished its intended purpose of encouraging me to start moving again. Movement is my life, and I've come to a firm realisation that overall wellbeing, both mentally and physically, is all about movement. Regardless of the circumstances, the imperative remains the same: you must keep moving.

In 1987, I made the decision to move away from Sydney to live on the Sunshine Coast in Southeast Queensland. While my career had only really focused on retail entertainment to that point, I had little or no idea of the employment or industry options that the Sunshine Coast might offer me. Despite the relatively shorter distance of around 1000 kilometres, compared to my earlier move all the way around the world to head down under in 1981, this decision was an enormous leap of faith and, with it, another exciting adventure and exciting new chapter in my life. After spending a week on the Sunshine Coast with my girlfriend, I fell in love with the area, especially Buderim, a volcanic mountain situated just a few kilometres inland from the Coast's glorious beaches. You may already know that Buderim is famous for its Ginger, celebrated for its health benefits, and for its distinctive homes perched on wooden or steel poles to accommodate the steep terrain of the mountain. By the end of that week, my heart was set on purchasing a quarter-acre of land at the base of Buderim, which was not yet titled. To inspect the land, I had to pick and fight my way through some dense bushland amongst the towering undergrowth and trees, and I couldn't shake the thought of encountering a venomous snake. As it turned out, my fears were not unfounded, as we would later frequently encounter snakes while clearing the land by hand. The process of obtaining the block of land's title would take an additional six months, during which I patiently waited to settle the purchase and make the payment. The land was worth thirty per cent more at settlement - a rewarding outcome considering I had not needed to pay the settlement balance until then.

Before long, we made the move up to Buderim, settling into a small, rented house at the mountain's peak and settled into a new life. In 1987, the Sunshine Coast had a population of roughly 120,000 people, with its economy heavily reliant on tourism and tourist dollars. This economic focus significantly narrowed the scope of employment opportunities available, prompting me to rethink my initial plans to engage in retail or start a business in that sector, potentially for another day.

As I weighed my options, I found myself gravitating toward the realm of finance and financial services, an area that had long intrigued me despite extraordinarily little experience. Scanning through local newspaper advertisements, one particular opportunity stood out: a position at Capita Financial Group, advertised by the regional manager, Lance. I phoned Lance, and we met a few days later. Lance took me through the role, responsibilities, objectives and pay, which was commission only. Despite the uncertainty of commission-based income, I was eager to dive into something new. Within a mere week, my first day in financial planning arrived—a day that marked the beginning of a career spanning over three and a half decades. By the second day, I found myself fully immersed in the challenges of the financial planning world, forced to adapt quickly and either sink or swim. I swam.

Later that year, I tied the knot and transitioned to married life, settling into a house I had acquired in Buderim. Within 15 months, our son, Alexander, entered the world, ushering in a period of profound transformation. Life changed completely. Alex faced his fair share of challenges, including frequent sleepless nights that tested us both to the limit over the next couple of years. A few years down the line, after designing and constructing our dream home, our daughter, Emma, came into the world.

Amidst these significant life changes, I made the decision to rekindle my passion for soccer. Joining the Buderim team in the Sunshine Coast's first division league, I played with fervour until I eventually hung up my boots at the age of 33. Throughout this journey, we clinched numerous premierships, and I secured several player awards. My soccer journey culminated in the grand finale of 1996, which we won in extra time. While my return to the sport was marked by its share of injuries, the only broken bone I sustained was my nose.

DAILY PRACTICE ACTION

Own Your Legacy

Imagine you are 65, retired, and sitting in your armchair with a cup of tea at age 65. Based on your accomplishments to date, how will you feel about your life?	
If you could accomplish anything, what achievements would fill you with pride?	

My greatest fear, surviving the frenetic chaos at the start of an
Ironman Triathlon.

UNLIMITED IS BUT ONE CHOICE AWAY

"May your choices reflect your hopes, not your fears."

— Nelson Mandela

Embracing change isn't a walk in the park; it demands the reshaping of our daily habits. It's no surprise that change can be quite unsettling for most individuals, mainly because it requires us to make sacrifices, exercise discipline, and opt for the more challenging path. The catalyst for substantial and positive behavioural transformation often arises from a life-altering event or a self-propelled epiphany prompted by a moment of deep introspection – a time when discomfort prevails, much like the unease I felt when reflecting on my own legacy some 25 years ago. In the face of such situations, a single decision can tip the scales. A single, well-considered choice has the potential to forever change our lives for the better. And that's precisely the transformation I underwent.

The complex nature of the human mind is something I'd never claim to fully grasp. So, bear with me as I simplify one of its most powerful components – decision-making. I do, however, comprehend the power of cultivating your mindset, empowering you to achieve anything and attain the seemingly impossible. Whether a decision leans toward reason or emotion, it holds the power to dramatically shift one's life in an instant. Decisions are rarely confined to one realm – they're often a fusion of conscious and subconscious, rational and emotional facets.

Research tells us that our brains handle as many as 35,000 decisions every day. While this might seem a little exaggerated, especially as you consider the decisions you consciously acknowledge making in just one day, let's provide some context because your awareness of important discretionary decisions is vital. Many of the decisions we make are critical, and they protect us from harm. Often, these are instinctive, such as gauging traffic before crossing a road or choosing which way to step out of a lift. However, in my experience, beyond essential functional or safety decisions, the utmost pivotal and life-altering choices are typically discretionary and can be boiled down to simple yes-or-no judgments. Often, they revolve around the decision to follow the path of greater challenge or the path of least resistance. While not life-threatening, these decisions can be life-changing, as they often involve individuals choosing the easier route to remaining within their comfort zone.

Hence, opting for the easier alternative might, at best, maintain the status quo for a while. However, over time, this path could lead to a decline in various aspects like circumstances, emotions, physical wellbeing, mental health, or overall happiness. On the contrary, selecting the more challenging route will alter your path and potential. That initial pivotal choice to embark on a journey demanding more effort, dedication, or compromise will shift your perspective from the impossible to the possible. Staying committed to the tougher option can bring about a complete transformation in your life for the better.

Upon reflection, have you encountered a situation in the past day, week, or recently where you opted for a less demanding path, avoiding greater effort than usual? That was me. I'm raising my hand here, too. Now, picture this: what if you added the nerve-racking proposition of confronting your most significant fear and choosing to confront it head-on? Well, that's exactly what unfolded one day in 1997 when a colleague and friend of mine named Rob and I were having a chat over a cup of coffee. During our conversation, Rob mentioned that he was forming a team for a corporate triathlon and asked if I wanted to be part of it. While I had heard about triathlons, I wasn't entirely sure about the specifics, so I asked Rob to elaborate. He went on to describe the race involving a 300-metre swim, a 12-kilometre bike ride, and a 3-kilometre run. Rob was planning a corporate entry with employees from Westpac Financial Planning. Initially, it sounded like a fun venture, and considering I could do the 3-k run standing on my head, I agreed to join. I started training, and a few weeks later, Rob and I met again to discuss strategies, or so I thought. As our conversation unfolded and Rob shared his triathlon experiences, he noticed my growing expression of concern.

"What's up, mate?" Rob asked.

"I had the impression we'd each handle one leg, and I'd be taking care of the run, not the swim or the bike. Are you saying I have to do all three?"

Rob laughed and said, "Of course, that is the point of a triathlon". An impending sense of doom washed over me, a fear that I hadn't experienced in years.

"Rob, I can't swim at all. In fact, I have a fear of putting my head underwater, even for a short distance in a pool. Plus, I haven't ridden a bike since I was a kid, and that was over 20 years ago. I don't even own a bike."

He glanced at me, gave a smirk, and said, "Come on, Dunny, you've got this. We need you."

And so, that was the pivotal moment, THE decision that changed my life. I chose to take the hardest road, confronting not only my intense fear of drowning but also my next greatest fear, failure. I was committed, and there was no turning back. All I needed to do was teach myself how to swim, borrow a bike, and start training as much as possible. It might sound straightforward, but it turned out to be a monumental challenge. Given that much of my life story relates to competing in triathlons and the significance of facing my two greatest fears that would completely change my life trajectory, it would be prudent to first explain the essence of a triathlon.

Triathlon is a multisport endurance event that comprises three distinct disciplines: swimming, cycling, and running. While there are many different triathlon distances, competitors progress through these components in sequence, with transitions in between. The event begins with a swim, followed by the first transition (T1), then the cycling segment, followed by the second transition (T2), and finally, it culminates with a run. Although the Ironman race popularised triathlon in the 1980s, the origins of the sport date back to the 1920s in France, where events involving running, cycling, and canoeing were held. The modern concept of triathlon took shape in 1974 with the inaugural race held in San Diego, California, featuring a "run-cycle-swim" format. The first Ironman Triathlon, the now-famous "swim-cycle-run" arrangement, was established in Hawaii in 1978.

It is quite clear then that the order of sports in a triathlon is not a necessity. However, if you consider all the consequences of a particular order, the current format becomes the obvious one. Among the three disciplines, swimming poses the greatest safety risk, and it is during this leg that most casualties occur in triathlons for obvious reasons: if you stop swimming, you drown. Given that triathlon events involve a large number of athletes with varying skill levels, opting for the swim leg as the starting point mitigates the risk of exhaustion-induced drownings. In fact, this approach has been shaped by past experiences, as earlier triathlons that scheduled swimming as the final leg resulted in tragic fatalities. Ironically, while writing this book, only a few weeks ago, two competitors died during the swim leg of a half Ironman race in Ireland. If you've ever observed the Tour de France, you're aware of the inherent risks, particularly during the final sprint. In those last moments, when athletes are exerting their last ounce of energy for that final push to the finish line, it's not uncommon to witness crashes occurring within the last kilometres of the race – a compelling reason to avoid concluding a triathlon with the cycling leg.

In most triathlons, drafting (following too closely to another competitor to gain an advantage) is illegal and prohibited. If a race were to commence with a mass bike start, regulating drafting would become an almost insurmountable challenge. A bike start would make no sense for all non-drafting triathlons (such as Ironman) and would take out any spectacle from drafting races (such as ITU). So, while not definitive, I hope you can appreciate the logic behind the order of events in a triathlon.

That evening, I contemplated the enormity of the challenges that lay ahead. I concluded that I probably couldn't die on the bike, but swimming amongst a large group of athletes in a tidal ocean river in Noosa, well, that was a different story. As I started to break down the problem of how to avoid drowning, and, assuming success in that, the next worst outcome would be suffering the embarrassment of needing to be rescued from the river in front of hundreds of spectators. Ironically, this fear would become a reality in another major race, a tale I'll recount in a subsequent chapter. For the moment, I set aside the prospect of humiliation and embraced the reality that I had a mere 10 weeks to shape my fate and evade death by drowning. To temper my deep-seated fear, I realised I needed to cultivate my confidence and belief in my capability to conquer a 300-metre swim. The path ahead was clear: I had to embark on a gradual journey, steadily building my prowess until I could confidently tackle that 300-metre distance within the span of about 7 weeks. The following morning, in preparation for my imminent visit to the swimming pool, I acquired swimming trunks, goggles, and a nose clip. This tactical approach was vital, given that I hadn't yet mastered the skill of breathing solely through my mouth. This was true even during my teenage years when I managed a rather clumsy 25-metre swim.

Throughout the course of that workday, my nervousness gained momentum, occasionally setting my heart racing at the mere

thought of stepping into the pool. It might sound irrational, but the very idea of heading to the pool had the uncanny ability to evoke such intense fear within me. Finally, as the clock struck 6 pm and darkness had descended, I parked my car outside the entrance of the indoor 25-metre swimming centre, fully aware that my next challenge awaited me within. Drawing in deep breaths in an effort to calm my nerves, I sat inside my car. The sheer magnitude of my fear immobilised me, that I sat there for a full ten minutes. My hands were sweating as I tried desperately to convince myself not to start the car and drive away. While the gravity of these passing minutes and the obsession over a decision wasn't immediately apparent, I did grasp the significance of this pivotal moment. It's possible that deep within me, I sensed the potential for life-altering change. For now, though, there was a battle raging in my mind. *

The voice of fear kept telling me to just go home and relax, that we could do this tomorrow when we were feeling more confident. It reasoned that with a generous ten-week buffer ahead, there was ample time to acquire the skill of swimming. I felt so sick that, at one point, I started the engine and shifted the gear into reverse. But something suddenly stopped me. It was the growing voice that represented my shame and my regret at flaunted opportunities, at decisions I had made to take the easier road. That was the voice that taunted and mocked me these days when I looked in the mirror. The very voice that emerged from my subconscious depths and inundated my senses within moments of sharing with a colleague or even a stranger—maybe during a social gathering with a drink in hand—the notion that I could have attained more, that I could have been someone successful. It was a declaration crafted to impress; one meant to showcase my inherent talent and capacity, yet, paradoxically, it communicated quite the opposite; I had the raw materials of talent and capability but lacked the heart, the bravery, and the discipline required to translate that dormant potential into tangible accomplishment. Right at this moment, this was the conflict that raged within me.

Later in life, I honed the skill of condensing crucial decisions into a mere four-second span, especially when it comes to the choice between taking the easier path or embracing the more challenging road. Four seconds evolved into a precious commodity, one that helped curb or nullify any inclination to procrastinate. Yet, it also fine-tuned my capacity to follow my gut, which, more often than not, proved accurate. With ample practice, this will become instinctive. But for now, I was still sat in the damn car.

Undoubtedly, this was yet another "sliding door" moment. To the casual observer or to anyone attempting to understand this seemingly small decision, this would not have seemed like a pivotal life-changing moment. However, that perception likely stems from their lack of conscious awareness of the significance of their own decisions to take their easier road. What I was acutely aware of at that moment was that succumbing to my fears would deal a fatal blow to my ongoing battle to feel good about myself. I also recognised that if I chose to step into that swimming centre, it would set off a chain reaction, necessitating countless decisions—perhaps even thousands of them—to consistently opt for the tougher road whenever confronted with challenging decisions to be made.

Fortunately, the voice that advocated for my need to change permanently couldn't be ignored. With a decisive turn of the ignition, I snatched my bag and strode towards the entrance. This was the moment—my opportunity to prove to myself that I could become more than I had been. The pool was packed with swimmers during the peak end of the working day period, with many lanes occupied by squad swimmers gliding through the water with grace while recreational swimmers crammed the remaining lanes and hustled for clear water. This was my worst nightmare.

I took a few deep breaths and slipped into the chilly water as a small space appeared between swimmers. I ducked under the water, pushed off with my feet, and I was away. In an instant, another swimmer's arm brushed my head, startling me to the surface. I gasped for air before submerging my head again and resumed my journey toward the opposite end of the pool. It felt like an eternity until I touched the other end of the pool, sucking in oxygen as I clung to the steel poolside handle and spat out some of the chlorinated water that I had swallowed. My swimming style—or lack thereof—demanded significant effort just to stay afloat and propel myself through the water. But I had achieved it. I had conquered 25-metres with my head submerged. A new realisation swept over me, silencing my doubts and fear— I could do this.

Five minutes elapsed as confident swimmers executed tumble turns beside me, completing laps in succession. Finally, I gathered my resolve, pushed off again, and set off towards the other end of the pool. Even in that relatively brief span, there were moments when I teetered on the edge of feeling overwhelmed, the looming possibility of drowning causing panic to surge within me. The urge to halt, to break the surface and gulp down air, was tantalisingly strong. Yet, I resisted. Two laps were under my belt, fifty metres conquered through two separate endeavours, and I launched into my third lap. Three down, just one more to go. My heart raced, a blend of adrenaline, fear, physical exertion, and panic coursing through my veins. Amidst this, a fellow swimmer behind me repeatedly knocked against my foot, prompting me to momentarily stand mid-pool and gasp for air. Allowing them to pass, I resumed my course, plunging back underwater to complete the final 12.5 metres. Crouching on my knees, I removed my goggles and released the nose clip, sucking in lungsful of air as my heart fought to reclaim its regular rhythm.

I had done it. One hundred metres, divided into four distinct attempts—undeniable progress towards that magical 300-metre target. While the drive back home was accompanied by the lingering scent of chlorine, doubts still clouded my mind. Could I possibly transform a safe, pool-contained swim into a 300-metre feat in a tidal river, free-for-all effort, without lane markers or the reassuring guidance of a lane rope? As my confidence wavered, I made a conscious choice to quell those uncertainties, redirecting my thoughts towards the outcome I wanted and desperately needed to accomplish.

"What is the outcome you must achieve?" I asked myself. This was an incredibly significant moment - representing the first instance where I transcended the tendency to become enmeshed in circumstances, an evolution from someone ensnared in the mire of problems to an individual who directed their energy toward outcomes. Little did I realise the magnitude of this epiphany at that precise instant. It was a revelation that would gradually evolve into a transformative practice—a life-changing one – that I will delve into shortly. Following a sleepless night, I embarked on a run the next day and rendezvoused with Rob to collect the road bike he graciously offered to lend me. As I loaded the bike into my car, I recounted the experience from the day before, which amused Rob greatly.

"She'll be right, mate," he declared through the window as I hopped into my car.

As I immersed myself in work and focused on learning to ride a bike again after a hiatus spanning over two decades, persistent flashbacks haunted me. They constantly reminded me of the impending return to the pool—where I would confront, once more, my profound dread of drowning. Despite these intrusive thoughts, I remained resolute. The following day, I replicated my routine, arriving at the pool at 6 pm, shrouded by darkness. I sat in the driver's seat for yet another ten minutes as I psyched myself to venture inside. Eventually, I took the plunge, and encouragingly, it took me slightly less time to achieve this time around.

My second session mirrored the first in many ways, though I made an effort to apply a fundamental rule I had come across concerning the development of fitness and endurance. The rule was simple: restrict the increase in training intensity to no more than 10% each week while structuring this progression within a 3-week cycle comprising two gruelling weeks and one week of reduced intensity to facilitate recovery. The fundamental principle at play here is that your body, particularly your muscles, demands a three-week period for recovery following a maximum training exertion. In contrast, recuperation from a significant endurance race can span up to two months. One of the most challenging concepts for many athletes to embrace is the necessity of providing their bodies with adequate rest. Strangely enough, this aspect proves to be one of the most challenging psychological adjustments. The truth remains: rest equals growth. This forms a cornerstone concept that many individuals either fail to recognise or opt to disregard, often to their detriment.

The psychological challenge in this context stems from athletes associating physical progress or advancements solely with maximal physical input and effort. Unfortunately, it's impossible to sustain increased volume and intensity over an extended period without providing the body with the necessary rest and recovery. This mistake is a common one, often committed by individuals returning to exercise. They tend to overdo their initial training schedule during the first week, driven by enthusiasm that transforms into overexertion—a challenge many are ill-prepared to face, considering their prolonged absence from exercise. This invariably leads to soreness, and if persisted upon, it can culminate in injuries. Such setbacks not only dampen or extinguish enthusiasm but also bring any newfound exercise routine to a grinding halt, with little likelihood of it ever being resumed.

So, here are my recommendations for success if you are returning to exercise or in the initial phases of your fitness journey:

- Exercise a maximum of three times per week for the 1st few weeks.

- Always leave a day in between each session.

- Limit exercise during this period to between 30 to 45 minutes

- Exercise at a moderate intensity – if you feel overexertion or a high heart rate and breathlessness, reduce your intensity.

- Do not increase volume for at least two weeks, then only 10% more week on week.

- Ensure you have a nutritious breakfast – skipping breakfast can have a detrimental effect on your physical and mental capabilities during the late afternoon, typically between 4 and 6 pm, on the same day.

- Make sure to replenish all essential nutrients within 20 minutes after completing your exercise. Your body functions as a sponge during this critical window, typically lasting between 15 to 30 minutes post-exercise. During this time, it efficiently absorbs nutrients, including carbohydrates, proteins, amino acids, vitamins, and more. When you get this right, your body will recover quickly and rebound faster, ready for the next session.

- Practice flexibility. Ultimately, it is the window to exercise wellbeing, enhanced capability, and healthy longevity. Whenever possible, consider scheduling a deep tissue massage every two weeks or on a monthly basis. This practice serves as a crucial component in maintaining your body's health and provides a lovely reward for your dedication and hard work. Another practice that significantly improves flexibility is the act of regularly rolling different parts of your body using a variety of rolling balls in various sizes.

- Eat well. Many individuals tend to consume more food than necessary, often of the wrong kind and at the wrong time. I'll revisit the significance of diet and share some effective dietary practices later on. However, it's crucial to understand that your overall wellness is heavily influenced by what you eat. In fact, approximately 80% of your wellbeing can be attributed to your dietary choices.

- Go to bed to sleep before 10, or better still, 9.30 pm, and then rise early.

- If possible, prioritise morning exercise to kick-start your day with enhanced cognitive function and improved circulation. Exercising in the morning can significantly enhance your overall wellbeing, setting a positive tone for the rest of your day.

In preparation for my upcoming swim training session, I had already devised a strategy to boost my progress. Instead of swimming the first two 25-metre laps separately, as I had in previous sessions, I aimed to complete them in a single, continuous effort. I planned to implement the same approach for the final two laps as well. My primary goal was to enhance my confidence, given the deep-seated fear I grappled with. Once I successfully accomplished this, my subsequent session would closely resemble the previous one, with the addition of an extra twenty-five-metre solo lap at the end. This incremental approach allowed me to gradually enhance both my fitness and confidence, ultimately working my way up to swimming twelve consecutive laps, achieving a total distance of three hundred metres. The car park ordeal repeated itself before the next two planned sessions, though the duration of my internal debate gradually dwindled. It went from twenty minutes to ten, then further down to just five minutes before I finally implemented the four-second rule I had devised. About five weeks before the race, I achieved a major milestone by completing my first continuous three-hundred-metre swim. This accomplishment brought immense relief and significantly bolstered my confidence. However, the importance of maintaining a calm and composed mindset, especially on race day, in case things didn't go as planned, remained at the forefront of my mind.

The big day had finally arrived, and I embarked on a nervous journey to the race start at 5 am on that Saturday morning. The BRW Corporate Triathlon held great significance back in those days, boasting over 1,500 total competitors, with thirty-five teams from our banking division alone. Consequently, each wave set off with all three team members together, meaning 105 individuals would start in my wave. Feeling somewhat bolder, a trait that had often led me astray, I positioned myself at the front of the group, anticipating that my swift running abilities on the beach and into the water would provide me with a strong head start.

The starting gun sounded, creating a sudden wave of bodies in motion, with everyone initially sprinting and then executing quick dives in and out of the water, progressing until the water reached waist height. A final dive brought us all to a horizontal position in the water. As I had anticipated, I found myself in the lead when we initially dove into the river. However, my flawed strategy quickly unravelled within the first 40 metres or so as we approached the first turning buoy. It descended into chaos, with 105 swimmers converging and jostling for position at the turning point. In that moment, I found myself engulfed by a frenzy of thrashing arms and legs, pushing me underwater and triggering panic as I fought to keep my head above the surface. It must have appeared quite peculiar as I resorted to a backstroke and frog kicking, all while navigating the buoy and contending with the flurry of arms from other swimmers. I probably resembled a dying turtle as I rounded the buoy, eventually rolling over onto my back—a move that served both as a survival instinct and a means of regaining my composure. To my disappointment, my position in the race was far from ideal, with only about 20 of the 100-strong field of swimmers trailing behind me. Nevertheless, I swiftly flipped back over and began swimming as if my life depended on it, which, in a way, it did.

The swim in Noosa River that day felt interminable as if it had stretched on for an hour. Although in reality, it was only six minutes. I raised my head periodically to ensure I wasn't veering off course across or upriver until I eventually encountered the last buoy, signalling the need to turn back toward the riverbank. At last, my hand brushed the river's sandy bottom as I tried to stand upright, and my lungs seemed determined to escape my mouth in their frantic quest for air. My exertion had caused much of the blood in my body to concentrate in my upper body and arms, making me wobble and stumble back into the water as I attempted to rise. With the knowledge that hundreds of spectators were watching from the shore, I turned around to see how many competitors were still behind me. Unfortunately, there were none, not a single one. For a brief moment, I felt deflated and embarrassed, but then a surge of elation washed over me as I grasped the significance of two achievements: first, I hadn't drowned, and second, I didn't require rescue by one of the attending lifeguards.

"You can do this", I encouraged myself, finding motivation as I sprinted toward the transition area where my bike awaited. By the time I had rolled my bike out of transition and hopped onto the saddle, my legs had regained their sense of belonging to me, and I pedalled with determination. As the bike leg progressed, I continued to overtake numerous competitors in my category until I dismounted and hustled into the transition zone one final time.

"You've got this, Jason," I whispered to myself under my breath as I slipped out of my cycling shoes and attempted to launch myself into the run. It's a strange sensation you can only truly appreciate if you've ever competed in a triathlon. You've been pedalling as hard as you can during the bike leg, using entirely different muscle groups that require an entirely different blood flow. You soon understand this phenomenon when you've raced for the first time. In a nutshell, your legs don't feel like they belong to you – not an easy thing to navigate when you're trying to run fast. One training technique I picked up later in my triathlon journey, like many serious athletes, is the "brick" training session. In a brick session, you ride for about 5 minutes, hop off the bike, and then run a kilometre. You repeat this several times to help your body adapt to the transition from cycling to running muscles.

As I made the transition to the running portion and started over-taking fellow runners, my excitement surged, almost intoxicating. With each runner I passed and the increasing speed as the race progressed, my enthusiasm grew. Crossing under the finish arch to complete my first triathlon was every bit as exhilarating as I had imagined. I collapsed onto the grass, rolling onto my back, waiting for the encouraging cheers of my teammates. Strangely, they didn't arrive as quickly as I expected. So, I sat up and scanned the area for them. They were nowhere to be seen.

After a couple of minutes, I spotted Rob crossing the finishing line, followed shortly by Dan. In my adrenaline-fueled state, I had managed to pass them both during the run leg without even noticing. We shared stories from the race and basked in the morning sunshine as we watched other participants finish their races. Among the diverse crowd, there were people of all shoe sizes, body shapes, backgrounds, and cultures, but they all shared a common goal: to finish the race and be their best. We took the obligatory team photos, wearing our bright red Westpac spandex singlets and equally vibrant red swimming trunks, an outfit that was somewhat embarrassing. After packing up our gear, we headed into Noosa for a celebratory breakfast before making our way home. A sense of euphoria filled the air, not just because I had finished, but because I had finished strongly, securing the 8th place in our category after exiting the water dead last in 105th position.

By that evening, my mind was already consumed by thoughts of "what's next" and "how can I do better." I was undeniably hooked, and my life had taken a dramatic turn. The sense of accomplishment was genuinely intoxicating. In the following weeks, life settled back into its usual routine, but my hunger for challenges, coupled with an insatiable curiosity about what

I could tackle next, consumed me. As I returned to my training regimen, I began searching for my next meaningful and demanding challenge, one that would test my limits, excite my mind, and push every boundary I could imagine. Then, one day in April, as I relaxed on the couch sipping coffee and smoking a cigarette while watching Australia's leading sports program, "The Wide World of Sports," my attention was suddenly seized by the commentator's introduction to the next segment of the show:

"Well, there is one endurance sporting event that is often hailed as the toughest one-day sporting challenge on the planet. In recent years, it has captured the world's attention with its displays of courage and superhuman strength, epitomised by the unforgettable moment when Julie Moss repeatedly collapsed near the finish line on Ali'i Drive during the Hawaii Ironman Triathlon World Championships. She crawled on her hands and knees to reach that elusive finish line. This event consists of a staggering 3.8-kilometre ocean swim, followed by a gruelling 180-kilometre bicycle ride through the harsh and windswept lava fields of the Big Island of Hawaii, and then culminates with a marathon-length 42-kilometre run through the scorching temperatures of the Energy Lab. And all of this in one day and all as fast as you can go".

"Wow," I exclaimed, my eyes glued to the screen. This is it. This is what I must do. While I had heard of this legendary event in passing before, I had never truly grasped its significance. Now, it had my undivided attention. For the next hour, I sat transfixed as I watched both professional athletes and amateur age group competitors push themselves to their absolute limits and, in some cases, well beyond. One athlete, in particular, captured my imagination—an Australian named Chris Leigh.

Chris was racing among the professionals and found himself in fourth place as he made his way down the iconic Ali'i Drive toward the finish line, where so many dreams become reality. However, as he approached the finishing carpet and ramp, something went terribly wrong. He began to wobble and stagger, his arms flailing uncontrollably, until he finally collapsed onto the pavement. What happened next was a display of sheer determination and resilience. For the next six agonising minutes, Chris fought with every ounce of strength left in him to finish the race. He would stand, then fall, crawl, and even vomit repeatedly, but despite the relentless screams of encouragement from the crowd, he could not muster more than a few metres at a time. But he would not quit.

In the end, to spare his health, race attendants gathered around him, lifted him onto a stretcher, and carried him over the finish line in fifth place. Chris's body had completely shut down after enduring eight and a half brutal hours of racing at top speed under the scorching Hawaiian sun. Chris recovered, but his road to recovery was not easy, requiring urgent surgery to remove the four inches of intestine that had died due to the race's extreme demands.

The extraordinary courage and determination on display during this legendary event had me utterly captivated and inspired. I was completely committed to this audacious goal, hook, line, and sinker. Right then and there, I made the firm decision that I would one day qualify for and compete in the Hawaii Ironman. Later that very same day, I documented my goal and began to dream, even though I had no inkling of how I would bridge the gap between a 300-metre swim and the demanding 3.8-kiloetre ocean swim, let alone magnify the 12-kilometre bike ride by a factor of 15, and then endure a marathon run that was 14 times the length of the 3-kilometre run in the BRW Triathlon. All of this was to be undertaken in the scorching heat and the unrelenting trade winds, which could gust up to 80 kilometres per hour and abruptly change direction during the day, subjecting athletes to punishing headwinds on a 180-kilometre bike ride. The path ahead was daunting, but my determination burned brighter than ever.

That night, I was brimming with enthusiasm as I delved deeper into planning. My new goal was to qualify for and compete in the Hawaii Ironman within the next 5 years. What seemed like an impossible feat just weeks ago was now firmly, in my mind, possible and within my grasp, thanks to my previous choices of taking the tougher road. I was on my way to becoming unlimited.

To make this dream a reality, I needed to first qualify at a full-length Ironman event, which meant I had to excel at a half Ironman. So, my sights were set on the Australian Ironman in April 1999, pre-ceded by the half Ironman on Stradbroke Island in Queensland, scheduled for December 1998, approximately six months away. I started to craft my planning strategy and develop a 90-Day High-Performance Plan (HPP), a technique I will share in later chapter. The HPP would become my essential companion for achieving peak performance in sports, life, and business from that day on. Once I was able to perfect this process, I would enable hundreds of other people. My strategy was to create a meticulously designed schedule that progressively increased training volume and mileage, aligning with races that grew in length and difficulty, marking specific milestones along the way. To optimise their potential through the 90-Day High-Performance Plan and the subsequent daily practice.

Identifying a series of local races that slightly surpassed the challenges I had faced in the Noosa Corporate Triathlon, I eagerly registered for the Noosa Triathlon. This renowned event encompassed a 1500-metre swim, a 40-kilometre bike ride, and a ten-kilometre run. The timing was perfect, with only five weeks remaining until the Stradbroke half Ironman.

A few days later, I came across news of a new half Ironman event set to take place during the Australian winter in one of the country's hottest climates, Cairns in North Queensland. It dawned on me immediately that this would serve as an ideal test for the half Ironman qualifier scheduled for December 1998. The race would kick off in the picturesque coastal town of Port Douglas, located approximately seventy kilometres north of Cairns, commencing from the stunning yet challenging Four Mile Beach. I was unaware at the time of signing up that Four Mile Beach was one of the most formidable places to swim, mainly due to its residents—giant saltwater crocodiles, various large sharks, sea snakes, and deadly stinging jellyfish. However, the race organisers had wisely chosen June for the event, ensuring it fell outside of the stinger season at least.

On June 7, 1998, I packed up my gear and took a flight to Cairns. This marked my first encounter with packing my bike for air travel. I secured it within a sturdy, thick cardboard bike box borrowed from a local bike shop, hoping it would endure the journey unscathed. My good friend, Trish, met me at Cairns airport and couldn't help but notice my anxious demeanour while I waited by the oversized baggage counter tucked in the corner of the airport. I waited and waited as Trish attempted to lift my spirits. On that day, I learned for the first time that bikes often take their sweet time to emerge from an aeroplane's cargo hold. When the dented and battered box finally slid through the oversized luggage exit door, my heart skipped a few beats. "Oh shit, perhaps they tossed it off the plane," I remarked as I retrieved it using the hand-carry holes punched into either side of the sturdy cardboard box. In the parking lot, we grappled with the box until most of it was securely nestled in Trish's sporty hatchback, and then we tied down the rear hatch to the locking mechanism to keep it in place. Luckily, the drive to her house in nearby Trinity Beach only took about 20 minutes, and soon, I was unpacking the box while silently praying that there was no damage. Fortunately, everything was in perfect condition.

That evening, we talked about the race over dinner. Our conversation revolved around the upcoming race, and I shared some details of the course. Trish couldn't help but laugh as she described the array of creatures that frequented the waters off Four Mile Beach, including enormous saltwater crocodiles, various species of sharks, and the notorious box jellyfish. As if I didn't have enough to worry about already. Over the next few days, our journey took us to Port Douglas, where my nerves kicked into high gear. With a multi-discipline race of such epic proportions, combined with the vast distances and the unpredictability of nature, there is always an endless list of potential obstacles that could derail your efforts, even if my mind and body were in top form on race day. My confidence took another hit as I strolled along the beach, observing the powerful waves and the challenging swell that followed the sets, which would pose a considerable challenge for navigation and survival. It was all the more daunting considering I had absolutely zero experience swimming in the open, untamed ocean. Nevertheless, I needed to focus on what I could control.

Race morning arrived with surprising speed, following my usual pattern of fragmented sleep as my mind ran through every detail I could possibly obsess over. When my alarm finally broke the early morning silence at 4 am on Saturday, I felt a mix of exhaustion and

exhilaration, likely fuelled by adrenaline. With the car loaded the night before, we hit the road by 4:30 am, eating a silent breakfast en route. The 45-minute drive was subdued, almost eerie, but Trish understood that I needed this time for introspection and left me to my thoughts. This was the moment I'd been building toward, and today, I'd need to summon everything I had to conquer this formidable challenge. This was finally it.

The weather forecast predicted mid-twenties temperatures with 85% humidity and strong, gusty southerly winds, which would create a choppy swell. Hopefully, the swell wouldn't pick up too much until after we completed the swim. However, a relentless headwind over the seventy-kilometre coastal route and through the cane fields was a likely prospect. Amidst the bustling preparations in transition, I focused on the myriad of tasks at hand, attempting to block out the factors beyond my control. The weather and its potential impact loomed over us as we approached the moment to head down to the beach. Race mornings are always charged with intensity as everyone follows their individual routines, many immersed in music to prepare their minds. Finally, the time came for me to remove my headphones, shuffle quietly toward the starting line, and let the race begin.

Six hundred souls, each driven by their unique reasons, stories, motivations, inspirations, or perhaps inner demons to confront, had gathered at the water's edge, anticipating the starter's gun. It was the calm before the storm, that fleeting moment before chaos erupted. Then, as if on cue, the gun resonated through the air, and we surged collectively into the rolling surf. "You've got this, Jason," a reassuring voice echoed in my head as I dove through the first wave, then the second, my feet leaving the sandy bottom and my arms propelling me forward with each stroke.

In the midst of this, a massive stingray glided beneath me, mere inches from my body, catching me off guard and eliciting a moment of panic. I instinctively raised my head, gasping for air, until a fellow swimmer accidentally clouted me in the head, snapping me back to reality. To regain my composure, I focused on my strokes, determined to avoid swallowing mouthfuls of saltwater as I settled in beside a couple of other swimmers. "There's no turning back now, Jason," I reminded myself. Today, I would succeed.

It was going to be a long day, albeit not as gruelling as a full Ironman, yet both races hinged on the crucial element of self-pacing. My strategy was clear: race smart, stick to my carefully planned pacing, and resist the temptation to let adrenaline and my well-rested muscles from tapering over the last three weeks push me to go too hard too soon. I needed to avoid getting caught up in bravado and the excitement of competition and maintain restraint during the initial hour or so of the race. Pacing, however, had always been my nemesis and would prove to be my greatest adversary in my journey of competing in ultra-endurance events. Pacing is the Achilles' heel that plagues most individuals participating in races lasting longer than 25 minutes.

The swim turned out to be more challenging than I had initially expected. Not only was it the longest distance I had ever attempted, but ocean swimming in strong swells, without the reassuring presence of lane ropes to guide you, adds another 25% in difficulty and distance. Nonetheless, I felt a rush of elation upon completing the swim, thinking that the toughest part of the day was behind me—at least, that's what I believed at the time. After making the long run from the receding tide to the T1 transition area in the beach car parking, my transition went relatively smoothly with no immediate hiccups. I hopped onto my bike for the two 10-kilometre loops around Port Douglas and then onto the daunting 70-kilometre stretch heading south towards T2 in the heart of Cairns along the scenic boulevard.

As I left Port Douglas and merged onto the coastal road, which would run alongside the ocean for the next 50 kilometres or so, I felt reasonably good. The scenery was nothing short of breath-taking along this picturesque coastline, offering stunning vistas for the first part of the ride. The road meandered and undulated, presenting its own set of challenges, particularly in segments frequently exposed to the increasingly fierce winds that were growing stronger by the minute. Eventually, the relentless gusts began to take their toll on my legs. With about 25 kilometres remaining until the transition to the run leg and amidst the cane fields, we were completely exposed to the prevailing wind. Some gusts were so forceful that they almost brought my bike wheels to a standstill. The sight of the cane plants, typically standing upright, now bent almost parallel to the ground, left no room for doubt about what we would need to endure until the completion of the bike leg.

Traffic added another layer of complexity. Unlike most half, and full, Ironman triathlons that are afforded the luxury and relative safety of being closed off to vehicles, at least in the direction of the cycling route, the coastal road was the sole main route between Cairns and Port Douglas. Consequently, it could not be temporarily closed to traffic. Lost in deep concentration and reflection, I was abruptly jolted from my thoughts when Trish drove by on the coastal road. Her words of encouragement not only lifted my spirits but also rekindled my focus. The last twenty-five kilometres of the bike leg turned into a taxing mental and phys-ical challenge that required every ounce of energy I had left in my locker. As I approached the outskirts of town, the throngs of people lining the route grew significantly as we reached the

Esplanade along the shoreline. The Esplanade was typically bustling with tourists and locals throughout the year, making it a popular spot for walking, biking, and running. Today, it was alive with people who had come to witness the intriguing spectacle unfolding in their own backyard.

On this muggy day, many were enjoying the adventure pools built along the Esplanade, a response to the presence of dangerous creatures lurking in Cairns' waters year-round. Regardless of how drained you feel during a race like this, a large and enthusiastic crowd of spectators can lift your spirits, even if only for a few precious moments, especially when you're at your lowest. Transition 3 (T3) was now in sight, and it was time to shift my focus to the transition process, replenishing my energy with nutrition, and making the necessary moves to prepare for the run. While not scorching, the temperature had reached 26 degrees Celsius with 90% humidity, which was enough to sap the life out of you after three or more hours of intense exertion. To put things in perspective, experts consider the ideal temperature for running a marathon to be around 7 degrees Celsius, as seen at events like the Boston Marathon, and humidity levels ranging from 30 to 50%. So, while I would go on to race in considerably hotter conditions during my career, this was far from ideal and distinctly hot for my first ultra-endurance event.

The first 200 metres of the run seemed manageable, buoyed by the energy of the cheering crowds lining the streets after spending two and a half hours cycling virtually alone and the relief of completing two of the three disciplines. However, this initial surge of exuberance quickly gave way to the harsh reality of exhaustion and the daunting prospect of a 21-kilometre run on already fatigued legs in the sweltering Cairns afternoon. After about 10 kilometres, as I wrestled with my thoughts, calculating the remaining distance versus my level of exhaustion, the voice of reason briefly prevailed, and I decided to walk. About 200 metres later, I pushed myself to jog once more, running as far as I could before walking became inevitable again. The scorching heat was making my head spin, and I could feel the pressure building within my skull. This pattern repeated itself twice more before I managed to summon the strength for one final push to run across the finish line. I had completed it! I could endure a half Ironman distance. This achievement filled me with confidence as I began to strategise how I could compete at the required pace in the Ironman qualifier on Stradbroke Island in a few months, with the goal of earning a spot in the Australian Ironman the following May.

Every Ironman race is the same distance, despite often vastly different conditions and terrains they present. From the chilly fresh waters of Lake Taupō on a February morning to the 95% humidity and 37 degrees Celsius of Malaysia or the scorching heat and unforgiving lava fields on the Big Island of Kona, Ironman consists of a 3.8-kilometre open water swim, a 180.2-kilometre non-drafting bike ride, and a 42.2-kilometre marathon run.

These days, there are fifty-three qualifying races held around the world, attracting around 100,000 athletes. Many of these athletes have already qualified through pre-qualifying races, and they compete for 2,500 coveted spots at the Hawaii Ironman World Championships. Back in 1999, when I first raced, there were fewer spots available, and they were in extremely high demand. In fact, each year, 10 places were auctioned off to the highest bidder. It's quite staggering that the demand to participate in this historic and legendary race was so high that individuals were willing to pay up to $50,000 US to secure a spot on the starting line.

Balancing the demands of work, family, home life, and an inten=
sified training schedule to build confidence and achieve the
necessary fitness and speed for Ironman qualification presented its
own set of challenges. My mindset had to shift from simply finishing
a long race to competing with others for coveted qualification
spots. This shift in focus led me to prioritise technique improvement across all three disciplines, as well as incorporating speed
work and hill training into my routine—lots of hills. Fortunately,
living atop Buderim Mountain offered a multitude of hilly routes,
with approximately seven different roads leading up to various
points across the mountaintop, providing plenty of options for
gradient selection in my training regimen.

The Stradbroke half Ironman rolled around quickly, and before I
knew it, we were travelling over on the ferry from Brisbane across
Moreton Bay. After checking into our hotel, we decided to explore
the island and take a look at the bike course, half of which ran
through private land not available to the public, so we couldn't
access it before the race. The run course, on the other hand,
consisted of a multi-lap, undulating route with plenty of steep
hills, which was just the kind of terrain I favoured and would help
compensate for my nemesis, the ocean swim. The day before
the race, nerves set in as I tried to relax and stop worrying that
everything was organised for this crucial test. I reminded myself
of the hard work I had put in and the reasons I was racing, urging
myself not to worry about things beyond my control.

The next morning, after meticulously checking my bike and
equipment in transition, we embarked on a long walk down the
beach. The tide dictated that we would have to start the swim
from the beach, head left to swim alongside the shoreline, then
turn left again and head back towards the beach. Memories
of Four Mile Beach came rushing back as we strolled along the

1.5-kilometre stretch of beach. When the starting gun sounded, an army of around 1,200 athletes threw themselves into the waves, repeatedly duck-diving until the sand disappeared below. I lost count of how many mouthfuls of salty water I swallowed due to my inexperience with ocean swimming. But I kept reminding myself that I had to get through this, and then everything would be okay. It wasn't until I exited the water and ran into transition that I had any idea of my position in the field. There were still enough bikes racked, so I knew I wasn't last. We all sped along the long stretches of road, aided by a healthy tailwind, and I settled in to focus on catching as many riders as I could. Midway through the return leg, my back began to tighten up and spasm, a problem that would persist throughout my triathlon years due to the hours spent in the aero position. Much later, this issue would develop into a severely bulging disc pressing into my spinal canal. The worst bouts of this condition would leave me in the hospital paralysed for a few days, and on one occasion when I flew to Melbourne for an overnight business trip, it would necessitate me contorting and trying to drag myself up for an hour or so to stand in the morning. Occasionally, the pain was simply too much, and I would pass out. It took six days before I could manage a return flight back to Sydney.

The bike leg was challenging, as is typical in any 90-kilometre non-drafting ride, where you're averaging over 35 km/h. I had to dig extremely deep on the final return. When I exited the transition for the run, my legs were tired but filled with determination. I knew this was my strongest leg, and my mission was to catch as many people as possible. I imagined that the next person in front of me would take my qualifying spot if I didn't catch them. The constantly undulating run course, weaving its way around the town and local residential streets, took its toll on many runners as they struggled to find their rhythm. I was flying, however, and eventually finished strongly, though completely exhausted from giving it my all. I had no idea where I had placed in the field.

Jen and I had to get back to Brisbane that night for work on Monday morning, so we left straight after the race and headed home on the ferry. The next few days brought a mix of delight at finishing the race well and some anxiety as I waited for the results and the final Ironman allocation slots. This nervous wait would become synonymous with Ironman racing, as each year from now on, I would have to go through the same process to qualify for the local Ironman event. In this particular race, athletes who had opted to qualify would be notified and then had to confirm their acceptance within 24 hours. If they didn't confirm, the spot would roll down and be offered to the next-placed person. I knew I was two places away from qualifying, and I needed two people to decline. I stayed close to my email inbox during those two days until I finally received the notification I had been so desperately waiting for – I had qualified!

Qualifying for the Ironman was an incredibly significant step for me, both in terms of my confidence and the fact that I had finally booked my place in my first Ironman race. Within a couple of weeks, my body had started to recover from the race, and with the impending holidays, it was the ideal time to increase my training volume and intensity to all new heights. I had allowed for a three-to-four-week taper leading up to the Ironman race in May, which gave me four months to go hard until then. I needed to build enough confidence and fitness to finish the Ironman in a reasonable time and in reasonable physical condition. This would be no small feat, and I was fully aware of the monumental challenge ahead.

It was the 20th of December, and the Sunshine Coast greeted me with a splendid day. The weather forecast predicted a pleasant 32 degrees Celsius, and my plan for the day included a moderate speed fifty-kilometre recovery ride following my recent race at Stradbroke. Later, I intended to join my children and Alex and Emma, for a trip to the beach, making the morning feel promising and bright. As I cruised over the Maroochy River bridge en route to Coolum Beach via the Sunshine Way, it was 8 am, which counted as rush hour, or as close as it gets on the Coast. At this juncture, I must confess I have always loved the feeling of warm sun on my skin, particularly when at the beach or during my runs.

That said, this was the first, and soon to be the only time, that I had ridden my bike shirtless. Cars cruised past as I turned onto the Sunshine Way, and there were no noteworthy incidents to report. Why is this observation pertinent, you may wonder? Well, it's because training in Queensland has often proven challenging for me. I've encountered unprovoked hostility, harassment, aggressive motorists pushing me off the road, and even objects thrown at me from passing cars at high speeds. Try to imagine the impact of being hit by an apple thrown from a car travelling at 110 KMPH. However, on this particular morning, everything seemed to be going smoothly.

The technique that I practised most during my rides was positioning myself forward in an aerodynamic posture using specialty aero bars. Ironman triathlons strictly enforce non-drafting rules, emphasising the critical importance of maintaining an aerodynamic position. However, this stance presents its own set of challenges, which are magnified in Ironman as opposed to cycling in general. Most cyclists rarely adopt this awkward and compromising position, especially when riding in groups, as they don't receive significant benefits from it. This specialised position is typically reserved for athletes preparing for time trial competitions, a rarity unless you're a professional. Frequent use of this aero position, as required for most of my Ironman pursuits, takes a toll on the back, sometimes leading to severe issues and spasms. Furthermore, riding in a tucked aero position with extended aero bars compromises bike handling capabilities and reduces overall awareness of one's surroundings, as you are hunched over and less agile.

On that particular morning, I relished the sensation of the air flowing around me, basking in the warmth of the sun on my skin. The ocean appeared exceptionally beautiful as I pedalled along Coolum Beach before turning around shortly thereafter to spin home. As I departed Marcoola and approached the turnoff leading to Twin Waters Resort, I couldn't help but think that the world felt like a wonderful place. This feeling persisted as I navigated the wide, sweeping bend.

Then, bang!

A loud noise broke the serenity. It was the sound of scaffolding bouncing on the steel bed of a large flatbed truck approaching from behind. In an instant, I felt a hard impact, and before I knew it, I had vanished from the view of the following motorists. I crashed down onto the road, sliding along the asphalt on my backside and back.

Here I was once more, the victim of a serious accident, and jumping to my feet in shock. Concerned motorists pulled over to assist me as I skipped around in circles, still reeling from the shock. One compassionate man gently guided me by the arm to sit down on the curb to rest. My face had apparently turned pale as the blood drained from it, and I was beginning to feel dizzy. I hunched forward, resting my head in my hands, as another helpful individual doused water over my forehead to provide relief. Struggling to maintain my grip on consciousness, I overheard muffled voices behind me discussing the potential extent of my injuries. The lady who had initially come to my aid was now speaking with the ambulance operator in an alarmingly concerned tone, which left me with a sinking feeling.

"Yes, it's an emergency, and you need to get someone here as soon as possible," she urgently conveyed to the operator. There was a brief pause as she listened attentively to the instructions coming through the phone.

"Ok, good, yes, I will do that for him while we wait," she responded.

The instruction was clear: I was not to lie down under any circumstances, and they needed to keep me conscious.

"Oh, Jesus, it hurts," I moaned as the familiar pain began to set in once the shock started to wear off.

"It's ok, Jason, just try to relax and breathe, and the ambulance will be here very shortly."

"What have I done to myself?" I asked. "I can't see."

"You've hurt your back. Well, you've lost some skin," at which point I became acutely aware of the pain caused by sitting on my butt. Without notice, I stood.

"I can't sit down." I declared. To which the lady circled behind me to see what had caused me to suddenly jump up.

"Here, lean on one of us," she said as another guy moved to stand beside me. The lack of skin would have been alarming and raised more questions if I hadn't been preoccupied with the effort of remaining on my feet. I raised each arm one after the other to assess the cause of the searing pain in both my elbows. Due to the way I had landed on my rear, I had instinctively extended my elbows to absorb some of the impact when I hit the road. A quick glance confirmed the extent of the injury, with my elbows exposed down to the bone. This didn't help my already nauseous state, but I managed to avoid fainting before the ambulance arrived.

"What have you done to yourself this time, Jason?" echoed in my head, sounding eerily similar to the first words spoken by the paramedic at the scene. Bizarrely, there was a fleeting moment in the ambulance when I was thankful, I wasn't being transported back to Hornsby Hospital in Sydney, which was about a thousand kilometres away from where I was now. "This is serious," I thought as they needed to transport me while I lay on my stomach in the ambulance. Thank goodness for the Green Whistle, which I had both missed and not missed. "My old friend," I thought as I inhaled again, approaching Nambour Hospital.

As they admitted me and checked my vital signs, they inquired about whom they should contact. I knew that Jen would likely be occupied at that time of day, but I asked them to attempt to reach her. If that failed, I suggested calling my good friend George, a colleague from Westpac, who would be a reliable contact. As it turned out, it was George's voice I heard first when I arrived in the emergency room. The nurse had been delicately cleaning the areas around the primary abrasions, taking care to avoid the large open wounds that would require different care in the coming days. I was lying on my stomach, facing the wall, when another nurse pulled back the curtain. While all my injuries were stinging intensely, I don't think I fully grasped the extent of the damage until I heard George's immediate reaction to my appearance.

"Shit, what the bloody hell have you done," he exclaimed. "Oh god, you poor sod".

My heart sank instantly. From the moment I was loaded into the ambulance several hours ago, I had been convincing myself that my training wouldn't be disrupted for long and that I'd be back to exercising within a week, just as I usually did when facing severe injuries. George stayed with me for a while, providing company until the medical staff needed to attend to my wounds. This time, the nurses attempted to flush out some of the dirt, tiny stones, and bits of bitumen from the open wounds. The pain was excruciating, and I couldn't help but scream. To put my condition into perspective, I had four major areas where two or three layers of skin had been torn away. Both buttocks and most of my back had large sections of skin removed.

Fortunately, the Gods had been smiling down on me as there was no bone damage, and I had also escaped any substantial harm to my skull or neck. Instead of succumbing to self-pity, I immediately felt a surge of gratitude for not experiencing more severe and potentially life-threatening injuries. I had swiftly transformed my terrible misfortune into a deep sense of thankfulness. It's remarkable how you can influence your mind so effectively and rapidly when you've had enough practice and discipline. Gratitude, by the way, is one of the most potent promoters of wellbeing, and I would highly recommend incorporating gratitude practice into your daily life. I'll delve into this technique and its power more in the following chapters.

I was discharged from the hospital that evening, and my ex-wife picked me up, driving me back to the house in Buderim. I had to lie face down across the back seat, despite the strong pain-killers I had taken. Sleep eluded me that night, and by morning, I was utterly exhausted. There was to be no respite, though, as I had no choice but to stand all day to avoid putting pressure on my back or even sitting down, considering the substantial loss of skin. The following days were consumed by frequent trips to Nambour Hospital for wound cleaning and redressing. These dressings were exceptionally large and required careful taping and wrapping around my legs and torso. Adding to the complexity and discomfort, the scorching summer heat, with temperatures consistently above 40 degrees Celsius, made me sweat profusely. The combination of sweat, tape, and dressings sometimes caused them to shift and slide over my skin, producing additional discomfort. Within a few more days, as the large areas of my injuries began to scab over, any movement that caused them to flex would hurt greatly as well, often leading to the cracking of scabs on my buttocks.

During the Christmas holidays, including Christmas Day, I endured painful treatment sessions as the medical team worked diligently to remove any embedded grit or debris from my wounds. They used saline solution, delicate tweezers, and steroid creams for this process. As the healing process began, I was referred to a local specialist who had been conducting trials for synthetic skin gauze on behalf of the Queensland Government. This would make me one of the first recipients of the synthetic skin treatment. This trial would involve applying the synthetic skin to the areas on my back where I had lost multiple layers of skin and the holes in my elbows. The treatment was expected to facilitate skin regrowth without the need for grafting, potentially allowing me to return to training sooner. I did not hesitate when asked to participate in the trial. Once the synthetic skin gauze was applied to protect the most damaged areas, I began plotting my return to training and devised a schedule to get my Ironman race preparation back on track.

Just ten days after the accident, I resumed running without a shirt to minimise discomfort. Running shirtless, with my back covered in the white synthetic skin and covered in the white gauze that had now become part of my body, drew numerous strange and disconcerting stares from pedestrians and motorists as I ran along the Maroochydore River. I didn't care one jot – I was back training and focused on getting back in contention for Ironman.

The 4-second rule

There are two highly effective techniques that I have incorporated into my life over the past 25 years, particularly when making essential discretionary decisions. These techniques have played a significant role in my transformation and have greatly contributed to my success.

The first technique comes into play when I find myself pushed to the edge of my capabilities, often when the voice in my head relentlessly tells me to quit. When the only way forward is to muster courage from the depths of my being, I employ this technique. I will delve into this technique in full detail in Chapter 7.

The second technique I rely on is what I call the "four-second rule," which I briefly mentioned earlier. This rule is a crucial, time-bound principle that, with practice, can become a life-changing habit. It's important to note that not all decisions should be made within four seconds. I strictly apply this principle when it comes to discretionary choices, especially those that involve an easier and tougher option.

The rationale behind this technique is to eliminate apathy and prevent any opportunity for procrastination or delaying decisions. By not allowing oneself to entertain the idea of choosing the easier path, you can eradicate any potential patterns that could lead to deferring tasks to another day, ultimately hindering progress. Let me share an example with you.

Imagine my alarm goes off on a chilly winter morning at either 5 or 5:30 am, and I have a small window of time to complete a scheduled run. Now, lying in my warm and cosy bed might seem very tempting, but that's not an option I can entertain. So, I count to four and then force myself to get out of bed. Surprisingly, within a short time, I'm up and running. Within ten minutes, I'm already grateful for my decision to get up and run. I feel invigorated, with blood pumping through my veins and a clear mind, setting the tone for a positive day ahead. But what's even more important is that I've taken another step toward achieving my seemingly impossible goal.

I've applied the four-second rule not only to my athletic pursuits but also in various professional scenarios, and I've coached others to do the same, leading to remarkable and sometimes even career-changing results. One standout example of this occurred during an offsite conference with a large group of colleagues. At this conference, the facilitator demonstrated a set of skills crucial for effective customer engagement. To reinforce these skills, the facilitator asked for volunteers to participate in role-playing exercises in front of the entire group. This situation used to be a source of fear and anxiety for me, as it is for many people. In the past, I might have avoided eye contact with the facilitator, hoping to escape this daunting task. However, on that particular day, I decided to employ the four-second rule. I immediately raised my hand high to volunteer and, within four seconds, was out of my seat and ready to participate. Incredibly, the fear dissipated almost instantly, and I felt empowered. How could I fail now that I had taken that bold step? From that day onward, I began applying the four-second rule to similar scenarios in my professional life. I've also shared this method with many colleagues and team members, leading to remarkable and sometimes even career-transforming outcomes.

DAILY PRACTICE ACTION
Choices

What decisions have you made in the last 7 days to take an easier road?	
What decisions have you made in the last 7 days that you would change if you could?	
What impact on your goals or legacy will your decisions have?	
What are the next discretionary decisions that you want to change so you take a different road?	

Running in the Athletics Australia 100 k Road Championships.

ACHIEVING HIGH PERFORMANCE

"The only way to achieve the impossible is to believe it is possible."

— Charles Kingsleigh

It's likely not surprising that setting specific, measurable, and time-bound goals, ones that are documented in writing, is a practice followed by only a minority of individuals. Many tend to limit themselves to New Year's resolutions, a well-known tradition notorious for its high failure rate, with approximately 70% of resolutions faltering or being abandoned within the first month, typically by the end of January. So, why is it that so few individuals embark on the journey of setting goals? And among those who do, why does their resolve often wane rapidly?

Furthermore, how can one stack the odds in their favour, increasing their likelihood of accomplishing their goals once they've been established? In essence, the prevalent issue I've observed is the gradual decline in motivation as the initial enthusiasm wanes. At this point, individuals often opt for the path of least resistance. This situation can be exacerbated when people fail to develop a comprehensive plan and, therefore, cannot see the daily routines that they will need to follow to get there effectively. It's essential to recognise the value and significance of each day, even when working towards substantial long-term goals that may be one, two years, or even a decade away.

Goals and your impossible

In this chapter, I'll be sharing my observations and research, as well as presenting the frameworks I've created. These frameworks are the bedrock of all the significant accomplishments I've achieved, including reaching my seemingly impossible goals. At the very minimum, these tools have empowered me to reach my fullest potential, and that in itself is an immensely rewarding experience.

The model I have followed, both in business and in sport, is as follow:

1. See your goal.
2. Understand your "why".
3. Quantify your goal.
4. Create a date to achieve it.
5. Make your goal visible every day.
6. Build a 90-Day High-Performance Plan.
7. Believe you can achieve your goal.

8. Be relentless, rise each day and carry out your planned tasks without making excuses.

9. Review the success measures of your 90-Day High-Performance Plan every 30 days.

See your goal.

What is your true desire? If you were to reflect on your life at the age of 60 or 70, what accomplishments would fill you with immense pride? A goal can encompass various aspects of life, such as career, family, personal development in education or the arts, contributions to the community, fundraising for a noble cause, or even sports achievements. When it comes to setting a goal, there are no strict rules except that it should challenge you and hold deep personal significance. In fact, it might appear insurmountable when you first envision it.

Quantify your goal.

It's essential to quantify your goal. Be specific about what you want to achieve, and make sure it can be measured.

Create a date to achieve it.

Setting a specific date for your goal is non-negotiable, but it should not be limited by any time frame. Larger goals may take several years to achieve, with various sub-goals to keep you on track. The date you set should motivate you to work toward your goal every day, ensuring that you stay committed to your daily actions.

Make your goal visible every day.

Life gets busy, right, and it's easy for other responsibilities to take precedence. You need to keep your goal alive and place a physical reminder in a prominent location. This reminder will serve as a regular prompt and remind you why you are making daily sacrifices, helping you stay motivated and committed to your goal, especially on challenging days.

Build a 90-Day High-Performance Plan.

If your ultimate goal is 1, 2, 3 or even 10 years away, it's crucial to establish measurable milestones or targets to keep yourself on track and maintain focus. Building these smaller, achievable goals will help you stay motivated and ensure that you're progressing toward your larger objective. I will soon share a method for creating a 90-Day High-Performance Plan, which can be applied to various aspects of your life, including health and business.

Believe you can achieve your goal.

Belief in your ability to achieve a significant, long-term goal is not always immediate from where you are now. In many cases, such goals may seem unattainable. Building belief requires creating a plan, setting milestones, and establishing the foundation for your journey. While setbacks and challenges are inevitable, both minor and major, this framework can help you maintain and rebuild your belief in your ability to achieve your goals, even when it comes close to being broken.

But you will get back on track with this framework. At this point, I am tempted to share many endless major setbacks and disasters that I have faced, but it would be a long and sad litany. Instead, I've chosen to highlight only a few to provide context and demonstrate that it's possible to overcome just about anything. Remember, believing in yourself and your goals is a continuous process that you can nurture and strengthen over time, even those seemingly insurmountable obstacles.

<u>Be relentless and carry out your daily plan without making excuses.</u>
Developing resilience is essential when pursuing your goals. It's
not just about toughening up; it's a skill that can be learned and
honed. Resilience involves building confidence and belief in
yourself so that when you face adversity, you have the mental
strength to persevere. It allows you to shift from doubt to belief,
from being overwhelmed by problems to focusing on solutions.
While the path forward might not always be clear, your resilience
helps you find a way. In extreme situations, like during long races
or challenging training sessions, you'll rely on your resilience
repeatedly. Imagine running for hours through treacherous terrain in the dark, feeling exhausted and alone, with every instinct
telling you to quit. Your inner voice may be screaming at you to
stop, but your resilience helps you push through.

"Stooppp! Just stop. You are smashed. You can barely put one
foot in front of the other, and you have 80k of running up and
down mountains to go. You will never make it. You can come
back another day." That's the voice of doubt and exhaustion
trying to pull you down. You need to shut that voice up! That's
where resilience and your "why" step in. "Keep going. You've
got this. You know why you're doing this. One step at a time.
Focus on your goal. You can do it." It's that inner strength that
helps you overcome the toughest challenges and stay on course
toward your goals.

To give this further context, say you have already run 100 kilometres and faced many mental battles in the process. That voice
has been at you all day to quit, but right now, it has become so
loud it is deafening. In this instance, it is futile to focus on the finish
because it is just too far away to comprehend. The answer is to
focus on what you can see and what your brain can accept is
possible. I have faced and endured these voices thousands and

thousands of times and have even lost on a handful of occasions, but that is a win-to-loss ratio I can live with. A DNF, did not finish, in a race is the most disastrous and traumatic outcome, and I have experienced this a few times. That said, perhaps the achievement that I am most proud of took its origin from a race in which I DNF'd in the 2004 Ironman New Zealand, which I discuss in more detail in a coming chapter.

When you find yourself stripped to your core, when the voice has become so loud that it is all you can hear or think about, you need to reset your goal to a micro goal, which might be what you can achieve in the next 2 minutes. Once you have achieved that micro goal, you can then reset. And so on. There have been many times when I have faced this situation, with many hours and kilometres to get to the finish line, where I have tasked myself with running to the crest of a hill or the end of the road that I can see ahead. At any time on any given day, you will be faced with situations where you lose belief, and that voice in your head is convincing you to quit. That is why you must be prepared with the mental tools and techniques to fight back as quickly as possible.

Review your 90-Day High-Performance Plan every 30 days.
90-Day High-Performance Plans are as they sound. They are designed to maintain your concentration on measurable objectives in the next 30, 60, and 90 days, including the relevant targets and specific tasks needed. The goal is to provide daily guidance and generate positive momentum, propelling you toward your target at an appropriate pace. These are small, attainable goals that, when achieved, should boost your confidence by hitting short-term stretch targets. Consequently, the daily actions become your daily reality.

Your 90-Day High-Performance Plan

The three key elements of a 90-Day High-Performance Plan (HPP) are:

1. Objective
Your aim should be your end goal, including timing.

2. Targets
These should be specific, measurable and time-bound within 90 days. To achieve laser-like focus, you can break these down into 30-, 60- and 90-day targets.

3. Actions
The actions you've pinpointed are the tasks you must accomplish daily or within each specified timeframe in order to reach your stretch targets and ambitious goals. When your ultimate objective lies a year or more in the future, it's possible for both your stretch targets and the associated actions to seem unexciting and inconsequential in comparison. However, it's crucial to recognise and embrace the fact that, especially if you're starting from scratch or a minimal starting point, these tasks are absolutely essential. Accomplishing them will begin to build confidence and lay a strong foundation for your long-term success, which is key.

To provide further clarity, let's examine a couple of examples.

Example 1: Work-Related Goal
Bob is one of three financial advisers in a well-established small practice, and most of his clients were inherited from a senior adviser, Sally. Sally has a successful referral partnership with an accountant she knows from school. Recently, Sally shared the

firm's growth plans for the next three years and assigned Bob the task of generating his own new client referrals externally. After careful consideration, Bob has decided to establish a goal and create a plan to present to Sally. Bob's main objective is as follows:

"To establish a highly successful, scalable referral partnership that can yield two new prospect referrals per month within 12 months."

Considering that Bob is starting from scratch, this is a significant challenge. Setting goals related to the final outcomes could be counterproductive because it might take a substantial amount of time to even receive a single new referral, let alone two, every month. Here's how Bob's 90-Day High-Performance Plan (HPP) might look for the initial 90 days:

Objective
Build a successful, scalable referral partnership that will generate two new prospect referrals per month by the end of 12 months.

Target

30 days
Identify and establish contact with 40 new proactive accountancy practices via email.

60 days
Secure four meetings with prospective accountancy firms who have expressed interest.

90 days
Reach an agreement with two firms to refer at least one client each by the end of the month.

Actions

30 days
Research to identify 40 suitable accountancy practices within the specified radius - and gather their email addresses.

Draft an email template.

Send 40 initial emails and, if there is no response within seven days, follow up with a phone call.

60 days
Call all non-responders.

Ensure that the Client Value Proposition (CVP) analysis is both clear and meaningful.

Prepare a pitch for the meetings you have booked.

Complete a minimum of four meetings.

90 days
Finalise agreements with at least two firms and request one new referral to begin working on.

90-DAY
HIGH-PERFORMANCE PLAN

Objective	Targets	Actions
Build a highly successful, scalable referral partnership.	30 days Identify and reach out to forty new proactive accountancy practices via email.	1. Search to identify forty suitable accountancy practices within your required radius - including email addresses. 2. Draft and email template 3. Send forty emails then follow with a phone call seven days later if no response.
	60 days Book four meetings with interested prospective accountancy firms.	1. Call all non-responders. 2. Ensure your CVP is clear and meaningful. 3. Prepare your pitch for the meetings you have booked. 4. Complete a minimum of four meetings.
	90 days Reach an agreement with two firms to refer at least one client by the end of the month.	1. Complete the agreement with a minimum of two firms and request one new referral to work on

Example 2: Sporting Goal

Jill, at the age of 38, hasn't been for a run since her high school days, a hobby she used to really enjoy. Her fondest memories of running are of the training sessions she used to have in the local park. Over the years, the demands of work, raising kids, and managing family responsibilities have left her with little to no time for herself. However, a chance encounter with an old school friend, Alice, who she hadn't seen in over 10 years, has inspired Jill and rekindled her interest in running. Jill bumped into Alice during a lunchtime break.

Jill was rushing to grab lunch to take back to the office while, as it happened, Alice was going for a short lunchtime run. As they hugged and laughed, they stood back to take each other in. Jill noticed how amazing Alice was looking as they began to chat.

Upon her return to the office, Jill found herself brimming with excitement and captivated by Alice's vibrant and healthy demeanour. Her encounter with Alice had left her feeling genuinely curious and eager to reconnect. That evening, unable to contain her curiosity, Jill messaged Alice and proposed meeting up for coffee or lunch later in the week.

During their arranged lunch, Alice shared her impressive journey with Jill. She revealed that she was currently preparing for her fifth half marathon, scheduled to take place in just two weeks. What's more, this half marathon served as a stepping stone toward her ambitious goal of running her very first full marathon, which she aimed to achieve in three months' time.

"How on earth did you manage that with your job and family? I can never seem to find the time," Jill asked Alice in amazement.

Alice went on to explain that a couple of years ago, a colleague at work had persuaded her to join a group of friends for a park run or walk, followed by some social time for food and drinks if time allowed. Alice fell in love with the experience and decided to set more ambitious goals for herself. She started planning out the steps she needed to take to achieve those goals. Jill found Alice's story truly inspiring, and it motivated her to create a 90-Day High-Performance Plan (HPP) based on her own goal, which was set for 12 months in the future.

Objective
Complete the Sydney Half Marathon on May 23, 2024

Target
30 days
2 x fast walks & 1 run/walk by the last week.

60 days
3 x 20-minute run sessions by the last week of the month

Ensure one 20-minute core and strength session is completed each week.

90 days
Enter and finish the Mother's Day fun run, completing it within 45 mins.

Complete 70 minutes total running in 1 week.

Complete one 30-minute core and strength session per week

Actions
30 days
Find 3 x 20-minute sessions per week and add to phone calendar.

Chat with Dave, and share my goals and plans.

3

Research to find suitable running shoes and purchase.

Weeks 1 & 2: 2 x fast walk and one run/walk session.

Week 3: 1 x fast walk, 1 x run/walk, and 1 run session.

Week 4: 1 x fast walk, 2 x run session. Complete calorie and nutrient plan

60 days

Week 5: easier 2 x fast walk and one run session.

Week 6: 2 x earlier 20-minute runs & 1 x hill walk/run session.

Week 7: 2 x usual 20-minute run session & 1 x short sprints session

Week 8: easier 2 x fast walk and one run session.

Complete one 20-minute core and strength session per week

90 days

Week 9: 1 x 20-minute run/walk & 1 x 20-minute run session & I x 30-minute run session.

Week 10: 1 x 20-minute run session & I x 30-minute run session 2 x earlier 20-minute runs & 1 x hill walk/run session.

Week 11: rest all week until the Mother's Day 7-kilometre fun run in July. (Run in under 45 minutes as a substitute for training for whichever week this race lands on).

Week 12: recovery 2 x fast walk

90-DAY
HIGH-PERFORMANCE PLAN

Objective	Targets	Actions
Complete the Sydney Half Marathon on 23 May 2023	30 days 2 x fast walks & 1x run/walk by last week.	1. Add 3 x 20-minute sessions pw to phone/calendar. 2. Shar goal and training with Dave 3. Research and buy new running shoes. 4. Weeks 3-1x fast walk, 1 x run/walk & 1 x run session. 5. Week 4-1x fast walk, 2 x run sessions. 6. Complete calorie and nutrient plan sessions.
	60 days 3 x 20-minute run sessions by last week of the month. 1 x core & strength sessions per week.	1. Week 5 - 2 x easier fast walk sessions & 1 x run session. 2. Week 6-2x 20-minute runs & 1 x hill walk/run session. 3. Week 7-2x 20-minute run sessions & 1x short sprints session. 4. Week 8-2x 20 minute fast walk & 1 x run session. 5. 2x 20-minute core and strength sessions.
	90 days Finish Mother's Day run within 45 minutes. Complete total of 70 minutes of running in a single week.	1. Week 9-1x 20-minute run/walk & 1 x 30-minute run session. 2. Week 10-1x 20-minute e run session, 1 x 30-minute run session & 1 hill run session. 3. Week 11 - rest all week until the MD 7 k run. 4. Week 12 - recovery 2 x fast walk.

There you have it. To maintain your focus, I highly recommend completing your template as soon as possible, then printing it out and prominently displaying it in two key locations, such as your workplace and home. Daily, refer to your high-performance plan to ensure you're staying on track. Use it to check off completed tasks and remind yourself of your daily priorities. Remember, you only ever get today, and there's no option to defer to tomorrow or another day.

Then, monthly, you should review your 60- and 90-day targets to ensure they remain relevant, especially if you've already surpassed your 30-day targets. You may need to reset them if this is the case, which will feel inspiring.

Significant or seemingly impossible goals often require extended timelines, typically set at a year or more in the future. In certain cases, like two of my own, these goals may span over five years or more, necessitating the completion of numerous sets of 90-Day HPPs over an extended duration to reach your goal. However, if you adhere to this process with discipline, you will achieve your goal.

Train harder than the game

No matter what your goal may be, you will need to find your best on the day. Whether it's excelling in a crucial exam, addressing a large audience at a pivotal conference, or delivering an outstanding performance at a special concert, the array of tests and challenges is diverse. However, regardless of the specific challenge, the keys to success remain consistent: you must always be well prepared, well trained, and bring your best mindset.

Over the course of many decades, while cultivating an unwavering and limitless mindset, or as David Goggins calls it, "a calloused mind" – a mindset characterised by unshakable determination and peak performance resolve that declares, "I will accomplish this" - I've embraced a steadfast philosophy: "I must always train harder than the game." This approach underscores the necessity of continuous and rigorous preparation to ensure that you can consistently perform at your best when the moment of truth arrives.

Thinking outside the box, adapting, and dedicated practice have been guiding principles that I've applied both in my sporting pursuits and throughout my career. One of my favourite career examples revolves around the art of presenting, an activity that many find incredibly daunting.

While possessing subject expertise is undoubtedly important, it is thorough preparation and relentless practice that truly allow you to shine on stage. In addition to honing your technical presentation skills, which help you structure your presentation, refine your style, and deliver your narrative and key messages effectively, it's equally crucial to allocate time for practising your pitch to at least one person, twice over. The benefits of practice are immeasurable, as it allows you to discern what works and what doesn't, giving you the flexibility to make necessary adjustments. Most significantly, practice builds confidence in your abilities and competence, which stands as the cornerstone of successful presentations before audiences of any size. When you commit to training harder than the game itself, you position yourself to be not only well-prepared but also remarkably composed when the adrenaline surges. This composure allows you to deliver your pitch with maximum impact.

In fact, when you've trained rigorously, you can confidently discard your notes and stop worrying about what you'll say a couple of days before your presentation. I've made it a personal rule never to carry notes onto the stage because it signifies you haven't mastered your material well enough and should have prepared more diligently.

So, here's a valuable tip: Challenge yourself to ditch your notes and train to the point where you're proficient enough to deliver your pitch without any prompts. This level of competence not only enhances your presentation but also demonstrates your deep knowledge and confidence in your subject matter.

Over the course of the last 25 years or so, I've undergone numerous adaptations in response to setbacks, injuries, failures, and challenges. I've also applied a range of training techniques that have allowed me to remain competitive across a wide spectrum of races in varying conditions, terrains, and climates. When you stand at the starting line of a race, you should approach it with comprehensive preparation and leave nothing to chance. It's wise to anticipate that unforeseen challenges will inevitably arise. Instead of merely showing up and hoping to get through, it's crucial to be fully prepared to tackle the race, the distance, and the conditions head-on. This level of readiness ensures that you give yourself the best possible chance for success.

For amateur athletes aiming to compete at the highest level, there are infinite challenges to navigate. Maybe you're striving to excel while juggling family responsibilities and a demanding career, and the same applies. Naturally, your top priority should always be earning a living to support yourself or your family, as well as providing them with love and care. In addition to these priorities, nurturing friendships and maintaining a social network also require attention. Balancing these aspects of life can easily consume your time and energy. Moreover, if your job demands more than the typical forty-hour workweek and includes after-hours commitments, the challenges ramp up.

If you want to achieve your set goals, you must find a way to surmount the challenges that undoubtedly arise along the way, just as they do in life. While problems are a part of everyone's journey, with some being more significant than others, what truly matters is our approach to these challenges and how we overcome them. How we process the problem and how quickly we move to a solution is imperative. Adaptation is essential, and in my experience, the capacity to reinvent my training, my mindset, and even myself in pursuit of improvement. We can't change the past, but we possess the power to adapt how we perceive what has occurred and, consequently, how we respond to it.

I've always chosen to train alone for several reasons. Firstly, time constraints have been a significant factor. My schedule often required flexible adjustments to the timing and location of my training sessions. This unpredictability made it nearly impossible to coordinate with others or join a group at a set time and place.

The necessity of frequent interstate and international travel presented additional logistical challenges on a weekly basis. Training alone was a blessing because it provided the freedom to tailor my workouts precisely to my needs without any compromises. For example, I didn't have to stick to a fixed running schedule on days when my body wasn't responding optimally or when my training cycle required a specific approach. While this choice meant I might miss out on the external push of training with others, it had its advantages. It forced me to develop the techniques and discipline needed for self-motivation and self-improvement.

I learned to rely on myself for motivation, cultivating self-reliance in my training journey.

Additionally, training alone spared me from the need to adjust my pace or wait for others who might not have been at the same level or stage of training as I was. However, it did come with its own set of challenges. The solitude of solo training could be isolating at times and posed safety concerns, especially during long training sessions that took me far from home, particularly while cycling.

While training for Ironman races over many years, my typical long bike ride, often covering a minimum of 150 kilometres, took place on the Bruce Highway, heading towards Brisbane and back on Saturdays. Riding bicycles on the highway shoulder was prohibited for safety reasons due to the high-speed limit of 110 kilometres per hour on the four-lane freeway. However, the relatively safe one-metre-wide shoulder justified the risk, as it allowed me to cover a substantial distance without having to share a lane with motor vehicles.

This route worked for me because it rarely required me to stop at traffic lights, allowing for a continuous flow. However, I had to navigate merging intersections carefully. It also provided an opportunity to adopt the race technique of riding in the time trial position. While the solitude of these rides was mentally challenging, it contributed to building mental resilience. Nevertheless, there were drawbacks to this choice, primarily the ever-present and life-threatening danger posed by cycling in close proximity to cars travelling at speeds of 110 kilometres per hour, and sometimes even faster. The most intimidating encounters were with large trucks, which produced immense power and wind velocity as they approached from behind and sped past. Typically, I could hear a truck approaching and had to brace myself to counter the wind force that threatened to draw me towards its wheels.

As I mentioned earlier, I experienced several accidents and incidents throughout my training journey. However, one of the most extraordinary and dramatic incidents occurred during my training for the Australian Ironman in the summer of 2001.

On a scorching day, with reports of small fires erupting in the Beerburrum Forest area near the Bruce Highway, I embarked on what would turn out to be an unforgettable training ride. Despite my wife's attempts to dissuade me from going out that day, I was determined to complete a specific long aero ride of 160 kilometres.

After covering about 15 kilometres, I reached the on-ramp to join the Bruce Highway at Sippy Downs. It was at this moment that I first caught a whiff of bushfire smoke in the air. Initially, I dismissed it, as I had encountered the smell of bushfires on previous rides. However, the scent soon intensified as I headed south, and within moments, thick smoke engulfed the highway, reducing visibility to less than 100 metres.

Within a few minutes, sirens wailed from all directions, and the busy highway quickly emptied of cars. Not a single vehicle passed me as I pedalled onward, crossing the last major turnoff that led inland to Caloundra at the southern end of the Sunshine Coast. Despite the limited visibility, the ominous red glow from the flashing lights of fire engines and emergency rescue vehicles stationed along the freeway sent shivers down my spine and raised the hairs on my arms.

Suddenly, the wind shifted direction, and I could clearly discern the vehicles. I had no doubt now that the freeway had been closed in both directions. I continued to cycle slowly along the shoulder toward the blockade, which now seemed no more than a token, as it appeared that all traffic had been halted and redirected.

There were no emergency teams present at the blockade, as they had likely rushed off to combat the fires. It was now clear that the fires had burned right up to the very edge of the highway shoulder. In the distance, the flames seemed to be inching perilously close, as if searching for a path to leap across the six lanes of bitumen freeway.

Out of the hundreds of times I had cycled along this specific stretch of freeway and the thousands of times I had driven it throughout the years, this journey felt the most surreal. The absence of any car created a bizarre scene, similar to the postapocalyptic world that is often portrayed in many sci-fi movies. Combined with the eerie glow of fires and the thick smoke filling the air, I felt compelled to take this once-in-a-lifetime opportunity to ride in the freeway lanes themselves, zigzagging backward and forward across them.

Over the next 10 kilometres of my southbound ride, I absorbed the surreal atmosphere and took in the destruction that was raging around me, intensified by the extreme heat I could feel over the left side of my body, emanating from intense fires burning only metres away. Eventually, by the time I had ridden through the southern blockade, onto the Bribie Island Road and back, both the fire and the drama had receded, and despite many plumes of smoke rising away from the highway, it was now back up and running with traffic. What a day!

Snakes were a common sight during my long summer Saturday rides, requiring constant attention to avoid running over them or getting entangled with them in my bike wheels. However, the most persistent hazard I encountered was the presence of small stones, glass, and debris on the road that could easily puncture my high-compression bike tyres. To prepare for these inevitable events, I always carried spare bike tubes and air canisters to inflate the tire after changing it. My rule of thumb was to carry two of everything, just in case. While most of the time, I only experienced a single puncture, on a couple of occasions the following year, I encountered two punctures during a single long ride.

Then, a few months before the Ironman event in April, I had an unfortunate streak of bad luck, experiencing three punctures during one ride. The first two occurred early in the ride, and the third fatal puncture happened around my turnaround point, approximately seventy kilometres from home. This left me with no other option but to hitch a ride on the freeway. Luckily, a kind-hearted fellow cyclist stopped, helped me load my bike into the back of his truck, and gave me a lift for 50 kilometres to a bike store in Caloundra. It just happened that the store owner was a bit of a character who found humour in my unfortunate situation but provided me with the necessary replacements so I could continue my ride and head home.

Since that day, I always carried four sets of tubes and canisters with me, although I never needed more than two during a single ride again.

The following year brought another long ride that would test my determination and ability to make positive decisions. I set out on my most familiar route, which led me to Sippy Downs to join the freeway heading south. It was another sweltering day, a predictable occurrence during Queensland's summer. I had only been riding for about twenty minutes when I glanced up and saw a brick that had fallen from a truck lying in the middle of the shoulder. I was travelling at approximately 35 kilometres per hour, and with the brick closing in too fast, I had no time to brake. I could only swerve to one side, clipping the edge of the brick and catapulting myself off my bike onto the searing hot bitumen - you could have fried an egg on the blisteringly hot road within 30 seconds – and it hurt like hell.

As I dusted myself down and assessed my injuries, I was fortunate to find that I had escaped any significant damage. However, I had lost a considerable amount of skin from my knee and hip. The bleeding areas began to sting in the sun as sunscreen mixed with my sweat. This was already a demanding ride in the sun, and suddenly, the prospect of completing it appeared almost unbearable. The voice in my head clamoured for attention, advocating strongly for throwing in the towel, heading home, cleaning up, and resting with my fresh wounds. It was a tempting proposition. "Screw that. No excuses, Jason." my thoughts quickly shifted to the consequences of quitting on that day and what precedent it might set for the next time I encountered a tough obstacle.

I promptly hopped back on my bike and rode in the blistering sun for another 5 hours. The significance of my decision that day extended beyond ensuring that I didn't miss one week's long ride. It was about refusing to accept defeat in the face of challenges and discomfort because these types of decisions recur many times in life, and how we respond to them is crucial. If you take the easier road, you set yourself up to make it a habit, and before you know it, you will take the easy route again. And if you make a string of decisions to take the easier road, you will become a quitter, and you will never achieve your goals.

While winter in Sydney is generally milder compared to many parts of Queensland, it can still have its uncomfortable moments, albeit of a different kind—typically, a chillier type of unpleasant. One year, as I was training for the National 100-kilometre championships, I came down with the flu. It was the middle of winter, and I found myself running twice a day in morning and evening temperatures hovering between eight to ten degrees Celsius. Yet, true to form, I continued training. Then, an unusual weather phenomenon unfolded—constant rain for three weeks straight, all day, every day. Undeterred, I persisted with my twice-daily runs, gradually growing sicker and sicker as a result. By the end of that week, I was diagnosed with Bronchitis. However, I chose to keep running regardless to get the miles ticked off. It was an awful period. I would never recommend emulating this, but back then, my determination was unwavering, and nothing would deter me from the pursuit of my goals.

Learning to swim was my own personal battle. My battles with swimming didn't stop there, though. Swimming posed my most significant training challenge due to frequent travel around the country. I must have swum in nearly every swimming pool in Queensland, a very large state. That's somewhat a liberal application of poetic licence, but it's well over 50 different pools.

The primary difficulty stemmed from the necessity to swim long distances in very short pools, such as those you typically find in hotels. Sometimes, these small pools were the only bodies of water available in certain towns or parts of a city. And by long distances, I mean somewhere between 2.5 and 4 kilometres in a single session. The small pool size presented several challenges.

First, I had to make turns every eight to ten metres, which meant that a longer swim could require covering 300 to 400 lengths of the pool. Additionally, small-town pools and hotel pools do not seem to ever have any water runoff. Given the frequency of turns, I found myself constantly swimming and turning back on myself hundreds of times, creating a virtual ocean swim experience with a constant swell. This makes it nearly impossible to establish any consistent stroke rhythm. There were a few lengthy sessions in pools like this that left me feeling practically seasick.

Travelling interstate, internationally and around some states for work added further obstacles to a significant and strict daily training regime. Whilst running was less of an issue than bike and swimming training sessions, it would often prove to be problematic. Alongside the demanding travel schedule, there were frequent evening work functions, presentations, client meetings, team dinners, sleep deprivation, and limited access to the specific foods I needed.

There were instances when I had to fly interstate for a day or overnight, which removed a vital evening training window. On such occasions, I made the unconventional choice to disembark from the plane at night, change into my running gear at the airport, strap on my heavy backpack, and run the 14 kilometres back home. This also created the added bonus of saving on a taxi fare. My colleagues often found it amusing because I would occasionally slip away to the restroom toward the end of a work function or dinner, only to reappear in my running attire, ready to run home. Sometimes, you have to do whatever it takes, right? I even resorted to lengthy treadmill sessions when I was confined to a cruise liner during one conference. This particular ship had outdated stabilisers, requiring me to master new skills to stay upright while running on the gym treadmill located at the bow. The few lively souls on board probably wondered, "Who's that tipsy guy on the treadmill?" as the ship swayed from side to side and pitched back and forth. I vowed never to attempt that again.

When it comes to preparing for a specific race, as in any other pursuit, and following the principle of training harder than the game, ultra-endurance athletes face several challenging physical elements during races. These include heat, cold, altitude, changes in elevation, distance, and terrain. Among these six factors, cold presented the most formidable challenge for me. I've never been particularly fond of cold weather, possibly because my body fat percentage hovers around only 3 to 4%. Extreme cold would cause me significant discomfort and pain, both during training and races. This discomfort often manifested as the loss of feeling in my feet, toes, and fingers, which would quickly go numb before transitioning into a painful, stinging and aching sensation.

As you've likely gathered by now, accumulating a significant number of cycling kilometres also increases the risk of accidents. To mitigate this risk, I alternated between road cycling and using a stationary wind trainer in my garage in Buderim for every other long training session. On the wind trainer, which had a fixed resistance roller, I could vary my sessions and benefit from the constant resistance provided by the magnetic roller. This was different from riding on the road, where you could occasionally stop pedalling and coast. On a wind trainer, you had to pedal continuously. Spending six hours training in the same spot presented its own unique mental challenges, helping to build mental resilience and exemplifying the philosophy of training harder than the game.

A couple of years before I adopted this training approach, I had read about Dave Scott, one of the most legendary Ironman athletes of all time, who was known for enduring six-hour wind trainer sessions in his basement, illuminated only by a single light bulb. By the way, he won the Ironman World Championships six times. Additionally, training in an enclosed garage in the middle of the Queensland summer created ideal conditions for heat training. Often, after a long session, I would find myself surrounded by a substantial pool of sweat.

So, what can you do differently or better to accelerate your performance?

To identify what you need to change or perhaps what you need to do more of, you will need to find some quiet time for reflection. Time devoted solely to thinking. I know all too well how it can be challenging it can be to find some quiet time, but I also know that everyone can. You can establish this practice by waking up earlier in the morning when the world is peaceful and quiet. With regularity, it will become a habit and a very beneficial one at that. It's likely that you'll also start going to bed earlier and enjoy better sleep. Personally, I've always found early mornings to be the most productive for thinking, reflection, and planning.

If you want to reach your best, you will need to think and do things differently. I've found that one of the most effective ways to bring about positive changes is by outlining the actions in your 90-Day High-Performance Plan. In fact, your key objectives and high-performance targets will drive you to find actions and solutions.

Daily Practice Action

Create at least one significant goal/objective and complete the 90-Day High-Performance Plan template below:

90-DAY HIGH-PERFORMANCE PLAN

Objective	Targets	Actions
	30 days	1. 2. 3. 4.
	60 days	1. 2. 3. 4.
	90 days	1. 2. 3. 4.

Acclimating for "La Ultra - The High" at 15,000 ft above sea level in the Himalayas on Khardung La, Ladakh, India in 2014.

7

THE POWER OF WHAT YOU EAT, SAY, AND THINK

"Beyond the mind, at the deepest level of consciousness, resides the spirit. This is the part of us that is eternal, unchanging, and imbued with pure unlimited potential. Tapping into this potential is what enables us to manifest miracles."

— Deepak Chopra

Your attitude and mindset are everything in life. They enable you to perform better, become a better person, or cope with life's setbacks while maintaining happiness. With a positive attitude, you can accomplish almost anything. The remarkable thing is that you have control over your attitude, regardless of others' actions or words and irrespective of external circumstances. A positive and content mindset is, undoubtedly, your most valuable asset if you nurture and utilise it effectively.

There are various methods to train your mind and improve your life. In this chapter, I'll discuss some of the frameworks and techniques I've learned and practised to pursue happiness, wellbeing, and the realisation of my dreams. I've also had the privilege of coaching others on their journey to achieving their best lives. To this day, I continue to refine and apply these techniques to make the most of each day. In this chapter and the next two, where I explore gratitude and resilience, my goal is to provide you with essential techniques that contribute to cultivating a positive mindset and happiness. Let's start by discussing the impact of your diet on your physical and mental wellbeing.

Don't kid yourself because you are what you eat.

There is extensive research regarding the impact of diet on physical and mental wellbeing, although I may not possess the scientific wisdom or education to conclusively validate my beliefs. What I can state with absolute certainty, based on continuous and relentless self-experimentation, is that everything you eat will contribute to your physical and mental wellbeing – guaranteed.

As an athlete who trains many hours a day, every day, you become acutely aware of the daily, and even hourly, performance of mind and body, along with the influence of everything that you ingest. Make no mistake, you are what you eat!

By today's standards, I grew up eating very well. My mum was a great cook and looked after our family as well as any mum possibly could. Back then, there were extraordinarily few takeaway food options, especially where I grew up in semi-rural England, aside from a few fish and chip shops and a local Chinese take-away. Fortunately, most foods were fresh, and processed food was not yet fashionable, so we primarily consumed a traditional English diet of meat and two vegetables. That was all fine, except for one thing: I despised vegetables. Back then, I still used the word "hate," a term I have since banished from my vocabulary. At every meal, I would devour the meat and potatoes and leave my vegetables until last, hoping to escape eating them altogether. However, Mum always made me eat them.

Ironically, in 2009, I made a pivotal decision to become a pesca-tarian and later a vegan, eliminating all animal-derived products from my diet except for some fish. My motivation for this change was twofold: I had become increasingly troubled by the cruelty inflicted on many animals held in appalling conditions, particularly battery hens and chickens, and I was motivated by health and performance reasons. Having always loved meat, particularly a good steak or a tasty sausage, this decision was challenging. However, not taking the easier option changed my life.

The final catalyst for excluding meat from my diet was reading the former US bestseller, "Born to Run." This book transfixed me with its many subplots, making it one of the most fascinating and remarkable true stories I have ever had the pleasure to read. Reading it changed my life in so many ways. Not only did it entertain and inspire me, but the book also altered my views on running and what to eat. "Born to Run" motivated me to reinvent the way I ran by occasionally ditching my comfortable cushioned running shoes to run barefoot on grass. This approach closely resembles how we ran as children and, I believe, aligns with our anatomical and physiological design for running. Undoubtably, modern, highly cushioned running shoes weaken the strength of our feet, which running barefoot rectifies by strengthening muscles and the arches of our feet. Another benefit is that running without shoes forces us to run on our forefoot and to take smaller strides, importantly increasing cadence. According to researchers, establishing a direct connection with the earth helps regulate your circadian rhythms, aligning your sleep-wake cycles with the earth's natural day-night cycle. Furthermore, walking or running barefoot on grass or sand reduces cortisol, a stress hormone, thereby facilitating more profound and restorative sleep. Eventually, my barefoot running practice built to a 30-kilometre barefoot run-on grass around a local cricket oval. Apart from the immense benefits of strengthening the feet, the part of the body that endures the most force and impact over the course of your life, running barefoot is a liberating experience that connects me deeply with the earth.

Becoming a vegetarian significantly improved every bodily function, including gut and intestinal function, digestion, blood pressure, and nutritional absorption, to mention a few. These numerous benefits collectively accelerated my recovery from intense physical training, allowing me to return to training sooner and feel stronger. Remarkably, I also began to observe that cuts and abrasions healed much faster after adopting a vegetarian diet. If I can inspire you to reduce or eliminate your meat intake, you will experience these health benefits almost immediately, making the act of reading this book worthwhile in itself. When I stopped consuming meat, I noticed my entire digestive system transformed within just four days. It was as if I had unclogged my insides.

There are countless studies, extensive research, and readily available documentaries that can assist you in making this life-changing, life-prolonging decision. Within days of giving up meat, you will also notice how much quicker your body digests food and improves the absorption of vitamins, minerals, essential amino acids, oils, and both long and short-chain amino acids. Additionally, you will feel a greater sense of wellbeing and compassion for the world when adopting a vegan lifestyle. The most striking piece of research I've encountered claims that we could resolve the world's water shortages by simply ceasing to consume the livestock that rapidly consumes the world's vegetation. And just in case you are thinking, "What about protein?" An animal must eat 6 grams of plant protein to produce 1 gram of animal protein.

A large number of studies have delved into the significance of diet and exercise, but one particularly astonishing study I recently came across involved nine women aged 45 to 59. Over the course of three months, these women committed to healthy diets, regular exercise, and improved sleep quality. The results were nothing short of astounding: the average biological age across the group decreased by an impressive 4.84 years, with one participant experiencing the most remarkable transformation, shedding an incredible 9.5 years from her biological age. Consider, for a moment, the prospect of reducing your own biological age by 9.5 years in just three months simply by embracing healthier eating habits, engaging in regular exercise, and prioritising better sleep quality.

Positive language – positive mindset

Around the same time that I made the decision to dramatically change the course of my life by changing my diet, I became acutely aware of the power of language and its impact, not only on those around me but, perhaps even more significantly, on my own psychology and overall positivity. In essence, you are what you say, both to others and to yourself and the words you use shape both your external image and your internal mindset.

To influence or transform your own mindset and capabilities, as well as how you present yourself via your demeanour to others, it's crucial to pay close attention to your choice of words and make the conscious decision to alter any negative language or self-talk - moving away from who you do not want to be and how you do not want others to see you.

From my own experience, there is absolutely no doubt that the words you speak to yourself internally and externally, and the way you think, have a profound effect on your ability to grow and achieve, especially when it comes to accomplishing seemingly impossible feats. For example, if you think or say that something is hard, it will be hard.

I began to pay close attention in my interactions with others, particularly those I needed to influence in my professional career and began to notice recurring patterns in their vocabulary. As I delved deeper into the significance of their language and its connection to mindset, I became increasingly convinced that I could gauge a person's level of positivity and their willingness to change based on their choice of words.

Consequently, I reached the conclusion that most people never come close to realising their full potential, let alone achieving the seemingly impossible, because they restrict and limit their own minds. You cannot achieve the extraordinary if your mind is constrained and hindered by negative conditioning from external influences. Many people live their whole lives without coming anywhere close to achieving or being their best because their mind has been conditioned or influenced by people and the world around them to react negatively.

As you practice and nurture a positive mindset while adapting both your spoken and unspoken language, you'll become increasingly adept at recognising the mindsets of those around you. You may find, as I have, that you can sense a person's mindset within just 30 seconds of meeting them. Once you've mastered your own language and thereby influenced your mindset, you'll easily identify those individuals whose abilities and potential will likely forever remain limited. These are the people who can drain your energy and positivity. If you lead a team, regardless of its size, just one person with a negative mindset can consume more of your time than everyone else combined.

These individuals are unlikely to reach their full potential, nor will they swiftly resolve problems or challenges. Instead, they tend to dwell on problems or issues and may attempt to draw others around them into their negativity, perhaps seeking comfort in shared misery. As the saying goes, "Misery loves company." I've come to accept that it's my responsibility to reach out to such people and see if I can help. However, if those people chose not to react positively to breaking free and to help themselves, then I quickly chose to move on and continue to surround myself with people who exhibit positivity, act with integrity, and embrace courage.

In 1999, I made a deliberate and conscious decision to change my vocabulary, which, in turn, transformed my mindset. Over the course of two weeks, I dedicated a significant amount of mindful effort to identifying words with predominantly negative connotations that I needed to eliminate from both my spoken vocabulary and my unspoken thoughts. The aim was to find 10 words.

The key negative and judgmental words that I identified:

Spoken and Unspoken Words

- Disappointed

- Hate

- Can't – relating only to myself.

- Hard – relating to the most common thought generated in my mind during training or racing.

As much time as I spent considering the 10 words, I was encouraged that I had failed at this task and could only find four words that I wanted to remove. This meant that I had already evolved an incredibly positive mindset and that there were only a handful of words that were holding me back. This is why I had to remove these words:

Disappointed

Disappointed is a highly emotive, judgmental, negative term that people often employ in various trivial situations or circumstances. They may not fully grasp the impact this word has on themselves and those around them, including family, friends, or colleagues at work - or perhaps they do understand its impact. Using *disappointed* strongly suggests that the speaker is greatly upset by someone's actions or inactions or a particular situation. It also implies that the actions or behaviours of the person being addressed fall far below the speaker's values or expectations and that they are at fault, potentially judged as substandard or immoral in the speaker's view. This word might be used excessively, possibly to harshly judge, belittle, or exert control over others. In essence, it conveys to the target of this judgment that they do not meet the speaker's standards or that the speaker considers themselves superior. Upon reflection, I seldom found the use of this highly damaging, judgmental word appropriate, so I consciously removed it from both my vocabulary and thoughts.

Hate

Hate is an especially malevolent and destructive term that evokes significant negativity and abhorrence. It should be reserved for situations truly deserving of such a venomous emotion. However, we often use *hate* too casually, allowing it to permeate our minds and emotional states with powerful negative influences. As you become more attuned to words like *hate* and their often inappropriate use, you'll notice how frequently people employ this word to describe inconsequential situations and scenarios. For instance, I often overhear conversations on the train, at work, or while waiting for coffee, where individuals exclaim, "God, the bus was 5 minutes late this morning. I hate that." In such instances, I immediately think, "Really, is that what you hate?" Allowing your mindset to be significantly affected in a negative manner by a minor inconvenience like a slightly late bus can diminish your day and overall happiness. Life is full of such occurrences, and reacting so negatively to relatively trivial matters can lead to a permanent state of negativity and victimhood. Therefore, I strongly advise eliminating the word *hate* from your vocabulary and your mind.

Can't

Can't means that you will not. *Can't* means that you are not prepared to try because it is too hard, or you simply do not believe that you can. *Can't* is the easier road that will retain the status quo, at best. But *can't* is only a choice, and it can be influenced by implementing several of the techniques that are covered in this book. First, though, you must eradicate this toxic word from your thoughts and your speech.

Hard

If you allow the voice in your head to say, "This is hard." Or you say that out aloud to somebody else, then it will be hard. The impact on your positivity will be immediate and most probably steer you away from the task, or, if you are amidst the task, it will severely impact your ability to successfully complete the task or challenge. If you allow the voice to repeat that thought, you will give yourself permission to quit – because it is hard, after all.

The encouraging news is that you have the capacity to alter this psychological barrier to achieve high-performance. If you observe, as I frequently do, one of the greatest and most extraordinary athletes in the history of sports, Eliud Kipchoge, the Kenyan marathon runner who accomplished the unprecedented feat of completing a marathon in under 2 hours, you'll notice some highly specific traits. Running a marathon in 1:59:59 is equivalent to sprinting 100m in just over 17 seconds, and this feat must be repeated 422 times consecutively. Astonishingly, on October 12, Kipchoge achieved an even faster time of 1:59:40. What's fascinating is that one of his famous mantras, and a personal favourite of mine that I often hear him repeat, is, "No human is limited."

Now, this might raise a brow or two when I say that I love to watch marathon runners, particularly Kipchoge, run, and I will happily sit down and watch a major marathon from start to finish. Boring, I can hear you mutter. Kipchoge, though, is a beautiful runner to watch. I would best describe him as poetry in motion. Aside from his seemingly effortless glide across this earth for 42.2 kilometres, if you watch Kipchoge closely, you will notice that when he pushes himself to his limits, when he is virtually stripped bare and running at his absolute limit late in a marathon, perhaps about to break another world record, he will do something quite remarkable; he will smile.

Commentators often remark and debate the nature of his expression, which borders between a smile and a grimace. It is, though, how Kipchoge transforms his extreme discomfort into a positive mindset that enables him to achieve the incredible. It is one of the techniques he utilises to unlimit himself. He smiles to affect and influence his mind, to completely alter his mind, to tame the pain and to harness reserves beyond anything you or I can imagine.

After seeing Kipchoge implement this many times, I adopted this very technique when I was struggling, often during an exceedingly long run training session of between 60 and 70 kilometres. Whenever that voice in my head begins to say, "This is hard. It is too hard", and it would be so much easier to stop, I just smile and tell myself, "There is no such word as hard." It is remarkable how this practice changes my mindset. Within seconds, the voice dissipates, and my mind and spirit change from exhaustion to one of a positive state and a sense of gratitude. Suddenly, I feel much better, and my thoughts turn to the wonderful things I have been blessed with in my life—thoughts of being able to do something that only a fraction of the people on this planet can do or even imagine doing. Consequently, the adrenalin and euphoria return until the next time I need to utilise this technique. This might be in another 10 minutes or an hour. I never know when it will occur next, but I know it will return as I constantly push myself further, and I am ready.

There are many words that can influence, alter, and shape your mindset, either in a positive or negative direction, and you have the power to moderate, eliminate, or enhance them to change the way you think – that's guaranteed. It's important to identify these words, whether spoken or lingering within your own inner thoughts, so you can instantly transform them. Why do this, you might ask? Well, this will ultimately determine whether you choose the path of least resistance or persist in pursuing your goals. Incorporating such techniques will significantly contribute to cultivating a positive mindset. Keep in mind that each technique that empowers you to make the right decision is vital because every instance in which you choose to quit or give up will gradually make quitting and giving up more likely. If this pattern repeats frequently, surrendering and quitting may become your default outcome and destiny. Therefore, eliminate *hard* from your vocabulary today.

DAILY PRACTICE ACTION
Diet and Language

What 2 food items can you stop, start, or eat more of today to improve your diet?	Stop Start More
Write 5 words that you can identify that are negative in your vocabulary that you would like to eradicate to create a more positive mindset.	1. 2. 3. 4. 5.

My bed for the night at the 2016 Vinnies CEO Sleepout.

GRATITUDE WILL EMPOWER YOU

"Gratitude is an antidote to negative emotions, a neutraliser of envy, hostility, worry, and irritation. It is savouring, it is not taking things for granted, it is present-oriented."

— Sonja Lyubomirsky

When you meet a genuinely grateful person, you know it instantly. While you may not consciously think, "This person is filled with gratitude," you will feel an overwhelming sense of happiness in them and attraction to them. Grateful people are not only beautiful, but they are often humble, too, which is one of my favourite human traits. Typically, they care deeply about others, and you can't help but feel like you just want to be around them and in their presence. In many cases, this trait is instilled during childhood by parents and family, shaping their formative years.

However, it's also possible to self-cultivate and nurture this quality through consistent, diligent practice.

Gratitude stands as the most significant contributor to happiness and the evolution of a positive mindset. It can serve as the **bedrock** for believing in your ability to overcome any obstacle and achieve anything you desire. Two decades ago, during periods of mild depression, I began to refine my process of finding gratitude until it became a daily practice. Without a doubt, this technique, coupled with consistent daily effort, not only helped me endure immense challenges but allowed me to thrive through them.

Surviving adversity is a dramatically different mindset to thriving through adversity. Thriving will shift your mindset forever and improve your recovery and confidence the next time you face challenges and adversity. Initially, my goal was to feel gratitude every single day, eventually progressing to feeling grateful multiple times throughout the day. A mindset rooted in gratitude wields unparalleled influence over genuine happiness, and once you attain this precious state, you'll be inspired to create positive change and uncover your best self.

One of the most effective techniques I've developed involves envisioning a pair of old-fashioned scales, the kind with metal plates used to balance and weigh objects. In this method, I start by visualising the issue or problem that is negatively affecting my thoughts or emotions. Then, on the other side of the scales, I begin placing all the things in my life that I am grateful for. Initially, this can include fundamental things like good health or having a roof over my head, which, fortunately, more than 99% of people in Australia have.

Every day, I wake up and pile as many positive things as possible on one side of the scales until it becomes so heavy that it tips over and rests on the table. From that point on, no matter what negative events occur during my day, they are never enough to outweigh all the positive aspects I've accumulated. Even when something significant happens, I quickly recall everything positive and add it to the grateful side. The goal is to experience gratitude every single day, multiple times a day. This mindset is genuine happiness and will inspire you to make a positive impact on others and achieve your life goals.

This technique has been my greatest superpower and the reason I feel grateful every day of my life. If you find it challenging to master this technique initially, consider drawing a basic set of scales on a piece of paper and physically practice it by writing down all the things you're grateful for in your life. You can continue to add to this list. Rarely will your scales tip to the negative side.

I wonder how many people in Australia feel blessed that they have a roof over their heads at night. In 2014, the United Nations released a report that estimated 1.6 billion people live in poverty or are impoverished, lacking access to essentials like shelter, medical care, or food. This staggering number serves as a stark reminder of how fortunate many of us truly are, even in moments of despair.

I firmly believe that, during times of distress, when everything appears to be falling apart, you can find solace and gratitude by comparing your circumstances to those of billions of less fortunate individuals around the world. This approach has consistently worked for me, allowing me to quickly shift my perspective even in moments of considerable stress. Sometimes, all it takes is changing the lens through which you view your life and circumstances. This change in perspective not only alters your outlook but also fosters humility and empathy toward others. It empowers and inspires you to extend help to those less fortunate than you.

As you master this technique, whether through mental visualisation or using a physical representation like a piece of paper with a line drawn down the middle or an image of scales, your positive and gratitude-filled side will start to outweigh the negative one. When I first began using this powerful method, I made it a daily practice to allow only positive thoughts into my mind as I woke each day. I filled my thoughts with the numerous things I had to be genuinely grateful for, essentially cramming my head with positivity. Over time, this practice became a powerful tool that determined my mindset and enabled me to find happiness every day, regardless of the challenges I faced—some of which were truly devastating.

You can create your own written inventory of gratitude and continuously build upon the positive elements. You might even consider starting your gratitude stocktake and making copies so that you can revisit and add new positive aspects as you identify them. I guarantee that, eventually, your positive side will consistently outweigh anything troubling you on a given day. With practice, you'll develop the ability to instantly recall these positive aspects in your mind.

Perspective – don't sweat the small stuff.

Our sense of mental wellbeing is greatly shaped by our upbringing and our responses to the events and circumstances that life presents to us as it progresses. Life often dishes up situations that can either enrich our lives in a positive manner or impact us negatively. Your ability to positively deal with events that challenge you will be decided by your optimism and governed by your perspective.

Have you ever noticed people around you who consistently seem to be positive, happy, and grateful? Conversely, have you encountered people who tend to respond to even minor problems or issues with negativity and pessimism? A degree of our individual capacity for this outlook is innate, formed by the attitudes and beliefs instilled in us by our parents, and this foundation is further reinforced as we go through life.

Alongside the techniques that have enabled me to practice gratitude every single day, I've also discovered another highly effective method that proved invaluable during the initial years of transitioning to a perpetually positive and calm mindset. This technique involves creating perspective in any given moment and has been invaluable to me, especially when faced with negative or stressful situations. I first encountered this technique during a corporate offsite approximately 25 years ago. This powerful tool will enable you to swiftly assess or defuse challenging situations, as well as reduce stress and anxiety.

Essentially, this technique provides a highly effective test for determining which issues are genuinely not worth your worry and stress in the grand scheme of life. In other words, this is how you learn not to "sweat the small stuff". As I've emphasised previously, effectively addressing issues, negativity, and anxiety is crucial for taking control and swiftly moving past obstacles that hinder you from becoming your best self.

To some extent, there is a similarity between the perspective technique and the gratitude exercise, but I've found that the perspective technique comes into play at a more fundamental level when you're dealing with stronger worries or concerns and need a rapid way to discount or deescalate them.

To explain this perspective technique, let me share an exercise conducted by a facilitator during that development day. He asked each participant to imagine the following wildlife scenarios and then instructed everyone to consider and align their individual concerns with one of the wildlife experiences.

Is your issue that:

1. You are floating in the middle of an ocean after your boat has sunk fifty kilometres from the closest shore. You are treading water, and there are multiple large shark fins circling you.

2. You have just been accidentally left behind by a safari tour amongst a cluster of nearby climbable trees while a lion pride circles around you.

3. You are walking along the banks of the Amazon when you trip and fall into waters that are populated with small groups of Piranha fish.

4. You are walking along a bush track when you are confronted by a venomous snake curled up on the path a few metres away.

5. You are spring cleaning and uncover a pair of nesting redback spiders.

6. You are walking past a garden gate when an overprotective Jack Russel scampers out and tries to bite your ankle.

7. You are gardening and unearth a nest of green ants that want to bite you.

8. You are sitting around at an evening barbecue, and the mosquitoes begin to bite.

The key to this exercise is to connect your issue with one of the scenarios to determine its actual severity. This ranges from scenario 1, signifying you will certainly die, through to scenario 8, indicating a minor irritation that will soon resolve itself and go away.

If you prefer a different scale, you can create your own set of scenarios that provide a relative and contextual understanding easily applicable to your real-life situation. When dealing with issues ranked from 4 to 8, which is the case for most when accurately assessed, you can appropriately address them as situations that are generally inconsequential and don't warrant the emotional or psychological distress they may have previously caused.

You only ever get today, so make it count.

"Live for today" is a common mantra, and it makes good sense, but its true power lies in the intent behind it. For some, it becomes a justification for indulging in temporary pleasures, like an emotional sugar rush that offers short-lived endorphins and quick fixes, creating a cycle of fleeting highs. While occasional self-reward is essential, habitual short-term gratification can be detrimental.

For me, this mantra is a motivation to engage in activities daily that enhance my life rather than seeking shortcuts or cheap thrills. It means not postponing challenging tasks because tomorrow never truly arrives; we only ever have today to make a difference. Delaying what you don't want to do can become a habit, leading to regret that consumes happiness, positivity, and legacy.

Harness the power of recognising that today is all you have by spending a few minutes each evening reflecting on what positive impact you've made during the day. Get your journal out and write down your thoughts. This daily discipline holds you accountable for actions from your to-do list or your 90-Day High-Performance Plan that you didn't accomplish that day and serves as motivation to avoid regrets and ensure progress.

This daily discipline should motivate you to change before your next review the following evening, eventually becoming a learned habit. Consider this exercise a significant self-investment that will help you become the best version of yourself. The choice is yours: take the easier road or the harder road. One will likely lead you to the same place you are now, while the other offers the potential for meaningful transformation.

Another significant benefit of this practice and mindset is the ability to be fully present in the moment. There have been times in my life when I failed to be fully present, wasting opportunities to embrace the day to its fullest. As you age, your self-awareness should make you increasingly uncomfortable if you don't make each day count.

Technology, with its constant communication and access to everything, has become addictive and pervasive. People are often consumed by daily life and distracted from the world around them. Just observe what happens in an elevator filled with people; chances are, most of them will be looking down at their phones. This not only hinders genuine interactions with others but also eliminates the need to make an effort to engage with people.

An extreme consequence of this distraction is evident when families go on vacation together. Holidays are valuable opportunities for families to interact and enjoy each other's company. However, it's disheartening to see many families spending too much time glued to their phones, missing out on precious moments of togetherness. People sit around a pool in a beautiful location, yet they are fixated on their phone screens. Or a family of four goes out to dinner while on vacation, but all four individuals are immersed in their phones, not communicating with each other or appreciating their surroundings, which are often beautiful or unique. This is a tragic waste of precious moments.

Many people have a habit of dreading Mondays as the start of the workweek or celebrating Fridays as the gateway to the weekend. Having worked in large Australian corporations, I can conclusively state that the vibe in an organisation is dramatically different on a Monday as opposed to a Friday. But why does this happen when they're just regular days with the same number of hours? While it's natural to look forward to the weekend, making Monday feel like a waste can cause you to miss out on life.

A wise person once told me something that completely changed my perspective on this. They said, "By the time you reach 70, you will have lived 10 whole years of Mondays. So, if you choose not to enjoy or make the most of Mondays, you'll have wasted 10 years of your life, and I'm sure you'd do anything to get those 10 years back. If Tuesdays aren't much better, that's 20 years wasted, and so on..." This wisdom struck a chord with me. For the past 30 years, I've focused on enjoying every day I'm given. The key to cultivating a positive mindset each day, regardless of the day of the week, is to start by recognising the positive aspects of your life and expressing gratitude the moment you wake up. This daily practice has allowed me to take control of my mindset and happiness, ultimately changing my day-to-day life for the better.

This daily practice will help you develop the skill of creating perspective. I also recommend replicating this exercise whenever you feel mentally affected by an issue, and it's even better if you write it down, referring to the incident table. As you become more proficient with this technique, you'll be able to use it instantly and efficiently in your mind.

DAILY PRACTICE ACTION
Perspective

What situation or events worried you and impacted your confidence or mindset during the last month or so?	
On a scale of one to eight (one being the worst), how do you rate your reaction?	
Based on the wildlife incident scale that I shared in this chapter; how would you now rate the impact given this new perspective?	

Starting now, take out a pen and spend a few minutes contemplating and noting down the many things you feel grateful for in your life, adding them to the positive, right-hand side of the scales. Next, dedicate a few more minutes to reflecting on and writing down what is troubling you or generating negative thoughts. I recommend beginning each day in this way until you've honed this technique and can visualise the scales and virtually balance the equation of gratitude.

DAILY PRACTICE ACTION
Gratitude

Things I am grateful for.	What I am worried about.
_____	_____
_____	_____
_____	_____
_____	_____
_____	_____
_____	_____
_____	_____
_____	

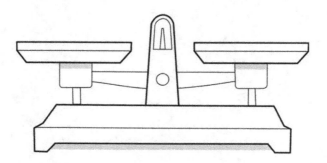

After 226 kilometres of racing the 1997 Hawaii Ironman World Championships, elite athletes Sian Welsh and Wendy Ingraham famously crawl to the finish line after battling it out for 226 kilometres.

RESILIENCE FORMS THE FOUNDATION OF EVERY SUCCESS

"The temptation to quit will be greatest just before you are about to succeed"

— Chinese proverb

Resilience

Resilience is generally considered to be, or defined as, the ability to cope with unexpected changes and challenges in life. These moments of adversity are inevitable for most of us, and they can range from minor setbacks to major life-altering events or trauma. We all naturally possess varying levels of resilience due to our unique life experiences and circumstances, but whoever you are, resilience is something you can develop.

Think about resilience as a rating on a scale from 1 to 10, with 1 being the most basic level of survival and 10 representing the capability to turn adversity into a meaningful, positive outcome quickly. Where do you see yourself right now on this scale? Rating your level of resilience is a valuable exercise that will enable you to identify aspects of your mental fortitude and resilience that you can begin to strengthen.

In the previous chapter, I discussed techniques for quickly assessing the significance of a situation, which is often the first place to start when you are confronted by challenges or trauma. The intent of this exercise is to place the situation in its rightful place,

The second technique is finding gratitude. Both of these exercises can contribute to a more positive mindset and reduce stress and anxiety. These techniques can help you recognise that many challenges and issues are not worth excessive worry or sleepless nights.

My view on resilience is that by mastering mindful techniques daily, you will soon score yourself between 8 and 10. This means that you will feel happy every day and always be positive about what you can achieve. You will move on from challenges quickly and switch to solution mode almost effortlessly. You will make positive decisions more quickly and, consequently, move forward quickly to find what you need to do to continue your stalled momentum and power towards achieving your goals.

Examples of resilience are abundant, and they often go beyond belief. While they are particularly evident in the world of sports, they are present in every aspect of life. Many individuals and teams have faced numerous setbacks and failures on their journey to ultimate success, whatever that may be for them. It's not challenging to find instances of people achieving remarkable success despite enduring countless rejections, failures, or setbacks. Consider Michael Jordan, arguably the greatest basketball player, who famously stated, "Every shot I missed, and there were thousands of them, was one small step closer to scoring and success." Then there's Stephen King, one of the most successful authors in history, who faced dozens of rejections before finally getting one of his manuscripts published, ultimately selling hundreds of millions of books.

As you can see, resilience is a mindset that can be cultivated and honed to overcome adversity. Once you've mastered the art of maintaining a genuinely positive mindset, you'll view any failure or setback as another step on the road to success. How empowering is that! To underscore the importance of developing resilience further, I've gathered several personal experiences from my life that I hope will illustrate the effectiveness of these methods in building exceptional resilience.

What doesn't kill you makes you stronger—or does it?

You've likely encountered this familiar saying before. Perhaps you've even uttered it yourself in moments of loss, defeat, substantial disappointment, or even tragedy as a way to maintain a semblance of positivity in the midst of adversity. The underlying philosophy here is well-intentioned but often flawed, especially in its common application. While it's generally accurate that loss, failure, trauma, and similar experiences impact those who face them, what isn't necessarily true, in my experience, is that these effects consistently result in individuals becoming harder, tougher, wiser, and more resilient.

However, the term stronger typically implies a positive outcome arising from a traumatic experience that enables a person to become better. But becoming better and doing so quickly hinges on a deliberate choice to improve oneself in the wake of loss, tragedy, or trauma—transforming these experiences into opportunities for personal growth rather than merely being better equipped to endure future challenges. The perspective that suggests merely surviving something inherently makes you better is fundamentally flawed, especially since behavioural or habitual changes won't occur without a conscious, mindful decision to change. True strength emerges when you construct a purpose-driven plan fuelled by your passion to derive value from your experiences, failures, or setbacks.

Throughout this book, I share numerous examples that vividly illustrate positive outcomes I've achieved, motivated by my greatest disasters. These stories will not only demonstrate your capacity to accomplish remarkable things but also help you find meaning and purpose during times of loss or suffering, empowering you to move forward positively.

So, have you ever encountered setbacks or felt like quitting? Have there been days when you've concluded that things must have gone wrong because you got out of bed on the wrong side? Or, that you must have crossed a black cat, or walked under a ladder and not realised it? Or you are just orOr you are just orHave there been days when you've concluded that things must have gone wrong because you got out of bed on the wrong side? Or that you must have crossed a black cat or walked under a ladder and not realised it? Or having bad luck? I am guessing that you do, as most humans do.

How do you respond to these situations, whether they involve minor misfortunes, significant disasters, or frequent bouts of bad luck? We all face adversity from time to time, but our responses can turn around our experience, which is usually a negative one or, at best, neutral.

The truth is your reaction to adversity plays a crucial role in your ability to overcome challenges and find solutions quickly. It will also influence your ability to grow. The longer you dwell on a problem, the less likely you are to recover and resolve it. Not only that, but consciously choosing to look at the problem from either a negative or positive perspective will significantly affect your happiness and demeanour.

If you consistently perceive problems as negative, there is a chance you will foster a victim mentality that holds you back in life and hinders your happiness. It will prevent you from achieving your full potential. On the other hand, decisively adopting a proactive, solution-oriented mindset allows you to navigate challenges, problems, and disasters more swiftly, leading to increased happiness. With practice, you'll naturally shift into problem-solving mode as soon as you identify an issue. Watch how others around you respond to your newfound mindset; it can be truly transformative.

Many of the greatest setbacks in my life include the thirty-plus times I have been hospitalised due to accidents or illnesses, some of which were life-threatening. It's almost become a running joke that if I were a cat, I would have long exceeded my nine lives. In an earlier chapter, I shared a few of the most serious accidents that put my life and determination to the test. However, there was also a peculiar period in my life when my family would playfully ask me each year what I thought might land me in the hospital during the upcoming Christmas break. This strange streak of events occurred consistently over seven years, always coinciding with the Christmas holiday season.

One strange consequence of such a brutal life is that whenever faced with a new medical situation, I'm asked to document my medical history. With so many incidents spanning several decades, I have little clue where to begin when faced with a medical history form, so I typically mark no to everything unless I can see a relevant significance or correlation.

The series of Christmas medical issues started rather bizarrely, although you might interpret the whole chain of events as unusual. It all started with a single bite from an unidentified insect. While I'll never know for sure, my doctor at the time made an educated guess that it might have been a bite from a toxic spider of some sort. He took a sample from the highly swollen area on my left index finger, stitched it back up, and sent me on my way with strong painkillers.

Despite regularly taking the medication, I spent the entire night tossing and turning in discomfort. Eventually, I couldn't bear it any longer, and at 4 am on Christmas morning, I decided to take action. Upon closer examination, as I got out of bed, I discovered that the stitches had torn through the skin at the tip of my finger due to the swelling. I must admit that neither my doctor nor my first wife was particularly thrilled with me when I called him at 5 am on Christmas morning, pleading for him to see me and either remove or cut the stitches.

The following year, while playing soccer again one night in December, my face collided with another player's head, which broke my nose. I didn't get it checked right away, and by the time I did, the fractured bone had already started to heal, making the process of resetting my nose particularly uncomfortable.

The year after that, I found myself in and out of Nambour Hospital multiple times due to the truck accident I described earlier while riding my bike. Then, a year later, I had my one and only pool accident. Given my frequent travels, I often had to switch swimming pools, most of which were large, deep Olympic-sized pools. However, my local pool in Buderim was only 25 metres in length and relatively shallow. One Christmas Eve, I arrived at the pool quite late and rushed to dive in so I could complete my laps. Unfortunately, I misjudged the pool's depth, and my forehead struck the bottom, catching on a tile and causing a gash that required stitches.

For many years, my training schedule was at its heaviest and most intense during the Christmas holiday period as I prepared for Ironman Australia each April. This was often preceded by races like Ironman NZ or Ironman Malaysia at the end of February or early March. Living in Queensland throughout this period meant enduring training sessions in the scorching Queensland summer, with temperatures frequently reaching 40 degrees Celsius or at least above 35 Celsius. So, when the hottest days fell on weekends, there was a good chance that I would need to train during the hottest part of the day, either running or cycling. Over time, staying properly hydrated became an ongoing challenge, and this no doubt took its toll.

On New Year's Day of the following year, at 4 am, I woke up with excruciating abdominal pains. As is my tendency with physical pain and discomfort, I usually tolerate it for as long as I can, hoping it might resolve on its own before seeking medical attention. So, in my infinite wisdom, I decided to tough it out and found myself eventually curled up in a ball on the bathroom floor, naked and sweating profusely as a kidney stone made its painful journey through my system. When the extreme pain finally subsided, my wife convinced me that I should go to the hospital to get checked out.

When I described my intense summertime training regimen, the symptoms, and the level of pain I had endured, the doctor didn't seem surprised and smiled knowingly.

"I believe you've likely passed a kidney stone. In fact, I would be quite certain that that is the case. So, I suggest you go home, sit somewhere cool, drink plenty of electrolytes over the next week, and absolutely do not exercise."

"Sure", I thought, as I smiled back and said, "Ok, no problem," although I already knew that I would be out training the next morning. And I was.

Amongst other hospitalisations, incidents like falling off a ladder and crashing through a glass window, suffering a hematoma in my knee, undergoing knee surgery, having tonsils removed, eye surgery, enduring 10 rib fractures from a single bike accident, ankle surgery, surgery for a groin hernia, and overcoming the life-threatening of severe ulcerative colitis featured among my physical setbacks. The purpose of sharing some of my setbacks and challenges is to demonstrate that you can overcome anything you choose to overcome. You simply must make the choice to win.

The harder you fall

Life's most important lessons are often learned through failure. The more significant the failure, the greater the value of the lesson. This also creates a huge opportunity to take that experience and make it count – really count! Most people in life view their fear of failure as the very reason not to pursue their dreams. Why sacrifice, commit, and take the harder road and expose yourself to the risk of failure? In some ways, I used to be one of them. Maybe that's you now, and you've gotten used to your comfort zone.

However, as I fortified my mind by seeking out challenges and overcoming obstacles, I embraced and internalised the motto: "If you don't fail, you're not pushing hard enough."

I draw on four of the most significant failures in my life and utilise the pain, frustration, and lessons to consistently push myself beyond my perceived limits and accomplish my most ambitious goals. These failures are etched so deeply in my memory that they could have occurred just yesterday. Perhaps it's because, during those traumatic moments, I made a conscious decision to engrave the emotional depths I had plummeted into with intricate detail. Even now, 23 years after the first disaster, I can shut my eyes and transport myself back to those very moments, and the heartache feels as real as ever. I also vividly remember the promise I made to myself during those times of disaster and failure—that they would ultimately have a positive meaning in my life.

To truly savour the elation of victory, and I mean victory as defined by your internal standards, not necessarily triumphing over someone else, you must first go through the despair and anguish of a corresponding failure. Just like in life, the things that hold the deepest meaning are often born out of struggle, unwavering effort, and relentless perseverance. You, too, can harness your most challenging experiences as the driving force behind your pursuit of greater accomplishments and the achievement of seemingly impossible feats.

18 June 2000, Nice, France

Every year, the International Triathlon Union (ITU) organises the ITU Long Distance World Championships, featuring categories for Elite Professionals, both Men and Women, as well as age group competitors in both the Men's and Women's divisions.

Each registered nation must select a maximum total of 20 competitors across all age groups while adhering to strict qualification criteria. With only two Ironman races under my belt at the time, my chances of being selected were apparently quite narrow.

Two weeks following the Australian Ironman event in Forster, the applications for the Australian team selection came to a close. Just two days later, the team roster was unveiled, and I was delighted to find myself among the chosen athletes for the Australian age group team. This opportunity carried even more significance than my previous selection to represent Australia as an age group competitor in the Duathlon World Championships in the US. It was a larger-scale race, featuring a higher number of competitors and boasting greater prestige. Undoubtedly, my strong performances at the Stradbroke Half-Ironman and Forster events were instrumental in securing my spot on the team.

We arrived in Nice, my new partner, Jen and I, a week before the race, and everything was going well up until four days before race day. I woke up with a sore throat, blocked sinuses, and a head full of mucus, which made breathing heavy. This was my worst nightmare.

Despite my attempts to stay positive, I was seriously sick, and I knew it. While medication could have been a partial solution, I had reservations about taking anything so close to such a significant race. There were concerns about the safety of my health, as some drugs mask the symptoms of illness, and also the risk of violating ITU regulations by using unauthorised substances.

I made every effort to rest in the apartment with my feet up, hoping for a miraculous recovery. However, as race morning arrived, my condition had worsened. A dry cough had developed, and my breathing was now extremely laboured. Despite my best attempts to put on a brave face, in my heart, I knew that my condition was far from ideal for a race of this magnitude. A race that I had trained so hard for over the last twelve months.

After setting up my bike and running gear at the solitary transition area along the Esplanade, I joined approximately 2,000 international competitors on the rocky beach. We were all gathered for a mass running start into the water.

Even as I stood on the beach, my breathing was already laboured, but I was determined to give this my best shot. The starter's gun sounded, and we all ran a few metres into the water, waded a few strides, then dived in and began swimming. Much of the next 150 metres was a blur, but I recall being pushed under many times and consequently gasping for air within 50 metres of swimming. By the time I had reached 150 metres, I was in real trouble, gasping for air, taking on mouthfuls of water and could not breathe. My heart raced. Reluctantly, I raised my hand to signal that I needed to be rescued by one of the official race dinghies, which approached rapidly. They came alongside, pulled me into the rubber dinghy, and sped toward the beach.

Even though I was incredibly ill, the most painful part was the anguish in my heart, closely followed by the blow to my ego and dignity as I was helped from the raft and up the stony beach, with thousands of spectators still gathered and watching along the shoreline. I had suffered an epic failure on a grand stage.

After a thorough check by the race medical team, I made my way back to my bike and gear in the transition area. At this point, I not only felt physically ill but also mentally shattered and deeply distraught. In that moment, I knew that this had to count for something. I realised that I needed to absorb and bottle the devastating emotions, using them as fuel to motivate and drive me towards making amends for this monumental failure in the future. I was determined to find a purpose for my pain and avenge this catastrophic day.

I had to fight the strong urge to pack my bike and gear and go back to the apartment right away, but I knew that would only make me feel like I was running away. Instead, I sat down next to my bike and, over the next 45 minutes, watched as other competitors returned from their swim and continued on their way to achieving their dreams. That stung.

Once everyone had finished the swim and embarked on the main course, I gathered my gear and headed back to the apartment for some rest. As the bike leg neared its end with the elite athletes returning to Nice, we positioned ourselves near the transition area and observed all the competitors as they made their way back over the next couple of hours.

After that, Jen and I sat in a café. I didn't say much as we watched the competitors run past on the two-run loops that made up the twenty-kilometre run. It hurt to watch everyone successfully achieve their dreams and goals on one of the biggest stages, but then that was the point; it had to hurt.

Later that day, we sat down to eat dinner outside at a restaurant in one of the quaint back streets. There were people everywhere, mostly buzzing from the adrenalin created by the race.

The final part of the ordeal was watching the embraces and effusive smiles of athletes, shiny finisher's medals around their necks as they wandered around Nice. Mission complete. I would draw on those emotions hundreds of times in the coming years, especially over the next five or so...

Ironman NZ, Lake Taupō

In 1985, the New Zealand Ironman became the second-ever Ironman race around the world, behind the legendary Hawaii Ironman World Championships in Kona. It has a rich history, starting in Auckland and now firmly established in Taupō. Taupō is a picturesque location in the heart of New Zealand's North Island, hosting many significant sporting events, including triathlons, cycling races, and long-distance running events.

I picked Taupō to be my first Ironman race outside of Australia for several reasons. Some of my triathlon friends were entering this race, given its proximity to Australia. Also, because there were some who believed it might be slightly easier to qualify for the Hawaii Ironman there, compared to the Australian race. The timing of the race aligned with my qualification goals, taking place in early March, about five to six weeks before the Forster Ironman. The principle being that this could prove to be the perfect preparation for me to go fast in the Australia race, if I didn't pick up any injuries.

The week in Taupō passed quickly, and with it, my confidence grew. However, the prospect of swimming for over an hour in the cold 16 degrees Celsius waters of Lake Taupō was not something I was relishing. I had trained rigorously and gained valuable experience from previous Ironman races, making me increasingly bullish and optimistic about my chances of qualifying for Hawaii. I had planned the race meticulously in my head, envisioning a successful qualification.

However, I had yet to learn a critical lesson—no one is bigger than the Ironman race. It demands perfect training, pacing, nutrition planning, execution, and, most importantly, respect. I was about to face a race day where I would get four out of these five essential elements wrong, all in one day.

On race day, despite this being a wetsuit swim, I stood up to my waist in Lake Taupō freezing cold.

As daylight broke, there was a stirring welcome by the local first nations Māori people – I would have loved to have seen that ritual from the banks of the lake as a spectator without the start of race nerves. But my mind was somewhere else. This was my race now. I was going to blow this race apart and qualify for Hawaii.

As soon as the cannon perched high on the lake's bank sounded, 1,500 athletes waded into the dark waters, ready to find their rhythm. No matter how many times I had experienced the chaotic start of a big race, I never felt adequately prepared to handle the situation. My original fear of drowning made it challenging to remain calm amidst the chaos.

The turbulent water, coupled with the feeling of claustrophobia from battling for a clear space for at least 5 minutes, triggered waves of panic in my mind and body. In my desperation to escape the mayhem, I expended far too much energy, trying to distance myself as quickly as possible from the commotion. This led to my heart rate soaring far beyond what it should have been, akin to burning unnecessary energy. I've often heard this described as "burning too many matches too early."

Compounding the issue, I had gone out too hard, and within a few minutes, I began to hyperventilate, causing me to momentarily consider swimming sideways and giving up. I bobbed in the water for about 10 seconds while I tried to convince myself to calm down and continue.

Seventy minutes of swimming in cold freshwater, which provided little to no buoyancy compared to saltwater, took its toll on me – someone who has practically no bodyfat and sinks like a stone. I exited the water and embarked on a long transition leg. The transition from swimming to running felt surreal, as most of my blood had shifted to my upper body, and my lower legs felt numb from the icy water. I finally thawed out after a few hundred metres of running barefoot across concrete and bitumen surfaces.

Finding my transition bag, among many others, I quickly changed into my cycling gear, mounted my bike, and set off. The air was now around 12 degrees Celsius, feeling even colder when wet and racing on a performance bike. Thank goodness for adrenaline. As I climbed the hills heading out of town, my speed slowed, and I began to question my initial pace. The constant uphill grind of the "false flat" started to wear me down, and I realised I might have overexerted myself during the outbound leg. The turnaround point would reveal the impact of my initial pace.

By the time that most of us had climbed up the hills heading out of town, onto one of the main roads out of Taupō, our core temperatures had lifted as the morning temperatures edged their way up. An hour into the bike leg, I was already feeling that I may have gone out a little too quickly, but my desire and instinct to compete overrode my logical thoughts, and I powered on. The scenery was quite beautiful as the outbound leg of the first lap progressed. Then, suddenly, the turnaround was there. I checked my time and pace at the turnaround and felt encouraged. Today, I was going to qualify, I told myself. For sure.

As I rode back towards town and the headwind picked up, I became aware of the constant uphill grind of the seemingly never-ending false flat, a term they use in cycling to explain a low, gradual rising climb that appears to be flat but is not. My speed slowed, and it began to dawn on me that my outward pace would have been somewhat exaggerated by the slight fall in elevation plus the tailwind we had experienced on the way out. The only way to evaluate the impact of this pace would be to wait until I had fully completed the 90-kilometre first lap as we passed through Taupō again.

Fortunately, the last few kilometres heading back into town were all downhill. As you transition from hours of virtual silence and spectatorless highways on which you are often sent during the middle of the bike leg into the populated areas of the town from which you started, where there are thousands of supporters, you increase your adrenalin, which falsely overstates your physical state. It feels so good, though, until the commotion and cheering dissipate into the background, and you are once again virtually on your own on a lonely highway with only your thoughts. It is an extreme high, followed by the corresponding low. That is exactly where I was, riding the climbs Back to the low.while heading back out to town. Then back to low. It was then that I took stock of my physical situation and the cumulating effects of racing now for almost 4 hours versus the six remaining hours to go.

This mental reconciliation, which I've come to recognise during strenuous exertion, involves a constant inner debate about the likelihood of achieving your goals, whether it's at your current pace or at all. It's a process by which your brain assesses and regulates your physical output to safeguard against potential harm or even life-threatening situations. These mental games pull your thoughts in various directions and intensify the battle of wills within your mind. They become more frequent, testing your determination and resilience to the absolute limit.

For now, I was hanging in there, although I had started to realise that I had not stuck to my food and drink plan, perhaps because the weather was much colder than I was used to. Perhaps also because I did not want to waste a second during my quest for qualification. I would come to realise, though, that the Ironman is always an exceptionally long race, and the worst mistake you can make is to go out too quickly, followed closely by not following a race nutrition plan.

There is a remarkably simple and valuable piece of advice that I would give to anyone who is participating in a race that is at least 40 minutes in duration, and that is to tell yourself during the first half of the race that there is always time to catch up in the second half. In fact, in most running races, achieving a negative split (running the second half faster) often indicates that you've executed a nearly perfect race strategy.

An extensive analysis was conducted, covering 26 marathons, and examining the results of 876,703 participants comprising 754,851 runners. The study aimed to compare the performance differences between positive splits (going slower in the second half of the race) and negative splits (running the second half faster). The findings revealed that only 13% of finishes were characterised by negative splits, with an average positive split of 8.25%. It's worth noting that, in my experience, my best marathon performance was characterised by a negative split, but I rarely competed in standalone marathons of that distance. However, when it comes to races spanning 100 kilometres or more, achieving a negative split has proven to be a challenging feat for me.

As the outbound leg progressed on the second lap, I picked up speed again with the stronger tailwind, but I could feel my energy levels waning and an empty tank approaching. The sun had warmed up a bit as we approached the turnaround point for the second time, the point that would lead us back to Taupō and the transition to the run. Within just 100 metres of making the turnaround, my worst fears were realised as the wind picked up, and maintaining a decent speed became increasingly difficult. I had deluded myself with the assistance of the tailwind, which was now punishing me for my earlier haste. My legs felt heavy, my pace dropped, and that nagging voice in my head began to question why I was putting myself through this, wondering if I could even finish, and even tempting me with thoughts of quitting. The last turnaround point, which we had just passed, was about 50 kilometres from the end of the bike leg. This part of the race is often challenging, depending on the conditions, course layout, and how well you've managed your nutrition and pacing. Unfortunately, I hadn't done either particularly well. I had started too fast, gotten ahead of myself, and convinced myself that I could smash this race.

For the next 20 kilometres or so, I battled on, wrestling with the relentless voice of reason in my head. "Hey, just give up. You can go back and rest. There's no shame in stopping. You've given it your all today, and it's just not your day." Eventually, at around 150 kilometres into the bike leg, fatigued from climbing and battling against a relentless headwind, I pulled my bike to the side, dismounted, and sat on the roadside, waiting to be picked up by the race sweeper vehicle. The voice had won. I had lost.

Ten minutes later, with my bike loaded into the sweeper truck, I was on my way back to Taupō. A sense of unease settled in. I had already started crafting my story, the narrative I would tell my family and friends. The reasons why I had been forced to withdraw. To quit. Despite my attempts to reassure myself, I knew that I had quit. I was a quitter. It was all my fault. The 30-kilometre ride back to town felt like an eternity. I was physically comfortable and warm, but I must have questioned my decision a hundred times during that short journey. "Could I have finished? Should I have finished? Could I have just pulled over and taken a few minutes to rest? Why didn't I pause my decision for a moment? Why did I quit for good?" The questions swirled in my mind, and deep down, I knew the answers. I had once heard a wise person say, regarding quitting a race, "You can convince everyone around you why you quit, except for yourself. You know the truth, and it's only your truth that matters."The 30-kilometre ride back to town felt like an eternity. I was physically comfortable and warm, but I must have questioned my decision a hundred times during that short journey. "Could I have finished? Should I have finished? Could I have just pulled over and taken a few minutes to rest? Why didn't I pause my decision for a moment? Why did I quit for good?" The questions swirled in my mind, and deep down, I knew the answers. I had once heard a wise person say, regarding quitting a race, "You can convince everyone around you why you quit, except for yourself. You know the truth, and it's only your truth that matters." The truth was already starting to sting, and it would only get worse.

When faced with failure, whether it's due to factors within your control or beyond it, you inevitably start thinking about the consequences. Dealing with the former outcome is especially challenging because it likely means you're responsible, and the potential consequences weigh heavily on your mind: "Does this mean I might quit again when things get tough? What about the sacrifices my family made over the past year for me to be here? What about the countless hours of training I've put in? What about the expenses of travelling to the race? Does this mean my dream and goal are shattered? How will you ever qualify for Hawaii, Jason?" The questions kept coming. While my family was understanding of my failure and why I had stopped, which offered some comfort, I couldn't escape the deep sense of discontent that welled up inside me like an illness. There was no hiding from my own self-assessment, regardless of what others thought or said.

As the day wore on, we returned to the race and watched some people realise their dreams after persevering through whatever challenges they had faced that day. Unlike me, they had stayed the course. While this was uplifting in a sense, the emotional pain and disappointment in myself, yes, disappointment, a word I had intentionally removed from my vocabulary, ran even deeper. Late that afternoon, I sat in our motel room and gathered all my negative emotions, so I could bottle that feeling, just as I had done in Nice a couple of years ago. I needed to preserve it for a time when the temptation to quit once again seemed irresistible. This epic failure must find a purpose, and, like Nice, I will use this to find redemption – no matter how long it takes me. I had to pull myself together and stop sulking, not only for my sake but for the sake of my family, who had stood by and supported me throughout the past year.

I went for a walk on my own along the lake shore. As I walked, I resolved to turn my dejection around, to stop blaming myself, to learn from this experience, from the poor decisions I had made, and to turn this pain and disappointment into something useful. Today's job was a long way from done. I decided that I would get up first thing in the morning and run the marathon of 42 kilometres, as I should have today, on my own. Then, I would refocus on the Australian Ironman, just six weeks or so away.

The next morning, I woke early and headed out to run 42 kilometres on my tired legs. Taupō and its surroundings were deathly quiet as most locals slept in on a cool, misty Sunday morning.

Meanwhile, many of the competitors caught up on the rest they had been deprived of for days. During most of that long run, my thoughts were determined, positive, and forward-looking. I knew I needed to move on quickly. A couple of days later, we were sad to see the beautiful town of Taupō disappearing in the wing mirrors of our hire car. For me, though, it symbolised much more than heading home. I had learned one of the most

important lessons of my life, and I knew, as I looked back, that I would be back here someday soon. Taupō would prove to be my redemption from this gut-wrenching failure.

Forster 2001

The 2001 Forster Ironman marked my fourth Ironman race and my third participation in the iconic Forster event, which also served as the Australian Championships. In the week leading up to the race, everything seemed typical as we enjoyed the sunshine, soaked up the event's atmosphere, and made final adjustments to my equipment and race preparations. However, the tone shifted when official race proceedings began with race registration two days before the event.

Registration is where all athletes officially check in and collect their race pack with number plates for the bike and other numbering. I stood in the moderate line, feeling relatively relaxed, and waited for my turn.

"Jason Dunn from Buderim, Queensland," I responded to the female volunteer who asked me for my name, then promptly found me in the database on her laptop. She studied my record and began to ask some questions to confirm that I was indeed who I said I was and that they had all my vital information correctly recorded on file.

"So, can you confirm the spelling of your name and confirm your date of birth?"

"And I note that you are not taking any medication regularly?"

"And I see that you don't wish to qualify for the Hawaii Ironman World Championship."

"WHAT!!!!!," blurted from my mouth as I sat bolt upright and virtually bounced out of my seat. "No, I most definitely do want to qualify for Hawaii, and that's what I ticked on the application form."

"Yes, see here," she remarked, swivelling her laptop around to display the entry record that had supposedly been extracted from the entry form I completed six months earlier.

Of course, there was no doubt in my mind, given that qualifying for Hawaii had become my life's purpose and occupied my thoughts every day for the last three years. My heart raced in those few moments that it took the race official to consider my predicament. No doubt, things in her world had been going smoothly that morning until that moment.

"Ok," she exclaimed after what seemed like an eternity, "I'll make a note here on the system and get someone to rectify this for you."

"Are you sure that will be fixed?" I asked as I scrutinised her face for any signs that indicated uncertainty.

"Yes, we will fix that."

"Phew!" My heart rate slowed as I felt the presence of sweat on my skin. I also felt a little nauseous as I got up from my chair and headed out with my competitor's race bags.

Race day dawned with ideal weather. My dad and Rhonda had made the drive up from Sydney to support me on this special day.

This would be the first time they would see me racing, and I was excited about that proposition. My epic failure in New Zealand consumed my mind while setting up my bike and transition gear. I had worked hard to move on from the negative aspects of New Zealand, and now I focused on redemption on this day.

The race director's gun sounded, and the river instantly turned from its still morning calm to a frenzied thrashing, as though millions of fish were all avoiding a predator at that one moment. I calmed myself as I sustained kicks and fisted blows to my head. "This will only last for 500 metres or so, Jason. Then you will find your space," I assured myself.

It came as no surprise to me that I exited the swim in 854th place and thought about what I had to do to make up for it in the bike leg and then the marathon. It would be fair to say that in 2001 my bike fitness and bike handling skills had come a long way, and I managed to complete the 180.2 kilometres in 210th place, advancing my overall position considerably.

"This is your time now," I thought as I blasted out of T2 and onto the marathon run course. Having competed here twice before, I felt that I had a strong enough appreciation of the course, where the tougher segments arrived, running the sharper hills of the back streets, and where to put my foot down if I was physically capable. Having everyone there supporting me along the way lifted my spirits and regularly spurred me on.

I cannot say that there weren't times during the run that the voice tried hard to persuade me to quit in exchange for something more comfortable or to just walk, but I fought him all day and managed to defeat him. During the last couple of kilometres, I soaked up the atmosphere and imagined how I would feel as I finished. This was going to be my fastest Ironman yet and potentially earn me a precious and, so far, elusive Hawaii qualifying spot. I crossed the line in 10.08 and pumped both fists above my head. Finally, it was time to put the pain and suffering aside and enjoy the euphoria that infuses your mind and body after a successful race that has pushed you to your limits for over 10 hours.

So, the post-race operating rhythm the day following every Ironman race around the world involves race officials posting the lists of the top finishers and Hawaii Ironman qualifiers on an official race board outside headquarters. After every race it is traditional for hopeful qualifiers to gather around the board area in anticipation of the results being posted. I had raced well in my 35-39, which accounted for by far the highest number of competitors in any of the age groups and, given that I was age 38, I would have been one of the oldest in my ag group. Consequently, as the number of Hawaii qualifying spots allocated to the specific race would be distributed according to the proportionate number of competitors. Although there were more spots allocated, this is the toughest age group though in terms of qualification.After every race, it is traditional for hopeful qualifiers to gather around the board area in anticipation of the results being posted. I had raced well in my 35-39, which accounted for by far the highest number of competitors in any of the age groups. Consequently, the number of Hawaii qualifying spots allocated to the specific race would be distributed according to the proportionate number of competitors. Although there were more spots allocated, this is the toughest age group in terms of qualification. However, it is not as simple as assuming that the top 16 competitors to finish in an age group, assuming 16 qualifying spots, will all go to Hawaii.

Fortunately, there are two other variables and unknown factors on the day after a race that can affect the final qualifying positions. The first is when an athlete simply chooses not to qualify when they lodge their entry form. The other is that for a variety of reasons, they decide not to accept their spot. So, you could conceivably be in the 21st or 22nd position and potentially qualify, although that is unusual. Interestingly, it's worth noting that these developments typically occur during the official presentation ceremony, and the scene is quite remarkable to witness.

It is the rule of every Ironman event worldwide that you must be at the presentation to accept your spot. No physical presence, no slot. There is no better example of how brutally this rule is applied than the drama that occurred only a few weeks ago when the outright winner at an Ironman race showed up 30 minutes late due, ironically, to the official race vehicle being delayed, and so his Hawaii spot was rolled down. If you have ever been to one of these, you will know how emotionally charged these occasions are.

The significance of this insight will become clear in a later chapter. I had raced well, and I knew that I was in with a chance if the places fell the right way or if a few people withdrew at the presentation ceremony. As we waited patiently for the results to be posted at midday on the race headquarters pin board, the volume of discussion began to build in line with the crowds' excitement.

Rather than wrestle with the usual crowd that gathers to survey the official results as they were pinned up, I held back for 15 minutes until I knew that I could easily access the board. Thumbing my way down the 35 to 39 age group columns to find my name, I was suddenly taken aback by my omission from the list of athletes who had selected that they wanted to qualify.

To my total horror, I could see that the last spot had already rolled down to someone who finished two places after me. Stunned and speechless as my brain tried to process what had occurred, I stood frozen. I quickly realised what had, or had not, occurred, so I rushed off hurriedly to find a race official or director who could resolve this. Within fifteen minutes, I had found one of the key race officials and explained the entire story to him. He looked guarded and would not commit to any resolution other than investigating the issue. "This might take a week or so", he declared. I was beside myself, but I had no other choice other than to walk away and wait.

A week later, I received an email from the head of the global Ironman organisation explaining that they had investigated my concerns and had adjudicated that, considering my application form had been completed indicating that I did not wish to qualify, as I hadn't ticked the right box, that they would unfortunately not be able to reverse or allocate a Hawaii qualification slot to me. I was devasted and spent the next week exchanging further correspondence to try to influence their decision. Devastatingly, they did not change their position. This was now my third heart-breaking moment in endurance racing, but there would be more.

I went on to race the Forster Ironman on another three occasions, completing in times of 10.14, 10.24 and 10.37.

Consequently, the three disasters supplied the fuel and motivation to atone for my heartbreak while training every day for many years. In fact, each of them fuelled my motivation and determination, no matter what I was doing every day.

Heaven and Hell – Ironman Malaysia 2002

Life after Forster was changing rapidly. Jen and I had gotten married, and we were also expecting our first child together. I had previously identified Ironman New Zealand as an ideal race because the timing was perfect leading up to the Australian Ironman, as well as being the closest other Ironman race in those days, as Forster was the only Ironman in Australia back then.

After the distressing experience of racing so well at the Australian Ironman but missing qualification over an unfortunate technical mistake, I found another race that was also relatively close and perfect timing again in preparation for the 2002 Australian Ironman. Ironman Malaysia on the Island of Langkawi also seemed like a potential race in which to qualify for Hawaii, albeit only about a third of the spots available in Australia would be available in this race. Also, given that our new child was likely to arrive at the end of April or the beginning of May, this presented a tiny window for us all to still be able to fly. And, lastly, the Australian Ironman in mid-April was also under a cloud of doubt, depending on when our baby decided to come into this world.

So, I signed up for Ironman Malaysia, which was due to be held in February, starting from and finishing in Kuah, Langkawi. The other benefit I felt might fall in my favour was that Langkawi would be oppressively hot and humid, so training through the Queensland summer would give me an edge against many of the people who would be racing from colder climates. That said, nothing could prepare me for the place that I would first get to know as heaven, then as hell, all in the space of a week. Arriving in Langkawi, we set about exploring the island and, as usual, the bike course. The island was a beautiful place with a unique blend of rural villages, mountainous terrain, and stunning remote beaches, creating a particularly challenging mountainous 90-kilometre bike loop that would need to be completed twice over. The Malaysian people were wonderful, and everyone made us feel so welcome.

Race day arrived all too quickly, and before I knew it, I was treading water in the pre-sunrise darkness of 30-degree Celsius water, surrounded by jellyfish. This swim was the most daunting experience for me yet. The idea of swimming out into the darkness for 1.9 kilometres, following a light on a boat across a major ocean shipping lane, was terrifying. There was no turning back now, though. And then, the race began. As we crossed this stretch of water, debris, hands, and feet frequently brushed against me, causing me to startle on countless occasions.

By the time we reached the halfway point, there was just enough light to see, and I had settled into my stroke, trying not to dwell on what might be swimming below me. Due to the warm water, I started to experience dehydration, and by the time we were exiting the pier, I was desperate for a large drink. I almost emptied the water bottle I had placed on my bike in one gulp, and then I was off down the road, with little time to settle before the first climb. The constantly changing landscapes, the cheers from local schoolchildren outside schools along the course, and the frequent sightings of packs of monkeys along the road all provided welcome distractions from the ever-increasing heat. Surprisingly, I drank eighteen 750ml water bottles filled with either water or electrolytes during the two-lap course, although nothing seemed to quench my thirst. My core temperature was soaring as I gratefully rolled back into town and then into T2 with 180.2 kilometres behind me.

I dismounted from my bike and jogged into the change tent with my run bag in hand. After filling my hat with ice and putting on my running shoes, I tried to stand up. However, I only managed to get as far as standing before practically every muscle in both of my legs cramped at the same time. They locked up completely, and I fell backward onto the bench behind me. Fortunately, a helpful medical volunteer stepped in and rubbed large amounts of ice on the backs of my legs before gently stretching them until I could stand upright and start running slowly out onto the three-lap run course.

It was hot, unbelievably hot, and no matter how much ice I shoved into my hat, it melted away within a minute or two, providing only fleeting relief. As I neared the end of the first lap of the run, I began to see stars in my vision, and the pressure inside my head had built up to the point where it felt like my skull might burst. Despite years of training in the sweltering summers of Queensland, I had never experienced such oppressive heat before. Should I collapse? Should I stop? Should I just walk? A few minutes later, I witnessed two runners wobbling, stumbling, and then collapsing in front of me onto the hot pavement. They appeared unconscious and completely out of it, but I had no choice but to keep running. Someone would care for them quickly.

By now, the temperature had reached 37 degrees Celsius with 95 % humidity. We were running in a furnace. Then my stomach suddenly turned. It was bad. I had to find a toilet. Pulling the door open of one of the portable toilets the organisers had placed around the course revealed not only a terrible odour but kiln-like temperatures from within. It must have been 55-plus degrees inside and none too pleasant at all. As I stepped in, I stumbled exhausted into the wall. The structure wobbled, and I panicked, hitting my head on the door handle before managing to catch myself and steady my body. Toppling sideways in a well-used porta-loo would have been catastrophic, as I am sure you can imagine. As soon as I had finished, I jumped out and headed off to finish the last 10 oppressive kilometres. I eventually crossed the line in 10.38 and collapsed onto the bitumen. The recovery marques were full of athletes on intravenous drips, which, fortunately, I managed to avoid. Another remarkably successful race was complete, and it was time to recover and relax.

The next morning, we headed down for the ritualistic inspection of the official results and Hawaii qualifying spots. I was delighted to discover that I had finished in 38th position overall but dismayed by the fact that I was only one place off qualifying in my age group. Ironically, I would have qualified in every other age group with my time, even the three younger age groups. So, it was back to the drawing board again.

As if the setbacks and pain had not been enough the year before, I decided to return to Langkawi in 2003, just before racing the 2003 Australian Ironman. And, if we had thought that the previous year was eventful, 2003 was going to take proceedings to a new level. By now we knew the MO for Langkawi, and we had also experienced the brutal, unforgiving conditions. We settled into life in Langkawi nicely, our 10-month-old son, Cal, did seem to be coming down with a cold the day after we landed. We knew from experience that Callum's colds can quickly deteriorate into viral pneumonia, so we kept a close eye that day for signs. Sure enough, that night his condition worsened and by morning we knew that we had no choice but to find emergency care. The hotel we were staying at informed us that the only option to get urgent care would be to go to the local Langkawi Hospital, so we headed straight there. Without knowing what to expect, we were shocked to find the huge waiting area packed with sick people waiting for treatment. The waiting area was so packed with people, that there were just as many people sitting on the floor as there were occupying the rows of seats. It resembled an emergency response centre in a rural area that had recently endured a natural disaster. To our relief, the triage desk expedited our consultation and charged us only two Australian dollars. Within ten minutes, we were ushered into the emergency treatment section, and shortly thereafter, a female doctor entered to attend to us. "What seems to be the problem here," she asked looking down at Callum.

As if the setbacks and pain had not been enough the year before, I decided to return to Langkawi in 2003, just before racing the 2003 Australian Ironman. And, if we had thought that the previous year was eventful, 2003 was going to take proceedings to a new level. By now, we knew the MO for Langkawi, and we had also experienced the brutal, unforgiving conditions. We settled into life in Langkawi nicely. Our 10-month-old son, Cal, did seem to be coming down with a cold the day after we landed. We knew from experience that Callum's colds could quickly deteriorate into viral pneumonia, so we kept a close eye that day for signs. Sure enough, that night his condition worsened, and by morning, we knew that we had no choice but to find emergency care. The hotel we were staying at informed us that the only option to get urgent care would be to go to the local Langkawi Hospital, so we headed straight there. Without knowing what to expect, we were shocked to find the huge waiting area packed with sick people waiting for treatment. The waiting area was packed with people, with just as many people sitting on the floor as there were occupying the rows of seats. It resembled an emergency response centre in a rural area that had recently endured a natural disaster. To our relief, the triage desk expedited our consultation and charged us only two Australian dollars. Within ten minutes, we were ushered into the emergency treatment sec-tion, and shortly thereafter, a female doctor entered to attend to us. "What seems to be the problem here," she asked, looking down at Callum.

We briefly shared Callum's medical history with her, and she requested that one of us hold him on the examination bed. After listening to his chest with her stethoscope for a minute or two, she asked us to lay Callum down and comfort him. Without much delay, she inserted a plastic tube down his left nostril, suctioning mucus from deep within as Cal screamed and cried while I did my best to comfort him. She then repeated this procedure with his other nasal passage before moving on to his throat. God, it was so incredibly traumatic, and tears filled my eyes. Once she had completed the procedure, she left briefly and returned with a rather strange-looking bottle of green medicine and a prescription. She then advised us to take Callum home and let him rest for at least the next few days, which we did, diligently tending to his symptoms day and night as he gradually recovered. Perhaps it was the unorthodox treatment or the strange green medicine that really turned him around so quickly. Previously, such bouts resulted in a 5-to-7-day hospital stay connected to saline drips and ventilators.

By the time race morning arrived, we were all ready to go. The swim, starting in the dark, was just as unpleasant as last time. As I embarked on the bike leg, I encountered an issue within minutes. While climbing the first steep hill out of town, I felt my saddle strangely shifting beneath me. To my dismay, as I stood, it tipped backward, pointing straight up at the sky. "Oh god," I muttered, fearing that this could spell the end of my race day. Without any tools on hand, I continued riding, constantly adjusting my position in a futile attempt to keep the saddle in a somewhat usable position. Unfortunately, each time I rose from the saddle, it tilted backward, reaching for the sky once more.

As I approached each aid station, I tried to locate tools, but the language barrier with volunteers who spoke little or no English and the remote course location thwarted my efforts. My only hope, I thought, was to find my wife, who was supposed to be waiting around halfway through the course on the other side of the island. Thankfully, she was at the 45-kilometre point, near our accommodation, and my relief was visible as I jumped from my bike to scour the car for Allen's keys. Amazingly, I found a set on the floor, just beneath the driver's seat. A frantic and flustered repair of my saddle followed, and I pedalled away vigorously to make up lost time.

Despite experiencing the same muscle cramps during the transition to the run at T2, I headed out on the brutal run, overtaking many athletes as the run progressed. Hours later, I finished the race three minutes faster than the previous year. Although I achieved a higher overall placement in 35th position, I missed the qualification by just one minute. It took me several days to overcome the frustration of the mechanical mishap, which had cost me at least four minutes. If not for these issues, I would have been on my way to Hawaii later that year.

DAILY PRACTICE ACTION
Building Resilience

How would you rate your positive resilience on a scale from 1 to 10 and what level would you like to target?	
What was the last tough setback that you encountered?	
How did you feel, and what actions did you plan to quickly overcome to build your positive mindset?	
What could you do differently next time to help improve your positivity?	

The Holy Grail; the finishing line on Ali'i Drive, Kona, of the legendary Hawaii Ironman World Championships.

TRANSCENDENCE

*"You cannot amputate your history from your destiny,
because that is redemption."*

— Beth Moore

I n the opening foreword, I briefly shared my inspiration from encountering remarkable individuals who achieved extraordinary feats they once deemed impossible. On occasions when I've had the opportunity to inquire what their response would have been if asked two years earlier whether they could achieve such feats, their replies were all something along the lines of, "You must be joking, right? Not a chance. Impossible!"

For every person I've met who has undergone this profound transformation, their energy is euphoric, and their demeanour is enthusiastic. They now hold an unshakable belief in their ability to overcome any obstacle. Their paths have been marked by setbacks and failures, all of which have elevated their experiences and accomplishments to a transcendent level, which mirrors my own journey. Life-changing and transcendent in every sense.

Your holy grail

Many of us have dreamed of achieving something significant, and often, those dreams extend to what might seem impossible – our own holy grail. If you've experienced this, you know that it stirs profound emotions and thoughts. Pursuing such a goal is truly worthwhile. For me, this was my holy grail.

There is probably quite a reasonable chance that you have heard of the Hawaii Ironman or seen its highlights or coverage on television. This one-day endurance event, known as IRONMAN, was conceived by Judy and John Collins, a couple who moved from California to Hawai'i in 1975. The Collins family participated in the Mission Bay Triathlon in San Diego on September 25, 1974, an event that is now recognised as the beginning of modern triathlon in the US.

In 1977, the Collins' involvement in organising a sprint run-swim competition in Honolulu planted the seeds of an idea to organise a triathlon event the following year. They aimed to create an event for endurance athletes, those who preferred longer races like the Waikiki Roughwater Swim and the Honolulu Marathon over short sprint races. However, there was still the question of where to hold the bike leg. The answer came to them in early 1977 when John thought of using a route from a local bicycling club. In a pact, Judy and John said to each other, "If you do it, I'll do it," and John famously added, "...whoever finishes first, we'll call him the Iron Man." This marked the origin of the Hawaii Ironman.

At the Waikiki Swim Club banquet in October 1977, Judy and John announced their "Around the Island Triathlon," scheduled for the following year. When John described the three triathlon legs, the swimmers in attendance found it amusing. The couple's vision was that many would embrace the challenge of swimming, cycling, and running non-stop for 140.6 miles. They aspired for their triathlon to become an annual event in Hawai'i. On February 18, 1978, Judy and John Collins witnessed the realisation of their dream with the inaugural Hawaiian Iron Man Triathlon. Little did they know then the profound impact their race would have and how many lives it would touch. In 1980, the founders, John and Judy Collins, granted ABC's "Wide World of Sports" permission to film the event, bringing worldwide recognition to IRONMAN. A mere two years later, college student Julie Moss experienced a dramatic moment during the IRONMAN World Championship. She collapsed just yards from the finish line and was passed by another competitor for the title but refused to give up. Instead, she crawled to the finish line, unknowingly creating one of the most iconic moments in IRONMAN history.

How your first impossible goal will feel!

In January 1999, my recovery accelerated after the truck accident, and my training for my first full Ironman entered a new uncharted phase. From this point on, I committed to training for eleven months of the year, every year, in a relentless pursuit of my goals. Overall, my training increased from 13 or 14 hours a week to 20 or more hours a week, every week - to put that in context, my long swims went from 1.5 to 3 kilometres, my long rides from 100 to 160 kilometres, and my long runs from 21 to between 33 to 35 kilometres each week. To reach this level, I applied the 10%

rule, which involves limiting weekly increases to a maximum of 10%. By incorporating this method and incorporating a lighter week into my schedule every 3-4 weeks, I was able to progressively enhance my endurance.

Ironman Australia in late May 1999 marked a significant change in the race schedule, as it started a full month later than usual. The transition from autumn to winter in Australia meant that race conditions would be even more challenging than the already demanding Ironman distance. As I arrived in Forster, I had no idea just how challenging race day would turn out to be.

During this period, although I had never trained with anyone else in my triathlon journey, I connected with a group of triathletes from a club in Brisbane through a friend named John, who was a few years younger and a great triathlete. This club's members had individual coaches, strict training plans, and dietary regimes. They frequently trained together, and I decided to join them for a few organised sessions leading up to the race. We also hung out together for meals, during parts of the day, and back at various lodgings. I figured that their competition, training, and race experience would be valuable as I counted the days down to race day. However, I was about to learn two extremely important lessons, one of which would take me quite some time to master.

The night before a major race is always one of the hardest nights for me to get a good night's sleep. Race day had dawned, and I woke up at 4:45 am. I had also woken up at 12, 2, and 3:30 am, but who's counting?

Ironically, the night after a race is even harder, as you're dealing with muscles and fibres that ache, acute discomfort, surges of adrenaline, and a mind consumed with replaying every moment of a 10-to-24-hour race. It's an intense high that's incomparable.

"This is it," I calmly whispered to myself as I climbed out of bed, determined to force away the unpleasant thoughts that tend to creep in when you're lying comfortably in a warm bed on the morning of a race, imagining yourself treading water in a cold lake, river, or ocean among 1500 other anxious souls. I knew that if I lingered in bed for too long, the comparisons, nervousness, and fear could become almost paralysing. This was the perfect time to apply the 4-second rule, and I hopped out of bed.

The house we had rented was shrouded in darkness and silence. I followed my usual routine, partially drawing the curtains to catch a glimpse of the weather outside and looking for any signs of rain. I then meticulously checked my gear bags one last time. Then, I prepared my race morning nutrition and mentally geared up for the day ahead in the dim light. These are the eerily odd moments in life when you can hear your own heartbeat, and life takes on an ethereal quality as you sit with only you and your mind.

The race day soundtrack I played, cueing my routine and motivation, filled my senses as I forced each mouthful of porridge down, chasing it with gulps of chocolate Opti nutrition. My mind was already fully immersed in the race, playing through the day's strategy, visualising each transition, my pacing plan, race day nutrition, and rehearsing the mantra that would echo in my head throughout the day, especially when things got tough: "Never Ever Give Up."

As we drove in silence to the race start, the music in my mind continued to play, and raindrops sporadically pelted the windscreen. I tried to distract myself from the miserable conditions, even though, as always, I had silently prayed for a rain-free race day upon waking. Any ultra-endurance race is challenging without adding adverse weather conditions to the mix.

As I slipped on my wet suit, my nerves continued to rise before heading down to the chilly river to start the biggest endurance test I had ever faced. Something I would have considered impossible only two years before. In fact, if you had asked me two years before if I could do this, I would have said that you were crackers for even asking.

Treading water among the 1,500 other athletes, I was about to pursue my impossible dream and continue to accelerate the life-changing journey I had embarked on just a year ago. In that moment, it was hard to believe it had only been 12 months. The starting gun went off, and chaos erupted in the crowded river. "Just survive, Jason."

As I fought for space and struggled to stay afloat, a feeling of exhaustion already crept over me. Six hundred metres later, at the first turnaround, I finally found some space. I reminded myself constantly of why I was here and that all I needed to do was stay calm and trust in my preparation. The swim felt like it went on forever. I was ecstatic when my feet finally touched the riverbed after 3.8 kilometres in the chilly water.

I glanced up as I entered transition and noticed that it had taken me one hour and eight minutes, including the time in T1, to complete the swim, leaving me in 738th place overall. I exited T1 as fast as I could under the dark, foreboding skies and light rain. My mind drifted to the long day ahead in these miserable conditions, wearing nothing but swimming trunks and a Lycra vest, and then, suddenly, the heavens opened. Hail, of all things! Huge icy lumps began to pelt my skin. Within minutes, my hands were completely numb from swimming in the frigid waters and being exposed to bone-chilling wind and hail on the bike. "Why am I doing this?" The voice rang out in my head. In these moments, knowing your why is pivotal.

Despite the harsh conditions, a surge of adrenaline, combined with my competitive nature and an innate desire to race, kicked in. Holding back from powering through the first stages of the bike section went against all my instincts, and I couldn't resist pushing hard on the bike. This was to be my undoing. The Forster Ironman features a great bike course, with constantly changing beautiful scenery rolling over undulating terrain. However, there were significant road hazards for many kilometres along the main stretch out of Forster, including frequent, deep potholes and an uneven, un-kerbed shoulder, making vigilance critical. I kept up my pace as I rode past an unfortunate athlete who hadn't managed to avoid one of the deep holes and sat injured and bloodied on the side of the road, his collapsed front wheel by his side and his day over.

I already knew my pacing was off, but it was further impacted by the rule against drafting. This meant you had to stay outside of the 4-metre zone behind another competitor. This meant making a decision when closing in on the cyclist ahead. You either had to accelerate and overtake quickly, often pushing you above your desired speed and burning valuable energy, and then keep up a slightly faster speed than the rider you have just overtaken. Or sit back and wait and risk an infringement penalty. This meant you had to dismount from your bike at a designated zone and wait for 4 minutes. I found myself constantly catching up to other riders and struggling to decide whether to sit and wait or overtake. As I repeatedly chose to overtake, I began to feel the consequences around eighty kilometres into the first long stretch back into the town of Forster.

Thousands of enthusiastic spectators lined the streets into and around town, which lifted my spirits just when I needed that encouragement the most. I sped up and was heading out of town in no time. Unchartered race territory now beckoned, and the second lap took on a whole new meaning for me. There were many moments when I struggled both mentally and physically, forcing me to constantly adjust my goals. "Just get to the next aid station" became my mantra.

With only one year of biking experience under my belt, which was as identically limited as my swimming experience, I maintained an average speed of thirty-two kilometres per hour for the 180-kilometre bike leg, finishing in 635th place. I had no idea how my legs would feel as I headed out of T2, but I was relieved to finally be off the bike and on my feet.

In the first kilometre, I was feeling smashed, but I was running at a decent pace and started overtaking other runners. There's nothing quite like the feeling of hunting down and passing hundreds of other athletes in the marathon segment of an Ironman.

I experienced cramps at various points during the run, and by the halfway mark, my sole focus was to reach each aid station without stopping or walking, just as I had done on the bike. The second half of the marathon continued in the same manner, with me allowing myself to walk for 10 seconds through each aid station to hydrate and refuel before pushing on to the next one.

And so, it went on. With 5 kilometres left to go, my spirits soared as I assessed my physical condition, ran the numbers in my head and realised I was going to finish strong. The final 3 kilometres were a pain-filled struggle, but inside, I was celebrating.

I had gone from being unable to swim at all, not having ridden a bike since I was a kid in the street, only an occasional runner and a pack-a-day cigarette smoker, and now I was about to finish strongly in the toughest one-day sporting event in the world.

My performance in the marathon that day placed me in 267th position, and overall, I finished 467th with a time of eleven hours and five minutes. This was the most incredible high I had ever experienced, and I became addicted.

Redemption

If you persist long enough, one day, your dreams will become a reality, and that moment will be the most transformative of your life. But there's something even more remarkable than achieving your dreams: it's called redemption. Redemption is a moment forged like steel – from all your struggles and failures, and every time you picked yourself up and tried again, coming together to transform you forever.

No matter how tough life gets in the future and the personal challenges you confront, you can revisit those moments, and everything will become clear. Pride and euphoria will wash over and through you, and you'll feel reborn. There's no drug on this planet that can compare because every drop of sweat and tear you shed suddenly has purpose and meaning. While I can vividly recall every major race I've finished, all lasting more than 10 exhausting hours with a thousand thoughts of giving up, there are a few that stand and live above all others.

The six months leading up to my second visit to Taupō for the New Zealand Ironman had been the most difficult period of my life. During this time, my son, Callum, faced numerous life-threatening bouts of viral pneumonia, which led to several extended hospital stays lasting five days or more. By the time Callum was two and a half years old, he had been hospitalised 13 times for various conditions and operations, with nine of those admissions stemming from the symptoms of viral pneumonia.

There were many occasions when I had to take Callum with me during my training sessions, and we would often embark on morning runs around Buderim, covering distances of up to 25 kilometres, with Cal securely strapped into his stroller. Getting to New Zealand for the Ironman was probably the toughest thing I have ever had to do. I owe a great deal of gratitude to my wonderful in-laws, Bob and Helen, who stepped in selflessly and without complaint to assist me in managing the demanding training volume required for my preparations. During these long training sessions, I often found myself reflecting on my relentless and obsessive pursuit of qualifying for the Hawaii Ironman. I also ruminated on the pain I had endured due to my previous failures, including the 2000 ITU Long Distance World Championships and, most painfully, the 2001 New Zealand Ironman three years earlier.

Mixing up my training routines and techniques from year to year proved invaluable. This approach not only made me feel stronger and faster but also bolstered my confidence that my dream was attainable. Encouragingly, my race results had been steadily improving, although my most recent Australian Ironman race had only marginally altered that trend by adding a few minutes to my finishing time.

A significant portion of my training efforts were dedicated to enhancing my core strength and extending the duration of my long indoor cycling sessions, which I needed to do due to the training constraints I faced at the time. While I had always been inclined towards hill running and frequently engaged in hill repeat sessions, I intensified my long hill workouts. I started training on the challenging Mt Gravatt Hill in Brisbane, which offered a substantial 195 metres of vertical elevation gain from top to bottom, complete with steep sections. Each Sunday, following a gruelling six-hour bike session, I would run four kilometres to Mt Gravatt Hill and spend the ensuing three hours repeatedly running up and down it. These sessions took place during the sweltering Australian summer, often in temperatures exceeding thirty-five degrees Celsius and humidity levels of eighty to ninety per cent. These intense workouts demanded a brief dousing of water over my head at the summit of each climb before I descended again.

Once a week, as I travelled to Brisbane from the Sunshine Coast to stay for a few days, I would also go out a couple of times and ride hill repeats, seated, on the same climb to the top. To build strength, I challenged myself to use the highest possible gear I could handle and powered my way up repeatedly.

As the race day drew nearer, I felt confident about my training and my prospects. However, I couldn't help but feel a twinge of anxiety as I was returning to the only major race where I had made the decision to quit, which had nothing to do with a major health issue.

My second tilt at this race was to be my eighth full Ironman, and for the eighth time, I harboured hopes of racing fast enough to qualify for the Hawaii Ironman. My original goal was twofold: to qualify and compete in the Australian Ironman and then to secure a spot in the Hawaii Ironman World Championships in Kona. I had achieved my first impossible goal, completing a full Ironman race within 12 months, right on schedule. However, after participating in seven Ironman races prior to this one, I found myself just shy of my five-year target to make it to Hawaii. While the 5-year timeline to qualify for Hawaii had lost its significance, my desire to achieve this dream had only grown stronger. Giving up on my dream was never an option for me, no matter the circumstances, ever!

This time, I was travelling alone with Callum to Auckland, where I had arranged to meet my father and his wife, Rhonda, who had kindly offered to come along and help. Once in Auckland, Cal and I would travel to Lake Taupō and meet up with everyone there.

My skills in finding suitable accommodations had improved significantly, and this time, we were staying in a spacious house right in town, offering uninterrupted, breathtaking views of Lake Taupō. After our arrival and getting settled, my father joined us, and we enjoyed some wonderful quality time together in the Taupō area. We had also coordinated with Dad's friend, Craig, an avid cycling enthusiast living in Auckland, to meet us on the morning of the race to provide extra support.

With the race fast approaching, my nerves once again grew. However, I remained completely focused on exorcising the demons from my previous experience in the 2001 race. I was well-versed in the Ironman race routine by now, especially in the context of this New Zealand event. Having qualified but been deemed ineligible at Ironman Australia and twice finishing with strong overall positions at Ironman Malaysia while qualifying in every age group except my own, I felt that I had paid my dues to the Ironman gods, and my time to succeed was drawing near.

Once again, a race morning greeted us with the characteristic chilly conditions of New Zealand. "Relax, eat, drink. Relax, eat, drink," I repeated to myself as I set up my T1 gear, including my bike while waiting for the dawn to break. As before, we, the athletes, moved in unison like a solemn procession towards the beach in Lake Taupō, shrouded in darkness and lost in our own contemplative thoughts.

Each Ironman race holds a unique meaning for every participant. It might be a personal challenge, a test of one's limits, a quest for victory, or the pursuit of a coveted spot in the Hawaii Ironman, as was my case. Some undertake this monumental endeavour to honour a loved one or someone who has passed away. Whatever the reason, this race is significant, deeply personal, and profoundly special.

I had heard that Ironman New Zealand this time around had more first-time participants, Ironman "virgins", if you will, than any previous edition. They were about to plunge headfirst into the unknown, embarking on their inaugural Ironman journey, and, with that, the opportunity to experience exponential personal growth, the kind that only those who cross that finishing line in an Ironman can know or understand.

John Collins, the founder of Ironman, once so eloquently explained the essence of the event. When asked why he conceived and raced the Ironman, he famously replied, "The difference between those who get it and those who do not, is that those who have, do, and those who haven't, do not." In simpler terms, if you haven't experienced it, you can't truly understand how it feels and how it changes your life.

48

I looked around, knowing that the lives of hundreds of these courageous individuals surrounding me would undergo a profound shift in the next 17 hours if they aspired to earn the title of Ironman or Ironwoman. It's worth noting that every Ironman race is restricted to a 17-hour time limit. If you cross the finish line one second after the midnight cutoff, you are considered a Did Not Finish (DNF).

The finishing line of an Ironman is unlike anything else in the world of sports. Over the course of about 9 hours, from the first finisher to the last, you'll witness a powerful and emotional spectacle as both professional athletes and everyday people achieve this herculean feat. In the last hour leading up to midnight, you might find yourself brought to tears. I encourage you to experience it as a spectator one day: it's an experience that's absolutely free.

"Deep breaths, Jason, deep breaths." I reminded myself.

The water was chillingly cold, serving as a stark foreshadowing of the challenges ahead. Suddenly, the cannon sounded, and 1,500 athletes surged forward, each one battling for a patch of clear water, chasing their dreams, and competing for whatever or whoever had motivated them to race. I had held onto the hope that the swim would unfold smoothly without any complications. However, the familiar feeling of panic overcame me as I jostled and wrestled for space, my breathing growing erratic, as I began to navigate through the crowd, swimming sideways to escape the melee of bodies.

My inner voice berated me, "What the heck are you doing, Jason? Haven't you learned anything?" It snapped me back to reality. "Just keep swimming. If you quit now, it's over. You might as well abandon this whole endeavour. Say goodbye to your dream. Just pack up and go home, accepting defeat."

This was the wake-up call I needed. Within just 4 seconds of finding a bit of space and treading water, I made the crucial decision to keep swimming. For a moment, everything could have come crashing down. However, I soon found my rhythm, peering into the clear waters of Lake Taupō. My sole focus was to reach each buoy, one at a time, during the long 1.9-kilometre outbound swim. Upon reaching the turnaround point, my focus shifted to completing the swim and mentally checking off the first leg. As expected, exiting the cold water left my legs feeling stiff and frozen, as if they might snap with any sudden movement. The run to T1 seemed longer than I remembered, and I needed the assistance of a transition volunteer to help peel my wetsuit off my legs. Glancing at my timing watch briefly, I saw that I had completed the swim leg in 1 hour and 15 minutes, my slowest time in all my eight Ironman races. I attributed this to the exceptionally long run from the swim to the bike transition and the different swim conditions without the buoyancy of saltwater, which was common in most other races.

The first 30 kilometres flew by, and I felt good and strong. But then again, I had felt the same way in 2001 when I went out too fast on the bike leg with a tailwind. I kept reminding myself to keep my pace and exuberance in check, although it had little impact on my actual output. On the return to town, I faced the stretch where I had previously quit, which sent me into a deep reflection on my past failure. The memories intensified as I rode past the exact spot on the side of the road where I had given up. In my mind, I pictured a white cross marking my previous defeat. I was determined not to fall into the same trap this time.

As I raced downhill and sped through town, my adrenaline surged with the crowd's cheers and the inspiration I drew from my midpoint time check. I was riding faster than I had planned, which perhaps should have raised a small warning flag. However, it didn't, and I was in full racing mode as I tackled the hills on the way out of Taupō toward the main road heading west.

The rain that began as I tackled the long stretch to the turnaround could have been a warning to ease up because tougher conditions lay ahead, but I didn't pay attention. I powered on with the wind at my back. However, as soon as I reached and turned at the furthest point of the course from town, I felt the headwind again. I should have known better. I should have conserved more energy because this was going to be a challenging grind to get back and see this race home.

The gradual uphill slope and the strong headwinds continued to take their toll, and my inner demons soon resurfaced. They echoed the same negative instructions that haunted me during my last failure on this course. They were familiar, but this time, I had developed a mental weapon to counter them. It was at this point that I discovered the power of a technique that would make a significant difference in many tough situations in my life – using pain as my fuel.

As I pushed through the headwind, I summoned the memories, feelings and pain of my 2001 experience. I vividly imagined sitting in the living room of the house we had rented, trying to justify to everyone around me why quitting was the reasonable thing to do – but deep down, back then, I knew I was a quitter.

I evoked memories of the shame and deep pain I had felt when I realised that my dream of competing in Hawaii was slipping away. I recall thinking it would never happen and that I would never achieve my dream because quitters never reach their goals.

Then, as I struggled to push harder on the bike and keep pedalling, my legs sore and aching, my mind drifted into a haze of exhaustion, and the battle in my mind over whether to quit or find a way to keep going raged on.

It was at this point that I employed a perspective technique my father had taught me many years ago when I was troubled by something.

He would ask, "Jas, do you remember what you were worried about this time last year?" My response was always, "No, why?"

His reply was a valuable lesson: "Because whatever you were worried about back then obviously wasn't worth worrying about in the grand scheme of things. Otherwise, you would remember it, wouldn't you?"

"Hmm, I guess so," I remarked.

With that perspective in mind, I pondered whether this challenging moment during the race would be a defining memory when I looked back from the comfort of my armchair at age 65.

His point was to contextualise the significance of your concern or worry and deal with it accordingly.

If you're worried about something, consider whether it's significant enough to remember a year from now. Chances are, it won't be. So why invest so much energy in worrying about it? In the grand scheme of things, it's not that important. Conversely, if it will be, then you better damn well make sure you make the right choice for your future reckoning with yourself.

In that critical moment, five hours into the New Zealand Ironman in March 2004, I realised that quitting would be a decision I'd remember and regret for the rest of my life.

I asked myself, "How will you feel tonight if you quit, Jason?" I knew exactly how I would feel—deep regret. But I also vividly imagined the elation and hope I would feel if I simply finished. The latter was what I desperately wanted. At that moment, I removed the option to quit from my mind.

"What do you need to do now, Jason?"

I wrestled with my options and the various scenarios that would follow by deciding to go on.

"Slow down, roll your legs over and make it to the end of the bike stage. Then, see how your legs feel. If they are dead and you must walk the marathon for the first time in your life, then so be it. A finish that is three hours longer is infinitely better than a DNF because of quitting. Infinitely!!! Just finish, Jason".

A wave of calm descended over my mind. I backed off the pace ever so slightly to enable my dead legs to recover for a short while so they could carry me back into Taupō. As I began freewheeling back down the hills into the town centre, I realised I had not lost much time. The waiting crowds were louder than I recalled them being before, and this lifted my spirits. I ran slowly after dismounting my bike, which the bike handler took from me, and I scampered into the T2 tent, all the while telling myself to jog slowly into the marathon to assess my physical state. Surprisingly, from a place in which I thought I might have to walk the marathon, my cadence was ticking over well as I glanced down at my watch. It seemed that my bike split, like my swim split, was the slowest of any previous Ironman race, which momentarily deflated me. My legs were good, though, much to my great delight, as at that same moment, I caught a glimpse of my son, Callum, with my dad and Rhonda. My sense of pride consumed me, and I felt determined to find strength and salvage something from this day.

With one kilometre done and 41.2 to go, I was running well. After two kilometres, I felt strong and began to reevaluate my goals and consider what I could achieve that day. Just staying in the fight had given me hope. For a long time leading up to this race, and as I stepped up to the starting line, all I had thought about was racing fast enough to qualify for Hawaii. At the five-hour mark, I found myself on the brink of considering quitting or entertaining the notion that simply completing the race, even if I had to walk, would suffice. Ninety minutes later, I was again reevaluating what positive outcome I could chase. Ninety minutes between despair - deciding to fight it out to the finish - to wondering if I could achieve something remarkable.

Looking back now, these were quite possibly the single most important decisions of my life.

My legs felt good. How could this change happen so quickly?

As I considered this, I rounded a turn, and there was Dad and Craig, shouting and pumped.

"You look awesome," Craig shouted. "So strong."

At that moment, my feet felt lighter than ever, and I allowed myself to dream big. What if I could transform the thought of quitting into not just walking a marathon for the first time ever but running the fastest Ironman marathon I've ever run? "Wow, wouldn't that be something," I pondered. I swiftly adjusted my pace and set new goals for achieving my fastest marathon at the end of an Ironman. Off I went.

The New Zealand Ironman run course holds a special place, both in terms of scenery and the supportive crowd. Unlike many Ironman races around the world, most of the entire 21-kilometre lap, which needed to be completed twice, was filled with incredible spectators cheering on everyone who had dared to take on this monumental challenge. As is customary in most races, competitors have their names printed on their race numbers. This allowed the enthusiastic supporters to call out your name as you passed by. "Come on, Jason, looking so good!" I heard frequently, and each shout injected new energy into my legs.

As the marathon continued, my quadriceps began to cramp, especially as I pushed the pace. A couple of times, they locked up completely, forcing me to stop abruptly and clutch them in pain before hobbling forward. Fortunately, the last time this happened, I was approaching an aid station. I quickly grabbed handfuls of ice and stuffed them down the back of my racing shorts.

At the turnaround point with seven kilometres to go, I knew I had the potential to run faster than ever before in an Ironman. This thought became my singular focus as I chased down many other competitors. In my mind, each person in front of me represented the competitor who had narrowly edged me out for the final Hawaii qualifying spot the previous year.

I could sense the elation building within me, followed by waves of euphoria and pride as I neared the finishing chute. The disappointment of missing out on Hawaii and my dream had faded into the background. What consumed me in that moment was an overwhelming sense of pride and joy. I had pushed through the toughest of challenges and made it to the finish line. Without a doubt, I had learned more in that single day than on any other day of my life.

It's impossible to fully convey the emotions that wash over you as you cross the finish line of a race of such immense distance and difficulty. After pushing your mind and body to places you never thought possible, it's a feeling that defies explanation. So, I won't attempt to describe it, but I can tell you that it's a truly transformative experience.

As I sprinted down the finishing chute, my dad handed Callum over the barriers into my arms, and we crossed the finish line together. I hugged and kissed my son, then collapsed to the ground, still holding him. The demons that had haunted me throughout the day had been defeated and laid to rest. In that moment, all that mattered was savouring the overwhelming feeling of triumph, a memory I wanted to etch into my soul forever.

Sleep eluded me that night, as it often did after races, but this time, it was exacerbated by the adrenaline that continued to course through my veins for at least 12 hours after crossing the finish line. Throughout the night, from dusk till dawn, I replayed every minute of the race in my mind, reliving the highs and lows, the doubts, and the determination.

The next morning, Callum's early wake-up at 6 am was almost a relief, as it forced me out of my discomfort and sleepless state.

Sometimes, when you're physically and emotionally drained, you just need to get up and start moving. I spent some quality time playing with Callum, and then I went for a reflective walk along the shores of Lake Taupō. It was a way to gather my thoughts and try to breathe some life back into my exhausted limbs.

No matter how physically drained you feel on the morning after a successful race, there's a unique high that comes from knowing you gave it your all. It's an incomparable sense of satisfaction after months of training, sacrifice, and overcoming countless challenges just to get to that starting line. Despite the fatigue and soreness, you practically feel like you're floating on air. That morning, I did float. I felt as though if it were to be my last day on this earth, I would die happy and content. So, I floated, blissfully unaware of what the rest of the day had in store for me.

We had a celebratory breakfast at around 9 am, and afterwards, I decided to casually run down and check over the qualifying spots for Hawaii at the race headquarters in town. I didn't think there was much chance of qualifying, but I wanted to confirm it. A small crowd had gathered and were craning their necks, eagerly searching for the results of their relevant age group categories. When a gap opened, I slipped through and found the 40 to 44 age group results. To my surprise, I had finished eleventh in my category, with nine qualifying places up for grabs.

I noticed that one of the athletes ahead of me had decided not to take a qualification spot, so it had rolled down to the next person. At that moment, I was just one place away from qualifying for Hawaii. One place! It seemed almost impossible that I was so close yet so far away. I checked the results repeatedly over the next five minutes, unable to believe the situation. When we all met up again, my face must have instantly revealed the unlikely chance that had suddenly become possible.

"So, what does that mean?" Dad asked as I explained excitedly.

"Well, it means that if one person of the nine in front of me does not accept their qualification place at the presentation night this evening, then I am in," I explained, struggling to hold back tears. When you've given your all in a race and have nothing left, your emotions can overwhelm you the next day. It's a strange phenomenon that's hard to explain, but my family understood. They knew how much this meant to me.

The rest of the day seemed to drag on forever as I constantly checked the time. We decided that Rhonda would attend the awards presentation, scheduled for 7 pm in the main auditorium in Taupō, while my dad looked after Callum. We arrived early, at around 6.30 pm, to secure a seat. The auditorium quickly filled up, and the excited chatter of hundreds of people waiting for the ceremony to begin filled the air. For the seventy people, plus their friends and families attending, this was going to be an incredibly special event. While a majority would already know that they had qualified, the anticipation was palpable.

Rhonda and I chatted while we waited, and then suddenly, the race director tapped the microphone to get our collective attention and began welcoming us all.

"Welcome everyone to this evening's New Zealand Ironman presentation of the Hawaii Ironman World Championships 2004 qualify allocation", he announced, to which the audience responded with a huge cheer.

"This evening marks the culmination of many years of sacrifice and commitment, no doubt, from all in attendance who have aspirations of racing the greatest race on the planet," he continued.

Every hair on my body stood on end. Could this, finally, be it? Have I finally made it? "Do not get ahead of yourself, Jason. Just know you have given it everything and that whatever will be, will be. You will be back."

Proceedings began with the qualifying allocation for the pro men and pro women. We clapped and cheered as the best of the best walked down, one by one, when their names were called to collect their certificates. Gosh, I had no idea it would be such an occasion, with individual names being called in turn, one by one, to see if that athlete would come down to the stage to accept their prize – a place in the most legendary and prestigious endurance event on the planet. Ten age groups and the two pro groups would be called, decided, and awarded before mine.

The tension and excitement mounted as the director ran through each in turn. Occasionally, there would be a nervous pause as an athlete's name was called, and the crowd waited expectantly to see if anyone rose from their seat and went ahead down the auditorium steps to accept their destiny. I guessed that each pause was around fifteen seconds, which seemed like an eternity, until the race director would recall the person's name, then move on to the next if there was no claimant of the spot. As each non-claimant was passed over, and there were only a few, the realisation by someone in the expectant audience was at once apparent as they realised, at that moment, that shortly, the opportunity would be rolled down to them as the next in line. I note that this was marked by a cheer or a cry of delight. The butterflies rose in my stomach as I dared to dream that it might be me. What would I do in that moment if it were suddenly me realising that I would be going to race in Kona? "Oh God, is this it? Stay calm. Please, God," I repeated in my head.

As things stood, I was eleventh in my age group, and there were 9 qualifying spots available. One person ahead of me had decided pre-race that they did not wish to qualify. That meant I was now only one place away from my major goal for the last six years. To add further context to how tough it is to qualify and how close and cruel it can be to not qualify, the next athlete after me was only one second behind me after ten hours and thirty-eight minutes of pushing themselves to the limit. In fact, the next three athletes after me were within ninety seconds of my finish.

As each age group closed out and mine approached, my hands sweated more. At first, I wished the race director would hurry up and reach the 40 – 44 age group, but then I hesitated, fearing that I might have narrowly missed out. I wanted to cling to the hope a little while longer, but my curiosity was eating away at me. The final woman in the 35 – 39 age group, despite the toll the race had taken on her body, practically bounded up the steps to join her waiting partner after securing her qualification spot, which had surprisingly rolled down to her. Her radiant smile painted the whole story on her face, spreading from one ear to the other as she made her way past other attendees. I couldn't bear to witness their joyous embrace, so I averted my gaze just as the race director announced, "And now, for the men aged 40 to 44." This was it, the moment of truth.

Rhonda looked at me and smiled. Even as I write this almost twenty years later, I can vividly feel the exact same emotions that I felt that night, and my eyes are glazing over. It's a fact that my age group and the 40 to 44 age groups are typically highly competitive, with some athletes in these categories also vying for top overall rankings. To illustrate, in that particular year, the first and second-place finishers in my age group achieved overall standings of eleventh and seventeenth, respectively, out of a field of nearly 1,500 participants. Both had previously competed at the professional level, reaching the pinnacle of the sport.

The race director announced, "First in the 40-44 age group and eleventh overall is Stephen Farrell from New Zealand." There was a brief pause, and Stephen rose from his seat, walking down to the sound of applause. Every athlete that night received applause from this sizable gathering of individuals who, more than anyone else, fully comprehended the significance of the moment.

"Next up, Scott Molina", a famous and highly accomplished pro Ironman. In fact, Scott was the Hawaii Ironman World Champion in 1988. A true legend. Scott rose to applause and jogged down.

Stuart Smith was announced, and he rose and accepted.

Three from three, my chances were diminishing.

Next came John Knight, who got up at once and hobbled down. He was ecstatic.

One more gone.

Richard Merrett sprang from his seat just a few metres away.

Five down. Only four more chances. My hope had diminished and was now delicately poised. Surely, this could not be me now. My thoughts turned to the athlete one place in front of me and to what I could have done differently to catch him. How could I have saved 96 seconds of time over the course of ten hours and thirty-eight minutes? That is all I would have needed to be assured right now that I was finally going to Kona to race. Then again, imagine how the poor soul, who was literally one second behind me, was feeling. I had run past him within metres of crossing the finishing line.

"Andrew Walker, come on down and collect your spot," announced the director. Silence. Nothing. My heart raced. And raced. "Please, please, please do not be here, Andrew." I looked anxiously around. The pattern was clear now, and every other athlete who had wished to qualify had virtually leapt from their seat at their name being called. Nothing. Was this it? It was. It is. You have. I clenched my fists, looked at the ground and held the tears back.

"Ok, Kevin Lawrence."

"Fu...!!!!!!" I had made it. Just three more names before mine would be read aloud. Guaranteed. Nothing could change it. Nothing could stop me now. Three more dreams come true, then me.

"Jason Dunn, come on down." Announced the director.

Never, and never since, has the calling on my name sounded this good; this special. I glanced sideways at Rhonda with that knowing smile. Rhonda beamed her wonderful smile back. I was so stiff from sitting for an hour or so that as I rose, I nearly fell forward. Everyone was watching, and I had already pumped the air with my fist. All I could think of was making it down the sharp row of steps to collect my ticket to the Holy Grail. I needed to have it in my hand to make it real. I had to hurry down and collect it before it was given away to someone else. As I shuffled sideways past others in their seats, everyone smiled broadly as I was facing them, while a couple of people extended their hands to congratulate me. Fortunately, I managed to make it down the flight of steps without falling and turning this euphoric moment into my greatest embarrassment. The next thing I knew, the certificate was in my hand, and I was striding back up the steps. I felt like Willy Wonka with the Golden Ticket. Rhonda hugged me, and again, I held back the tears that had built up over six years of trying, six years of sacrifice, six years of dreaming, every day, of my goal. We watched the proceedings for a little longer but soon decided to leave as I wanted to get back and tell Dad.

As soon as we got home, I shared the news with Dad, to his great delight. About an hour later, I went outside to sit on the steps from the deck of the house to ponder and reflect. As I sat, Dad joined me on the step. As he hugged me, I could not hold the torrent of tears back any longer. I cried with everything that I had. It was a final cathartic release of emotion. We all flew out the next day, Dad and Ronda back to Sydney and Cal and I back to the Sunshine Coast. In between entertaining Cal during the flight home, my mind turned to Kona and preparing for Hawaii. My relationship with Taupō had transformed into the epitome of bittersweet. What was once the site of my greatest racing failure had now become the backdrop for my greatest racing success.

Taupō Return in 2005 & 2006

We returned to Taupō twice more, in 2005 and 2006, which marked my last Ironman race ever. Equipped with the valuable life lessons I had learned from my previous races, I was determined to give it my all in 2005.

In 2005, we arrived in Auckland at the beginning of the week, picked up our rental car, and made our way to Craig's place in Auckland, where we met up with my dad and Rhonda. The following morning, we all headed to Taupō, with Craig, his wife Chelsea, and my dad and Rhonda following closely behind. This time, we surpassed ourselves in the accommodation department. Our home for the week was a stunning four-bedroom house situated on a rise next to Lake Taupō. For the remainder of the week, we enjoyed the glorious weather that Taupō had graced us with. In fact, it was so unseasonably warm that I ended up with sunburn.

Race morning arrived quickly, and the excitement in the air was palpable. At exactly 6 am, the starter's gun fired, and the race began. The 3.8-kilometre swim went smoothly, and I managed to improve my time by a couple of minutes compared to the previous year. On the bike leg, I felt like I had finally mastered the course, shaving an impressive 18 minutes off my time, thanks in part to more favourable wind conditions. I couldn't help but wonder if I had a shot at qualifying once again. Could I dare to dream with an 18-minute lead on my previous qualifying time?

As I transitioned to the run after leaving T2, my legs felt heavy. The warmer weather triggered frequent cramps, forcing me to slow down or, in some cases, come to a complete stop to stretch out the cramps as best as I could. Managing hydration had always been a challenge for me, and I struggled to drink enough during the race to prevent these debilitating cramps on the run. Despite the cramps, I fought with every ounce of energy to pick up my pace. Each small acceleration came with the risk of cramping, but I persevered. Running down the finishing chute was, as always, an indescribable feeling. I finished the race 11 minutes faster than my previous year's qualifying time, and I felt confident that I had secured my spot at the World Championships once more.

That night, we celebrated the day's achievements. However, my night was, as usual, sleepless as I replayed every moment of the race in my mind, analysing where I could have improved and where I had exceeded my expectations. But the thought of qualifying for Hawaii dominated my thoughts.

When I finally arrived to review the race results and my chances of securing a spot in Hawaii, I was disheartened to discover that I had placed lower in my age group compared to the previous year, despite my impressive 11-minute improvement. I was now four places away from the last of the ten available slots. Feeling dejected, I decided not to attend the presentation ceremony, as the likelihood of four slots rolling down to me seemed very slim.

It wasn't until two days later, back in Auckland, that I decided to check the results online to see if there had been any changes. To my surprise and horror, I learned that three athletes had not accepted their qualification spots, and the person who had finished only 19 seconds ahead of me had indeed secured the last qualifying spot. As it happened, the individual who crossed the finish line slightly ahead of me was the one I could have defeated if I had pushed a bit harder or avoided one last cramp, thus securing my qualification.

I struggled to come to terms with this tiny difference for a few days, but eventually, I found solace in the knowledge that I had only qualified by a mere second ahead of the last person to miss out the year before. It was a reminder that sometimes, in racing, as in life, the smallest margins can make all the difference.

In 2006, the following year, Jen, Cal, and I returned to Taupō for the fourth time, although I had no idea at the time that this would be my last Ironman ever – well, kind of. Little did I know that this race would turn out to be the most unusual Ironman I would ever experience.

The week leading up to my fourth attempt in New Zealand started much like previous years. However, things took a turn three days before the race when I woke up with debilitating stomach cramps. A visit to a local doctor confirmed that I had contracted a severe stomach virus. The doctor advised me to take a course of medication and rest for 4 to 5 days.

"This is going to take days to work through, so I want you to put your feet up and rest," the doctor recommended.

Sure, I thought, although the worried expression on my face must have shown that I was not relaxed after working tirelessly for the last year to compete at the highest level and perhaps qualify for Hawaii again. We returned to the house we had rented overlooking Lake Taupō, and I attempted to relax. By the day before the race, my stomach cramps had subsided, but the weather had taken a dramatic turn for the worse within the last twenty-four hours, and forecasts suggested it would worsen further.

A strong southerly low-pressure system had formed, bringing near-gale force winds to the region. The typically calm and placid lake had transformed, with waves surging as high as a metre across its expanse. The sight of whitecaps dotting the lake's surface was surreal and a stark departure from anything we'd seen in Taupō. My stomach issues, which had improved, were now overshadowed and reversed by the queasiness I felt when contemplating swimming 3.8 kilometres in these virtually cyclonic conditions. The concern weighed on me to the point where I began discussing the possibility of withdrawing with Jen as we made our way along the shoreline toward the emergency briefing held in the massive marquee tent set up for race head-quarters and the expo site.

Inside the marquee, 1,450 athletes cramped together, anxiously awaiting news about the race's fate, which hung in the balance— either cancellation or significant modification. While we stood there, the tent groaned and billowed, buffeted by the gusts of wind, with the ropes straining to anchor the entire structure and prevent it from taking off.

"Good morning, folks, what a morning we have in Taupō! We've been closely monitoring the weather forecasts, and the strong winds you're experiencing today are expected to intensify by tomorrow morning, with gusts reaching up to 100 kilometres per hour at times," declared the Race Director.

A collective moan swept through the crowd, and the room was suddenly filled with chatter.

"We have been collaborating with Ironman HQ in the US, and we've decided that the conditions on Lake Taupō are too dan-gerous to hold the swim leg as planned. Therefore, we will be removing the swim entirely from the race tomorrow."

Wow, never in Ironman history, anywhere, had the swim leg of a race been cancelled. This announcement brought a rapturous response from the crowd, and the director allowed the applause and cheers to continue for a minute or so.

"Yes, this is indeed the first time in race history where such a decision has been made," the director continued, "but I am sure that when you look out there this morning, you will understand that the conditions are simply far too dangerous to go ahead with the swim. And, folks, the conditions are going to be worse tomorrow morning. We will again review the conditions tomorrow morning, and we ask that you all attend a special race briefing here in the marquee at 6 am before the race starts. Thank you for your patience, and good luck for tomorrow."

The marquee filled with noise again as athletes passionately debated the outcome among themselves. However, there was no debate at all for me; cancelling the swim was a huge relief. I spent the rest of the day reading a book and trying not to look out of the window at the relentless rolling waves that extended across the lake for as far as the eye could see. It was a sleepless night indeed.

Gale force gusts rattled garden furniture and anything else that they could infiltrate during the night. At 3:30 am, I gave up trying to sleep, lying there in the warm bed, thinking about the cold, unpleasant conditions outside. Although it was pitch black outside, I could still see the trees in the garden bending in the wind despite them being quite well protected. My stomach was still unsettled, and I wondered how much strength the sickness had taken from my body. I would soon find out.

The atmosphere inside our car was palpably tense as we made our way along the lake foreshore toward the race start and headquarters. Once there, my focus shifted to preparing my bike. I diligently pumped the tyres, readied my cycling shoes, and attached nutritional supplies to my handlebars.

The weather low had intensified, and as anticipated, the wind had picked up considerably. Stepping into the marquee, which seemed on the verge of being uprooted at any moment, I couldn't help but contemplate the immense challenge that lay ahead, even without the swim. The bike leg, in particular, was a cause for concern as the winds were forceful enough to potentially knock a cyclist off their bike. Conversations buzzed around me as fellow athletes exchanged thoughts and apprehensions about the unfolding circumstances. By now, 6 am had come and gone, and it was evident that discussions were taking place among the race organisers.

"Welcome, one and all," announced the director. "Thank you for your patience at a time when I know you must be nervous and ready to go. As you can all see, the weather conditions have deteriorated, and we've been in continuous communication with the international governing body in the US this morning. Due to the rapidly escalating wind speeds, we've made the following adjustments: Instead of the planned two laps for the bike leg, we'll now race just one lap. Additionally, we'll be covering 21 kilometres for the run instead of the full 42. I want to assure you all that the qualification spots for Hawaii will still be awarded as per the standard regulations." The room erupted as he finished.

I found myself grappling with mixed emotions about the race adjustments. Relief was the dominant feeling, primarily because I wasn't feeling well. My heart wasn't fully invested in the race anymore, and I just wanted to complete it. Thoughts of still potentially qualifying for Hawaii lingered, but deep down, I knew I was far from my best.

An hour later, the race kicked off with a staggered start, athletes setting off from a standing start every 30 seconds on their bike, which was bizarre and an unusual departure from the typical mass swim start. This unconventional beginning set the tone for a day that was far from ordinary. The bike leg proved to be a battle against unpredictable crosswinds, headwinds, and tailwinds. Finding any semblance of rhythm felt challenging, especially when facing gusts of up to 90 kilometres per hour. Survival and safety became the primary concerns over the 90 kilometres, and making it to T2 without incident was a genuine relief. There were moments when the relentless wind seemed determined to dislodge me from my bike.

As for the run, it exposed us to the full brunt of the wind along the lake's edge, alternating between headwinds and tailwinds. Some might think that wind doesn't affect running significantly, but in these extreme conditions, it makes a noticeable difference.

I crossed the finish line in 194th place out of 1,248 finishers, but it was clear I was far from qualifying in my age group. To give you an idea of my lacklustre performance, I maintained a pace almost identical to the previous year. However, this time, I covered only half the distance on the bike and run, and there was no preceding swim. The stomach virus I had caught days before had sapped more of my strength than I had realised. A few days later, we bid farewell to Taupō and headed home, perhaps for the last time, from Taupō.

Training for races that are far from Australian shores presents its own set of challenges, especially when the bulk of the training needs to be done during Australia's colder winter months. Another significant challenge is transitioning from training in cooler conditions to preparing for a race in an extremely hot climate. Unlike preparing for the scorching heat of Malaysia during their summer, when it aligns with Australia's summer, getting ready for Hawaii means going from maximum temperatures of 15 to 18 degrees in Australia to a sweltering 55 degrees in the Energy Lab on the Big Island at 1 pm.

As I mentioned earlier, I've consistently incorporated extended bike sessions on my stationary wind trainer to develop both mental resilience and physical strength. However, this approach became the cornerstone of my bike training regimen as I prepared for Hawaii. Even in the winter, our garage would become quite warm during the midday hours, allowing me to simulate the heat conditions I'd face during the race. Additionally, I could layer on extra clothing to further challenge my body's ability to handle the heat. Furthermore, I made it a point to schedule my lengthiest training run of the week during the midday hours.

We had chosen to travel to Hawaii without Callum, allowing us to focus entirely on competing in the World Championships. Jen's parents graciously agreed to care for Callum during the ten days we'd be away. It's fascinating how the significance of what could potentially be your sole opportunity to participate in the World Championships can alter your attention to detail and amplify your tendency to worry about nearly everything or, at the very least, to zero in on anything that could potentially go wrong.

Sometimes, I wonder if this heightened focus can inadvertently bring about some of the issues you fear. I began encountering minor problems even before our arrival in Kona. During the check-in for our connecting flight, the airport security team thoroughly inspected my bike bag, an item I'm particularly protective of and somewhat paranoid about when travelling to major races. To my surprise, they decided to confiscate the compressed air canisters from my bag before allowing us to board. I was unsure if I'd be able to procure replacements on the island. This was the first time such an incident had occurred, and I had previously flown to 15 different countries for races with the exact same equipment without any issues.

At the Kona airport, I waited with bated breath for my bike to emerge. It was, without doubt, the single most crucial piece of equipment, and my anxiety would only dissipate once I had retrieved it without any damage and successfully reassembled it. The soft case containing my bike had clearly been handled roughly, resulting in the zipper opening. A swift examination confirmed that nothing was harmed, but it seemed that some of the contents had either fallen out when the bag was tipped sideways or had been removed due to the open zipper. Regardless, I planned to assess what was missing upon our arrival at our accommodation. After picking up our rental car and reminding ourselves to drive on the right-hand side of the road, we set off to collect our keys.

Choosing accommodation can be a bit of a gamble, and you never know how well you have picked until you arrive and settle in. However, the moment we stepped into our place in Kona, we knew we had picked an absolute winner. It was spacious, comfortable, and featured a large deck overlooking the ocean. Notably, it was peaceful, and even though it was conveniently close to the town's action, it was far enough away to offer respite from the race's hustle and excitement when needed. We were finally in Kona, and I absolutely adored everything about it. We took some time to explore the race expo, the race-related areas, and then the town itself. I had watched countless legendary races unfold on TV over the years, many of which took place right on these streets where we now stood. Ali'i Drive, which wound through the heart of the town and led to the bay where the race always concluded, held a special place in my heart and was my boulevard of dreams. And here I was, slap bang in the middle of it all, preparing to compete in my own race in just six days.

Later that day, I decided to stretch out my plane legs after the long flight. Spending hours in a pressurised plane cabin can take a toll on your body, so I decided to go for a run along Ali'i Drive, heading away from the town.

During my run, I crossed paths with several other athletes who were either running or cycling. It was the first time in my life that I began to doubt my own presence, my self-assurance, and whether I truly belonged here. I felt a bit intimidated and questioned my own worthiness as I watched some of the fittest athletes on the planet cruising by.

"Wow, look at that guy," I said to myself. "What are you doing here, Jason? What are you doing here?" said the voice of reason in my head.

By the time I got back to our unit, I was feeling like crap – like an impostor. My inner turmoil must have been visible on my face because Jen asked me what was bothering me. Was I injured? I opened up and shared the self-doubt that had crept in while I was running and my uncertainty about whether I truly belonged there. Jen responded with:

"You have sacrificed so much and put everything into this. You qualified for this. You deserve this."

While these words did not instantly change how I was feeling, within an hour or so, I was back to my normal self. "I did f**king…. deserve this."

Kona was buzzing like the greatest show on earth had just arrived in town. I was in heaven. Despite the exhilaration, it was becoming challenging not to lose sight of the monumental test that was rapidly approaching.

My favourite go-to spot for coffee and lunch quickly became Lava-Java, which boasted a view directly looking out on the ocean. There were moments when Ironman legends Norman Stadler or Peter Reid, both multiple Hawaii World Champions, visited Lava-Java while I was there, and it was nearly impossible not to stare with an open jaw in awe. These guys were my idols. We also made an effort to explore the island as much as possible, getting a feel for the bike and run courses, and immersing ourselves in the culture and heritage of the Big Island. It truly is a unique and beautiful place. Our apartment even had a lovely pool, and sometimes it was so easy to relax there that I momentarily forgot the reason I had come – to push my limits in just a few days. The contrast between the serene relaxation and the impending challenge of pushing myself to my limits was surreal.

As I patiently waited in the queue to check my bike in, a process that had extremely strict and limited time constraints and took place the day before the race, I suddenly noticed that my rear tire was flat. My heart began to race as I considered my options. The tyres I was using were expensive and specialised, and this unexpected issue threw me into a spin, as anything right before a race can. Except for the birthdays of my children, tomorrow was going to be the most significant and important day of my life. It was a day I might never get back in terms of this iconic race. Since I had already visited one of the local bike stores, I decided to head straight there to see if they could replace the tire. Carl greeted me with a smile.

"Hey dude, aren't you supposed to be checking your bike in?" To which I responded by raising the back wheel into the air.

"Bummer, I am not sure we have one of those in store. Tell you what, how about I slip that spare tyre on your bike so you can proceed to check in, and I will hunt around town for a replacement?" Carl suggested.

"It's a deal" I responded.

I checked my bike in just inside the cutoff time, and Carl came through with the tyre a few hours later. Everything was back on track. The tension of race day was building, and I didn't want anything to disrupt my preparations.

As usual, I woke up early on race day, and there's something truly inspiring about waking up somewhere in the world on race day when the weather is warm and sunny, as it was on this morning in Kailua-Kona. This morning, I approached my breakfast with the utmost attention to detail. The big day had finally arrived. I meticulously checked over my bike, pumped the tyres to 130 psi (which is quite high compared to the typical 32 psi of a car tyre), taped my gel nutrition to my bike's top frame, and then made my way down to the famous Digme Beach to get a feel for the water.

The water temperature was higher than the maximum allowed for wetsuits, so it was going to be a non-wetsuit swim. For someone like me who lacks buoyancy, is fat deficient, and tends to sink like a stone, these swims are particularly challenging. Wetsuits provide considerable buoyancy and minimise water friction.

As I stood there, gazing at the crowded shoreline and the rows of people gathered along the sea walls, I couldn't help but feel goosebumps. After watching this iconic race start for so many years, it finally sank in that I was here to compete. Wading into the water, I imagined the other iconic image associated with this race: aerial shots of nearly 2,000 athletes in this famous bay, all crowded together, starting with the firing of the cannon, and instantly turning the whole bay white with the churn from their thrashing limbs.

Then, the cannon thundered, and chaos erupted!

I was jostled, thumped, kicked, and pulled underwater for what felt like an eternity, about three minutes or so, until I finally found a bit of clear water. Suddenly, amidst the frenzy, a breathtaking underwater world below caught my eye with its colourful fish and vibrant coral. This was a magnificent swim, one of the most spectacular in the world, and it was a challenge to stay focused on the race with such a mesmerising underwater spectacle.

The rolling swell made navigation tricky. The buoys disappeared from view as I lifted my head to check my direction during each stroke, especially on the downside of the swell. I couldn't gauge the exact distance I swam that day, but it was longer than the scheduled 3.8 kilometres. When I pulled myself onto the ramp leading to T1 near the jetty, I glanced at my watch and confirmed my gut feeling that it was indeed an exceptionally long swim - the slowest Ironman swim I had ever done.

The transition area was quite a long and convoluted run around the jetty track from the swim exit. I had to grab my bag, change into one of the white tents, and then retrieve my bike. In races like this, a swift transition can make a significant difference, especially for the leaders. I quickly mounted my bike, and with a burst of energy, I pedalled away onto the bike leg. Kailua-Kona was filled with spectators and supporters, creating an electric atmosphere for the racers. I had never experienced such a rush of adrenaline in a race before.

We left town briefly to reach the first turnaround point, then retraced our path to tackle Paolina Hill and join the Queen K Highway, which would lead us through the mesmerising lava fields. Exciting the sharp hill out of town and onto the Queen K, I expected the cheering crowds, cowbells, and words of encouragement to continue, but instead, they vanished as we entered the silent, desolate highway that sliced through the treeless, moon-like lava landscape.

Then, the wind hits you. Wham. Take that. "This is going to be a very long day, Jason,"

I heard that voice in my head as I pedalled further out of town, and the wind grew stronger and more intense, gusting at a punishing 80 kilometres per hour. You know those days when the wind is nearly gale force, and even walking down the street is a struggle? Well, imagine riding a bike as fast as you can into that kind of relentless wind for the next three hours, and you're only halfway there. There were moments when I had to glance down at my wheels just to reassure myself that they were still turning. Coupled with the scorching heat, it was brutal.

During that exhausting stretch to the halfway point, I had moments of doubt, wondering if I would even finish the race, let alone in a decent condition. It's no secret that many athletes end up receiving fluids via intravenous drips in large recovery tents at the race's finish line. When things got incredibly tough, I kept telling myself that all I needed to do was reach the turnaround point at the top of the hill in Hawi. Once there, the same trade winds that were currently my tormentors would become my allies, propelling me back home as if I had sprouted wings. Or so I thought.

There was a brief respite as we made the turn for the major climb up to Hawi. Ironically, this year turned out to be one of the two toughest race days in the history of this legendary event. The turnaround at Hawi was a welcome sight, and the descent back down to the Queen K Highway promised speed, even though it meant no opportunities for drinking. The consequences of the gusting crosswinds on the descent meant you couldn't afford to take either hand off the handlebars to sneak a drink. The fear of being blown off the bike was ever-present. Not being able to hydrate for 40 minutes in a race like this, in such harsh conditions, could be disastrous from both a performance and health perspective, even literally fatal.

I had read somewhere during my research for the race that Kona is one of the few places in the world where the trade winds often change direction around midday. This natural phenomenon hadn't registered as particularly significant at the time, but boy did it now. I reached the base of the climb, then suddenly, and heartbreakingly, the wind gusted right into my face as the road aligned with the Queen K Highway.

"Jesus, surely not," I said out aloud to myself. "Not today, please, not today."

Before I knew it, I was back on the Queen K Highway, and sure enough, the winds had indeed turned around completely, now posing another 60 kilometres of headwind on the way to T2. I can't stress enough how heartbroken and deflated I felt. The next thirty minutes came and went as I battled my demons and fought just to keep the wheels revolving. I continually fought the voice in my head that kept questioning why I was doing this, again, and encouraging me to quit because this was just too hard, until about 10 kilometres from T2, and I knew that I would soon be off that wretched bike.

As the noise level rose while heading into town, I found myself running back along Ali'i Drive to the first turnaround. Despite feeling utterly exhausted and smashed, it was hard to hold back while running through the cheering crowds along this famous stretch of road. I had watched the greatest athletes in history compete for the title of World Champion on this very road. Running past our apartment, I made a point to seek out every hose I could find. Along this famous stretch, some homeowners had set up hoses with spray nozzles for runners to cool themselves as they passed by. I took advantage of this a couple of times before resorting to grabbing handfuls of ice at each aid station and stuffing them under my hat to melt.

There were many obviously important aspects to successfully completing this race, such as hydrating yourself well over ten to eleven hours of very strenuous exercise in the most oppressive conditions, ingesting sufficient calories while managing not to vomit them back up, and cooling a rising core body temperature was mandatory if you wanted to make it to the end in one piece. The latter, I have found, can be most successfully achieved by stuffing ice either under your cap, or down the front of your running shorts.

Downtown seemed to pass in a flash. Climbing the steep hill at Palani Road, with a throng of spectators on either side, cheering and shaking cowbells, was truly inspiring. However, within minutes, a strange silence enveloped me as I turned left at the top of the hill, entering the seemingly endless, rolling Queen K Highway. Instantly, the back of my thighs cramped simultaneously, a consequence of the steep hill's toll, and I had to take a few side steps to loosen them. Reaching the crest of that hill was an immense relief, but the stark emptiness of the highway hit me hard like a smack to the face.

This was, by far, the most instantly deflating and empty feeling I had ever experienced during a race, except for the disappointment of quitting the New Zealand Ironman a few years prior. I felt shattered, and there were still 28 kilometres to go, with 95% of the racecourse taking place on the Queen K Highway, in the Energy Lab, or on the long road to and from the Energy Lab. It was a brutally challenging race, and today, it was exceptionally tiring.

Despite contemplating it on a few occasions, I had never walked any part of a marathon before, aside for a few seconds to drink and walk through a running aid station, but I knew already that I would have to walk some stretches of the marathon today to the finish line. Sure enough, about four kilometres along the highway, I had to walk for a few hundred metres while drinking before picking up the pace again. I ran down to the Energy Lab with renewed energy, but by the time I passed through and turned around to head back, I found myself reduced to walking for another few hundred metres. It was 55 degrees Celsius in the shade!

With ten kilometres to go, I made a promise to myself: I would run and not stop. I needed to finish my race with strength, not on my knees, although I would have if there were no other option. Despite the intense pain and discomfort that I was enduring, I was determined to savour the final hour of the race, especially the last kilometre along Ali'i Drive, where I would hear the famous Mike Riley announce, "Welcome home, Jason Dunn, you are an Ironman," in his unmistakable, booming American accent. Mike had been the voice of this race for as long as I could remember and had become an institution in Ironman racing.

The cramps kept coming rapidly every time I tried to turn on a bit of extra pace in the last three kilometres as I made my way down into Kailua and onto Ali'i Drive. Completely shattered but filled with overwhelming emotions and a profound sense of accomplishment, I was heading toward the finish line along Ali'i Drive – a home like no other, the home of dreams. Thousands of spectators lined the streets, cheering me on. They understood what this meant; they knew the sacrifices and dedication required to reach this special place. Finally, finally, I raised my arms and pumped my fists above my head. No more "I could have," now I could proudly say, "I did it."

Supported on either side, I was guided away by two finish chute volunteers and into one of the massive recovery tents filled with athletes hooked up to IV drips. It resembled a vast WWII field hospital tent, I thought. They asked me what I needed, and all I could think about was lying down. I desperately wanted the physical pain to end, but at the same time, I didn't. You see, I've come to realise that pain is intertwined with feeling alive. Being alive. The 30 minutes following a major race are the most alive I've ever felt. The more pain you feel, the more you know you're truly alive. So, I lay on my back for a while, absorbing the magnitude of what I had just, finally, accomplished.

Suddenly, I became aware of the weight of my Hawaii Ironman finisher's medal around my neck, resting on my chest. I touched

it to make sure it was real. This large circular accolade was now my most valuable and treasured possession.

I didn't realise at that moment that there would be two medals that would come close and one that would equal it. But for now, I laid back and drifted into the post-race bliss.

Daily Practice Action

The objective of this exercise is to spend some time thinking about how you will feel when you achieve your impossible goal. Maybe you've always dreamed of writing a novel, or perhaps you want to make regional manager at work, or even climb Everest. Great! Whatever your goal, write down some feelings and thoughts to get clear on how your life will change when you achieve it.

DAILY PRACTICE ACTION
Unlimited

What positive impact will achieving your seemingly impossible goal have on your life?	
What other areas of your life will improve?	
What obstacle is stopping you or holding you back that you can now over-come?	
What actions do you need to take to overcome the obstacle?	

Summiting Khardung La over the highest motorable road in the world on
August 19, 2014, during La Ultra - The High.

YOU ARE UNLIMITED

"I can change. I can live out of my imagination instead of my memory. I can tie myself to my limitless potential instead of my limiting past."

— Stephen Covey

No human is limited. That is the mantra of one of the greatest athletes in history, Eliud Kipchoge, who I refer to in chapter 4. In essence, no human is indeed limited to their current state, other than by their mindset, which is the most significant inhibitor for most humans on this planet. So, if you haven't got it by now, you are only limited by your mind – so change it!

Once you have achieved your first impossible, everything suddenly becomes possible. This is the mindset that you may well develop and discover. And it is bloody effusive. It is empowering, and it evokes a sense of almost undeniable confidence. Not arrogance, but a sense of self-accomplishment and internal confidence. When I achieved my first impossible, the possibilities became endless, and I challenged myself to dream of my next impossible, reinventing myself over and over. It also pervades every aspect of your life and opens new doors and opportunities in other unrelated areas. In some respects, writing this book at age 60 is my next impossible.

The next phase of my reinvention started in July 2005 when we moved to Sydney, predominantly for career opportunities, and we chose to settle in North Sydney, which is only a stone's throw from the Sydney Harbour Bridge and the Sydney CBD. Consequently, this meant living in the heart of a large, busy city metropolis, which was not conducive to cycling 300 to 400 kilometres per week as was necessary to seriously compete in the Ironman Triathlon. As I considered what I had achieved in the Ironman Triathlon, I felt comfortable with parking my Triathlon aspirations.

It became clear that I needed a new challenge that aligned with our location in the heart of a major city and would ignite my passion for competing at a higher level than my previous age group Ironman events. It was seven years earlier that I had realised setting almost impossible goals, so far beyond what I could believe that I could do, was what truly motivated and inspired me.

I began running every day as this was as easy as lacing up my runners and heading out of the door to work. Conveniently, I could leave home in the morning with a backpack of essential clothing, run to work, shower, and change. Then home again in reverse. It was not long before I was running twice every day, and the kilometres were racking up.

The internet became a wellspring of inspiration, unveiling the burgeoning world of ultramarathons, one of Australia's and the world's fastest-growing sporting challenges. In recent years, long-distance races had experienced exponential growth, with the most prevalent series covering distances of 100 kilometres and 100 miles, whether on road surfaces or rugged wilderness trails. I found myself captivated by stories of races like the North Face 100k ultra series, held in numerous global locations, where 1,500 entry slots vanished within mere hours of online registration openings. This piqued my curiosity and transformed into an electrifying excitement. Could I run 100 kilometres, or perhaps even more, in one continuous, uninterrupted effort? And if so, how quickly?

As I embarked on my quest, I stumbled upon the Gold Coast 100 Super Marathon, a race that also served as the Athletics Australia 100 Kilometres Road Championships. Without hesitation, I committed to this challenge, applying my proven 90-Day High-Performance Plan. This method allowed me to reverse-engineer my training plan, counting down the days to the June 2006 event and providing me with a clear and structured path forward. Clarity was paramount, as it provided the certainty I needed to approach each day's training with unwavering determination.

In a matter of days, I began to discern the roadmap toward my newfound goal. Yet, before long, I found myself setting an even more audacious target – to secure a spot on the Australian Elite team for the 100 Kilometres World Championships within the next five years. To grasp the enormity of this ambition, consider that my farthest run to date had covered just 42.2 kilometres, and I had already crossed the threshold of 43 years of age. Kilometre by kilometre, I had now fixed my sights on completing

a 100-kilometre run, aiming to achieve it in under 8 hours, a lofty standard set by Athletics Australia. For those not inclined to crunch the numbers, that equated to nearly 2.5 back-to-back marathons, each completed at a blistering pace of around 3 hours and 20 minutes per marathon.

Contrary to the Ironman, which demands roughly twenty hours of exhausting training each week for eleven out of the twelve months, diving into the realm of running presented its own unique challenges. Running didn't distribute muscle fatigue across the body in the same way, making the training more demanding and potentially injury-prone. Nevertheless, the allure of uncertainty, the magnitude of the challenge, and the sheer adventure that awaited me were exhilarating.

In the beginning, my regimen consisted of running fifteen kilometres daily during the week, with a fifty-kilometre Sunday run. This totalled 125 kilometres per week, a volume I deduced from my research as the minimum necessary to build the endurance required for a continuous 100-kilometre run. Sundays took centre stage as the most critical training day, with a scheduled five-hour solo run. This rhythm soon became my way of life, a relentless pursuit of my goal to qualify for the World Elite Championships and other races that would push me to my limits.

My objective afforded me until the age of 48 to secure qualification, although I remained uncertain about how competitive I could be in my mid to late forties. Only time would provide the answer to that lingering question.

Training progressed well as I gradually worked my way up to 150 kilometres per week.

My long Sunday runs increased to 60 kilometres, spanning over 6 hours, which introduced a fresh set of challenges. These included ensuring I had adequate hydration and nutrition while mastering the art of eating on the run at a normal pace. Carrying enough water from the outset was a logistical puzzle, and looking back, it's almost a miracle that I'm still here, considering the countless times I relied on taps and water fountains to stay hydrated during my runs.

Sundays transformed into full-day training events, encompassing not only the run itself but also the preparation and recovery phases. On particularly hot days, I would even immerse myself in an ice bath for thirty minutes, both to lower my core temperature and to minimise muscle damage. As the race day drew nearer, I felt reasonably confident that I had done enough to complete the race. However, the leap from routinely running 60 kilometres at a moderate pace to facing a 66% increase in distance at a faster tempo remained a daunting prospect.

Race week had finally arrived, and we travelled to the sunny Gold Coast a few days ahead of the big day. At the pre-race briefing, the Race Director, Ian Cornelius, distributed race bibs and took a moment to introduce some of the more accomplished athletes, highlighting their remarkable achievements. Over time, I had the opportunity to get to know Ian quite well. He was a remarkable individual dedicated to inspiring others in the world of running. Ian also had an impressive track record as an ultra-runner in his own right.

To my surprise, I received a mention for my accomplishments in Ironman racing during the briefing alongside another first-time ultra runner, David Eadie, also known as The Running Man, and a fellow Hawaii Ironman participant. Dave and I would go on to become friends in the years that followed, often lining up together at the starting line of various prestigious races. During the briefing, I chatted with several of the other runners, and I quickly noticed that they were a distinct bunch compared to the typical triathletes I had come to know. They possessed a unique sense of friendliness, humility, and a down-to-earth nature that stood out in a positive way.

Race morning arrived, bringing with it the familiar pre-race restlessness I had experienced before Ironman events. However, this time, there was significantly less stress concerning race gear and preparation. Running seemed simpler in that regard, though there was the potential for more physical challenges, especially considering the enormous pounding my legs would endure. I set reasonably moderate expectations for myself on that day, aiming to avoid burning out early and risking a Did Not Finish (DNF) result. My primary goal was to finish the race within 10 hours, which meant sustaining a pace of 10 kilometres per hour for a continuous 100 kilometres. It sounded straightforward enough. Oddly, I couldn't help but feel like I had forgotten something, missing the usual meticulous preparation and the endless checklists of equipment that accompanied triathlons. At 6.29 am, we toed the starting line, and within minutes, we were away. To my surprise, a few runners surged ahead, which seemed quite ambitious given the daunting distance we had ahead of us. I focused on restraining my instinct to race and instead settled into a steady pace. The race began in a small athletics stadium, and we would return to it every 10 kilometres, completing a lap of the track before continuing. This would provide some much-needed encouragement along the way.

At the halfway 50-kilometre mark, I was ahead of my scheduled time, sitting in 10th place, with a time of 4 hours and 17 minutes.

My pace at the marathon mark was 3 hours and 29 minutes. However, my legs were starting to feel the strain, and I realised I needed to adjust my time expectations. At that moment, it seemed feasible to try to maintain a pace of 10 kilometres per hour for the remaining 50 kilometres, which would bring me to the finish in around nine hours and seventeen minutes. So, I backed off a bit to see how that pace felt. When I passed through the stadium again, 10 kilometres later, my legs had begun to cramp, and doubts about finishing this massive new challenge crept in. Most of the spectators were in or around the stadium, providing much-needed encouragement. For those few hundred metres, my legs felt a bit less heavy. However, once I exited the stadium and left it behind, the reality set in.

This was when the mental game of reframing began. I deliberately shout out, thinking about reaching the full 100 kilometres, as this would force my brain to contend with the psychological equation that starts to weigh your current physical state against the remaining distance and time. It's easy to feel defeated and want to stop when your mind can't conceive how you can keep going for the remaining distance. This is a fascinating topic that many high-performance studies of human endurance have analysed and debated for more than 100 years. Essentially, some popular theories and research suggest that we all have the capacity to evaluate our pace or effort to ensure we don't seriously injure or kill ourselves when running long distances. This evaluation combines experience gained from running tens of thousands of kilometres with our innate human instinct. For me, and many others, it's about finding a pace that I can first psychologically and then physically sustain for the remaining distance. So, I recalibrated my mindset and focused on completing the next 10-kilometre loop. After that, I would re-evaluate. I knew that this approach might eventually lead me to set even smaller goals, like reaching the next aid station or the end of a particular stretch of road. But for now, it was one more lap.

Running between the 60 and 80-kilometre mark in a race is often the toughest part. You're already exhausted, but there's still a long way to go before the finish line. It's a bit like being in no man's land because you're not yet close enough to the finish to unleash the full power of adrenaline and push you through. This made laps seven and eight the most challenging and slowest part of the race, with me grinding them out at a pace of around 10 kilometres per hour. However, as I reached the 80-kilometre mark, my spirits lifted at the thought of accomplishing something that was unimaginable to me just two years prior. This feeling was like the one I had experienced before my first Ironman race. Many people undergo this transformation when they decide to change their lives and pursue goals that once seemed impossible. Achieving that first major goal, something you once believed was beyond your reach, is a truly life-changing experience that lays the foundation for limitless personal growth.

Leaving the stadium for the last time, I was utterly exhausted. The temperature had reached its peak at 25 degrees Celsius, and the sun had shone relentlessly all day. Despite my physical and mental fatigue, I couldn't help but feel a surge of anticipation for the euphoria I knew was awaiting me at the finish line. This anticipation seemed to provide me with almost superhuman strength for my aching legs.

My pace quickened as I tapped into reserves of energy I hadn't known I possessed until I experienced a few painful cramps, causing me to slow back down to a hobble. But then, there I was, making the final lap around the track. I had completed the race in nine hours and eight minutes, securing ninth place. I was ecstatic. Floating on cloud nine.

Now, it was time to focus on recovery, attempt some much-needed sleep, and show up for the awards ceremony the following morning.

The following day, most of the runners gathered at the athletics track for the awards ceremony. We shared our race experiences and stories, greeted old friends, and made new ones. David Eadie and I had a conversation about the race, and David proudly shared that he had finished in 8 hours and 25 minutes, securing third place overall. Little did I know that David would go on to achieve remarkable feats in the world of running, eventually earning the title of Australian Ultramarathon Runner of the Year.

As I clapped the podium winners, I allowed myself to dream. I envisioned a day soon when I would stand on that very podium, receiving a medal at the Athletics Australia 100-kilometre Elite Road Championships. By the following day, I had set my sights on that new goal, replacing the one I had just accomplished. This achievement marked the beginning of my journey into the world of ultramarathons, with twelve races of 100 kilometres or more still to come.

The Western States 100

In 2006, Dean Karnazes released his book, "Ultramarathon Man: Confessions of an All-Night Runner," and helped introduce the world and me to ultramarathons. Well, technically, I was already an ultramarathon athlete, but I had never run an ultra-trail race, which, some might say, omitted the most important element of ultra from my CV. To be honest, I had never even read about these types of races, let alone participated in one. Additionally, I had never truly run on a wilderness trail, not even for training purposes. But more on that experience shortly.

I distinctly remember a book recommendation that had swiftly become a bestseller in the United States and, quite possibly, the most influential ultrarunning book up to that point and perhaps even since. It was a captivating read. As I devoured the pages, my emotions swung from awe and inspiration on one page to fear on the next. Yet, there was one race that both tremendously excited me and filled me with trepidation—the Western States 100-mile ultramarathon. It's the oldest organised and arguably the most prestigious 100-mile trail running race in the world, even though there are hundreds of such races.

The Western States Endurance Run, known commonly as the Western States 100, is a 100.2-mile (161 km) ultramarathon that takes place on California's Sierra Nevada Mountains trails each year on the last full weekend of June.

The race begins at the base of the Palisades Tahoe ski resort in Olympic Valley and concludes at the Placer High School track in Auburn, California. Runners tackle a rugged course that often includes snow on the highest passes and record hot temperatures throughout the course. Over the course of the race, participants ascend a total of 18,090 feet (5,500 m) and descend a staggering 22,970 feet (7,000 m) on mountain trails.

Given its extreme length, the race starts at 5 am and continues through the day, into the night, and into the following day. Finishers who complete the race within the 30-hour time limit are awarded a commemorative bronze belt buckle. However, those who manage to finish in under 24 hours receive a prestigious silver belt buckle, a distinction once regarded as the pinnacle of achievement in the world of ultrarunning.

The Western States 100 is one of the five 100-mile races that constitute the Grand Slam of Ultrarunning. This illustrious series also includes the Old Dominion 100, Vermont 100-Mile Endurance Run, the Wasatch Front 100-Mile Endurance Run in Utah, and the Leadville Trail 100 in Colorado. The history of the Western States Trail Run dates back to its early days as the Western States Trail Ride, an event that initially showcased the mountain course as a two-day march. In 1972, seven soldiers from Fort Riley, Kansas, accomplished the feat on foot, demonstrating that the course could indeed be traversed in less than 48 hours. However, the most significant moment came in 1974 when Gordy Ainsleigh became the first person to run the course in under 24 hours.

Ainsleigh was already familiar with the Western States Trail Ride, also known as the Tevis Cup, having completed it on horseback in 1971 and 1972. However, in 1973, his new horse experienced lameness issues and was pulled from the race at the 29-mile checkpoint. It was in 1974 that Gordy, inspired and encouraged by Drucilla Barner, the first woman to win the Tevis Cup and Secretary of the Western States Trail Foundation, decided to attempt the course on foot in under 24 hours.

Gordy's historic run took him twenty-three hours and forty-two minutes to complete, showcasing that a runner could cover the Western States trail in a single day. It's important to note that during this initial run in 1974, the course was not yet 100 miles long. It measured at most 89 miles until 1980, when it was extended to 93.5 miles. Finally, in 1985, the course reached its current distance of 100 miles. While Gordy Ainsleigh's achievement was groundbreaking, running 100 miles in a day was not an entirely new concept, as around 1,000 runners worldwide had previously completed this formidable feat on various tracks, roads, and trails.

Offering the sport's oldest and most prized possession, with its iconic sub-24-hour silver belt buckle, the Western States remains one of the undisputed crown jewels of human endurance. Capturing the belt buckle is what drove me. Out of the roughly 369 runners who typically participate each year, only 68.9% manage to complete the race within the 36-hour cutoff, and a mere 25.5% cross the finish line in under 24 hours to claim that coveted silver belt buckle. Gaining entry to the race has become virtually impossible over the years.

I guess I've never been one to seek out or rely on advice from others. Instead, I prefer to delve into extensive research and reading to understand and figure out what I need to know. This method served me well when I first started learning to swim, then cycling, and eventually expanded to other pursuits, including ultrarunning.

So, I began to research the Western States 100, and piece by piece, it revealed that the race posed five major challenges: altitude, vertical elevation change, temperature fluctuations, trail running skills, and foot care! Yes, foot care is a significant factor and a leading cause of non-finishes in events like the WS100 due to foot saturation from river crossings, snow, and the constant contortion of your feet over 40,000 feet of vertical change.

To put this into perspective, and for those of you who have tackled Heartbreak Hill during the Sydney City to Surf race - which has an ascent of 303 vertical feet. Compare that to the WS100, which features 18,000 feet of vertical change. That's nearly 60 times the climb of Heart Break Hill over 100 miles, and it's much steeper. Furthermore, the WS100 takes place at high altitudes and traverses rugged mountains, making it a far cry from the smooth suburban road surface of the city run. The relentless pounding on your feet, especially during descents, can lead to muscle and joint pain, as well as the risk of losing toenails.

In the book that inspired me to run the Western States, Karnazes describes crippling blisters that were treated intra-race by slicing them open with a scalpel, squeezing the fluid out, then inserting super glue into them, pressing them shut, before duct taping them closed. "Really", I thought, surely that does not happen. The prospect of continuing for hours with nail-less toes jammed into wet running shoes is a daunting reality for ultrarunners. It may sound extreme, but as I would soon discover, it's all too real in the world of ultramarathon racing.

To prepare myself for the scorching 100-plus-degree conditions of the Western States Endurance Run, I knew I needed to acclimate to the intense heat coming from the winter climate in Australia. After some research, I decided that the most effective training would be to sit in a sauna. My training plan involved 90-minute sauna sessions in a sauna set to a temperature of 55 degrees Celsius (131 degrees Fahrenheit). During these sessions, I followed a specific routine of spending 15 minutes inside the sauna, followed by a 10-minute break, and then repeating this cycle multiple times. Saunas are not that easy to find these days, much like squash courts, but I found one close by at the North Sydney Olympic Pool and I scheduled two sessions per week. Not surprisingly, this felt rather extreme in the middle of winter, but then that was the point.

The 2nd major challenge would be coping with altitude at the Western States 100, which starts at 6,500 feet above sea level and tops out at around 11,000 feet. For further perspective, the race commences at 6,500 feet and, within the first five miles, reaches 10,000 feet, even peaking on a snow-covered mountaintop. It's quite an intense way to kick off a 24-plus-hour day of running! That is 13.2 x the height of Heart Break Hill within 5 miles of the start. Considering that I had never ventured past 2,000 feet in altitude before, I was completely unfamiliar with the effects of high altitude. However, I learned that even at 6,000 feet, a human heart beats approximately 30% faster than it does at lower altitudes, so a 70-beat resting heart, which is typical of most active people, would beat at close to 100 times a minute just sitting still at 6,000 feet.

Of course, this magnifies as you exercise and as you climb towards 11,000 feet, which would ultimately take a significant toll on everything. At 11,000 feet, there is approximately 42% less oxygen in the air than at sea level. This meant that the entire day of the race would be spent running mostly between these two altitudes, putting significant extra strain on my body. While I did find a few altitude exercise chambers in Sydney, I made the decision to skip those sessions and face the consequences head-on. I had never even stood at a significant altitude point before, so I would have no prior experience, conditioning, or idea of what to expect at these altitudes when I raced at the WS 100. However, I would later be accepted into an exclusive race that claimed to be the highest-altitude ultramarathon on the planet, and I would have no choice but to run on a treadmill positioned inside a high-altitude chamber for more than three hours at a time to acclimate to the altitude.

YOU ARE UNLIMITED

Addressing the cumulative effects of climbing and descending 40,000 feet vertically, which is roughly 1.4 times the height from sea level to the peak of Mount Everest, I knew I had to train on hills extensively. Fortunately, I found a significant hill in Neutral Bay that had a 1.5-kilometre ascent and an equal descent, forming a 3-kilometre elevation loop. This became the site for my intense training sessions. I scheduled 6-hour, non-stop training sessions on that hill, going up and down repeatedly, even though the altitude change was only around 200 feet. It was demanding work, but I knew it was essential to prepare for the relentless elevation changes I would encounter during the Western States 100.

Single hill repeats have always formed the core of my training routines. I've embraced the repetitive, monotonous nature of this regimen because it built exceptional mental fortitude. I saw it as a way to prepare myself for race day when the stimulating terrain and thousands of other competitors would keep my mind engaged and inspired.

In addition to hill repeats, another strategy I deployed in my weekly training schedule to enhance my climbing strength and endurance was two three-hour workouts per week on the steps leading up to the Sydney Harbour Bridge. The session began with a two-kilometre warm up, then running up two steps in each motion to complete the up 60-step flight, then down again and repeating the process. By the end of the three-hour session, I would have conquered 20,000 steps. To add to this monotonous, leg busting session, I would aim to complete it at midday when the temperature was at its peak. Maintaining concentration was crucial to avoid tripping on the steps, especially as my legs turned to jelly as the three-hour session progressed.

When it came to the challenges of running on dark, unfamiliar trails while fatigued and potentially experiencing night blindness due to physical exhaustion, all I could do was trust in my training and hope the race gods looked down on me favourably on race day. Navigating treacherous mountain terrain with sheer vertical drops was a daunting prospect, and while I did manage to get in a few nighttime trail runs in the bush to prepare, I knew the true test would come during the race.

Dealing with the potential presence of rattlesnakes and mountain lions was another concern, and it was disconcerting to read reports of a runner being attacked and killed by a mountain lion just days before a recent Western States race. However, I had to put these fears aside and focus on the race ahead.

The challenge of navigating wild mountain trails, with their relentless rocks, undulating paths, precarious and unpredictable footing, large tree roots obstructing the trail, and ever-changing terrain, loomed large. These trails also presented the added challenges of snow and river crossings. To put this immense challenge into perspective, running 100 miles over the Sierra Nevada Mountain range was akin to covering at least 150 miles on smooth, paved roads, which equated to approximately 230 kilometres of road running.

Time is always a challenge when you have a family and a demanding career, which already places stress on everyone. Nonetheless, I sought an alternative solution that, while not perfect, allowed me to gain valuable trail experience. Once a week, I would set out from home equipped with a running backpack containing a hydration bladder and some food for replenishing calories during the run. My destination: a solitary 6-hour run, with approximately 4.5 hours of that time dedicated to exploring the trails within Lane Cove National Park.

While I would hardly call Lane Cove National Park a truly remote wilderness, it felt remote. For hours on end, I'd traverse rocky terrain, descend narrow trails, and conquer steep hills without encountering another human soul. However, the park was far from devoid of life; it was home to a fascinating array of creatures, including various snake species, which I'd occasionally encounter. Yet, there was one inhabitant I crossed paths with on a day I'd always remember.

On this day, I had been running solo for approximately four hours, immersed in the rhythmic beats of my headphones, and hadn't laid eyes on another soul for three hours. I was in a meditative state, each footfall a precise calculation to avoid losing my balance on the narrow trail high above the Lane Cove River in the park. The path was generally around five feet wide, but in some spots, it narrowed to a mere three feet or so. As I came around a blind curve, I abruptly came to a halt and froze. I might have screamed, but I certainly wouldn't have heard it over my blasting music. Why? Right there, in the middle of the track, only a few metres up ahead, was a colossal monitor lizard. Suddenly, we were locked in a staring contest, both contemplating our next move. These monitor lizards were no strangers to the park and could grow to be over six feet in length, complete with claws several inches long, incredibly sharp, and potentially menacing.

"Oh shit, what do I do," I thought out aloud as I stood motionless. I had read that startling these guys was a bad idea and that when scared, they would scale a tree with their sharp claws or perhaps a human if there was nowhere else to go. We faced off for a minute or so, which seemed like an eternity. This trail was my only path at this point, with a solid rock face to my left and a perilous vertical drop to my right. I decided to take a cautious step forward, hoping the lizard would retreat in the opposite direction or perhaps even over the edge, but instead, it suddenly moved towards me.

"F**k," I exclaimed, yelling out, startled as the colossal lizard immediately began to ascend a nearby tree on the path's edge, coming to a halt at head height. It now became apparent that this formidable creature was slightly larger than me, its gaze locking onto mine at eye level. Notably, a portion of its tail still rested on the trail. What left the most lasting impression on me during this tense standoff was the sheer magnitude of its claws gripping the tree's bark. In the five or so minutes that followed, we engaged in an unspoken duel of wills, pondering our next moves. The accumulating lactic acid in my legs intensified their stiffness, demanding that I decide. I opted to break the deadlock by stomping on the ground to startle the giant lizard into action. Without hesitation, he flinched and swiftly scaled the tree trunk, disappearing from sight. From that day forward, I remained keenly aware of my surroundings on the trail, although I never encountered another monitor lizard."

My training had been relentlessly intense, and I eagerly embraced the three-week tapering period as the race drew near. The gruelling regimen evolved into six-hour sessions of uphill and downhill running on a single hill one day, followed by three-hour sessions of stair climbing the next, and the repetition had begun to exact a toll on my left knee, which needed careful attention. Worries had crept in that this was becoming serious enough that my knee might deteriorate to a point where I wouldn't be able to endure the 24-hour non-stop run through the rugged Sierra

Nevada Mountains, complete with a staggering 40,000 feet of vertical elevation change.

Ten days before the race, we boarded a flight bound for the United States, heading to our pre-race destination, the pictur-esque Lake Tahoe in California. Our journey commenced with a few days in the vibrant city of San Francisco. We had an abso-lute blast touring Alcatraz, riding the iconic cable trams around the city, and enthusiastically exploring all that San Francisco had to offer. The highlight of our time there and our best day together came when we rented a couple of bicycles, with one featuring an enclosed trailer for Cal to ride in, and embarked on a memorable coastal journey that took us all the way to the Golden Gate Bridge. We triumphantly crossed the bridge before retracing our path back to the city. Though bidding farewell to San Francisco was bittersweet, it was time to continue our adventure, embarking on a four-hour drive in our rental car – on the wrong side of the road – to reach the breathtaking Lake Tahoe, our next destination.

Navigating the trip in those days was far from easy, especially since we didn't have the convenience of Google Maps, which we all rely on so heavily today. Navigating the sprawling free-ways with their multiple lanes and intricate exits was a bit of a challenge. However, once we finally reached the Sierra Nevada Mountains, any effort and stress we had encountered along the way quickly faded into the background. The stunning scenery before us left us breathless as we ascended to an altitude of 6,000 feet above sea level. As we continued our climb, the air grew thinner, causing our breathing to become more pronounced and our heart rates to rise noticeably. At one point, we had to make an impromptu stop on the side of the highway because we both began to feel sick and nauseous due to the effects of the high altitude. We parked the car, which seemed to be pointed straight towards the sky, and took a brief break to acclimate before resuming our journey.

Upon arriving in Lake Tahoe, we were captivated by its charming beauty. Our delight was further heightened when we settled into our luxurious mountain residence nestled among the fragrant pine trees.

The next morning, we made our way up to Squaw Valley, a place steeped in history as the venue for the 1960 Winter Olympics and the central hub for the WS100 race.

As we arrived, the atmosphere was abuzz with athletes, media personnel, and supporters all soaking up the atmosphere on this sunny day in the mountains. We parked our car and began walking towards the race headquarters, but it was impossible not to be awed by the towering peaks that loomed above us, knowing that in just six days, we would be ascending those very heights. We paused, shielding our eyes from the brilliant sun, gazing up at the majestic summits, and exchanged a knowing look. No words were necessary to convey our thoughts. The winding path leading up the main mountain seemed nearly vertical, ascending over 4,000 feet to reach the first peak at an elevation of 10,700 feet. And that was just the beginning, covering the first four miles or so of the race.

"Wow," was the only word that escaped my lips. It was probably best not to linger too long in awe, so we continued on our way towards the expo and race headquarters.

My heart raced with excitement and the effect of being 6,500 feet above sea level as I stood at the race start. We wandered around the expo for a while, and then, out of the blue, someone with a "Media" lanyard approached me and asked, "Excuse me, Sir, are you running on Saturday?"

"I am indeed," I replied proudly.

"Congratulations. May I ask where you are from?" She replied.

"Sure, we've come from Sydney, Australia."

"That's fantastic, such a beautiful place."

"It is" I beamed back.

"Well, we are filming a documentary on this famous race, and we would love to interview you before and after the race, if that would be ok with you?"

"Of course, I would love to," I replied. Within fifteen minutes, I was in front of their cameras and being asked questions about my training and my experience. I gladly answered every question for the next ten minutes. Then, the director came in and asked if he could throw a few questions my way. He sat down.

"So, can you tell us about your trail running experience? What other 100 milers have you completed?"

I hesitated for a moment, smiled, and said, "This is my first."

For a moment, there was silence. "You mean to say this is your first ever trail race?" he asked with a perplexed expression.

"It is indeed," I smiled back, uncertain if I had said the wrong thing.

"Wow, we haven't interviewed or heard of anyone racing here that hasn't run a major trail race before, let alone any trail races."

I wasn't sure how to feel at that point. Should I have been scared? Perhaps I should have been.

"Well, I do tend to bite off as much as I can possibly chew. And I do love a big challenge."

"Well, you certainly have our admiration, and we would love to interview you again after you have finished."

"You certainly will," I responded as I stood and shook his hand, and then we left.

That evening, I attempted to push the crew's surprise at my lack of trail racing experience out of my mind, along with the daunting image of the towering peak we'd have to ascend right from the race's beginning. Unfortunately, I didn't get much sleep that night.

In the following couple of days, we explored the Lake Tahoe area and its surroundings. We even went rafting on one of the rivers flowing from the lake, which was a blast and an exhilarating experience for us but not so much for Cal, who was petrified. I managed to fit in a few runs, not for training purposes but to keep my legs limber. However, my knee was growing increasingly sore and causing concern, possibly because of altitude.

Running the Western States 100 for the first time without any prior course experience was like walking straight into the wilderness, blindfolded. The added challenge of not having raced a major

104

trail event only heightened the difficulty. Yet, it was precisely this intoxicating challenge that drew me in.

Arranging for my family to follow the race, which could take up to 36 hours until cut-off, was a real logistical puzzle. The race route snaked its way through the Sierra Nevada Mountains and only really ventured into civilisation once at the 100-kilometre mark in the town of Foresthill. There were a few other potential points along the course where they could drive to, although navigating the mountain roads, driving on the opposite side of the road, and then hiking varying distances down trails to reach specific aid stations presented a significant challenge. Some of these aid stations were so remote that they required up to a 7-kilometre hike through the forest, and in some cases, supplies had to be airlifted in by helicopter. Estimating my arrival times at these locations proved to be a nightmare, so there was a real possibility that Jen and Cal might only be able to see me at one point during the entire race. Only time would tell how this would play out.

During the week leading up to the race, I had the opportunity to catch up with my friend David Eadie, who had also been accepted into the Western States 100. We chatted for a while, exchanging training insights and thoughts about how the race might unfold. It was clear that Dave was mentally prepared for a significant challenge.

Surprisingly, there were seven Australians competing in the race, which was quite an extraordinary number considering that only six Australians had ever completed the Western States 100 in under 24 hours in the 40-year history of the event, and so earned a WS handcrafted solid silver belt buckle; the most sought-after accolade in the world of extreme trail running.

Lake Tahoe, where the race was set, proved to be one of the most idyllic and picturesque places I had ever visited. It was a delightful surprise. One day, while exploring the charming village centre and looking for some fruit to take back for breakfast, I was astounded to walk into a McDonald's without even realising it. I later learned that Lake Tahoe was the only place in the world where McDonald's was not allowed to brand their store. I guess this epitomised the picturesque and quaint nature of Lake Tahoe.

At 3.15 am on race day, my alarm sounded, and my brain immediately kicked into action. The anticipation of the day's challenges filled my mind. The warmth of the bed was tempting, and I couldn't help but imagine what lay ahead once I started the day's journey. I knew that once I got up, there was no turning back. This was a day that required my full commitment, pushing my body and mind to their limits. No half measures. Over the next, possibly 36 hours, I will need to push beyond anything I have ever experienced.

With each step, I was reminded of the nagging issue with my knee. Would it become my Achilles' heel during the race? I hoped to God that it wouldn't. Jen also got up shortly after me, and we busied ourselves with gathering food and supplies. Meanwhile, we allowed Cal to sleep a little longer. We had packed the car the night before, recognising that our morning window was incredibly narrow to get organised, into the car and on our way along the dark, deserted mountain roads to Squaw Valley.

Our trial run drives to Squaw Valley had taken around 20 minutes, and there was little chance of encountering traffic at this early hour. So, as we drove through the pitch-black night, Jen took the wheel while I listened to music. However, as we turned off the main road toward Squaw Valley, something peculiar began to happen with the car. It started to stutter and jump, sending my heart into my mouth. Were we going to make it? We were in the middle of bloody nowhere at 4 am, with very little margin for error to reach the starting line of what would be the largest race I had ever competed in. This was the stuff of nightmares.

In fact, one of my most common dreams or nightmares over the past 20 years involved losing my way during an Ironman race or ultramarathon. It seemed that this fear had become one of my greatest conscious fears. We reduced our speed to minimise the car's jerking, hoping to nurse it to the race start. Ten minutes later, we arrived, bringing immense relief. However, this car issue could potentially turn into a disaster for Cal and Jen in terms of following the race or even getting out of Squaw Valley. For now, Jen went to ask around and find out where she could urgently get the rental car looked at.

After checking in, I started to prepare my gear amidst the bustling crowd of racers and their support crews. Time seemed to slip away, and before I knew it, the 10-minute horn sounded, prompting hundreds of people to spring into action and make their way toward the exit doors. It was still pitch-black outside as we gathered—389 ultra trail athletes, each with their own unique stories and reasons for being here, all united by immense respect for each other and the race. Then, suddenly, the countdown began: 5, 4, 3, 2, 1, announced the race director, accompanied by the assembled crowd. The countdown was followed at once by the traditional firing of a real hunting gun - as is customary. The air was filled with the excited whoops and cheers of runners as they took their first steps in this special race.

For those who had completed the WS 100 before, and some had done so multiple times, they were better equipped to handle the challenging conditions, anticipate what lay ahead, and pace themselves accordingly. On the initial steep ascent, pacing was crucial, and many opted for power walking as they tackled the long, arduous climb. In some places, the terrain was so steep that it necessitated the use of walking poles, or runners would press their hands against their thighs and pump them to maintain momentum.

Pacing has never been my strong suit, and today was no exception. Right from the starting gun, I kept up with the leading group until they transitioned into power walking, hands on their pumping legs, as we ascended. The temperature dropped steadily, and the air rapidly grew thinner as we made our way toward the snow-covered summit. The increasing altitude accelerated my heart rate, making my lungs crave oxygen as if I had just sprinted 400 metres at maxed-out top speed.

At only four miles into the one-hundred-mile journey, with 4,000 feet of elevation already conquered, I performed a mental calculation. It was the distance covered versus the distance left, contrasted with how my body felt, all equating to my confidence level in successfully completing this monumental task. As this internal dialogue was trending in the wrong direction, I decided to shut it down.

Upon reaching the summit, where we struggled to maintain our footing on the snowy slopes, we suddenly began a descent that took us through melting snow gullies that transformed into mud. The trail constantly twisted and turned, featuring complete switchbacks that wound their way down the colossal descent. I had never encountered such challenging terrain before. It demanded concentration, considerable skill, and an excessive amount of effort just to stay upright. This was tough terrain, all right.

Within five minutes of starting the descent, the constant jarring began to exact its toll on my left knee, sending shooting pain through my body as I descended rapidly. Immediately, this played havoc with my mind, rocking my confidence. This was just the beginning of an exceptionally long day. Would my knee hold up?

After the initial descent, I reached the first aid station at Lyon Ridge, which was 10.3 miles into the race. This station marked the end of the first major descent, during which I had descended 2,000 vertical feet. With one-tenth of the race now behind me, it was a relief to arrive at the aid table, where I quickly grabbed some refreshing watermelon and offered a grateful smile. The volunteers at these aid stations, who dedicatedly show up year after year, play a crucial role in making this race possible. Their enthusiastic support often makes the difference between fin-ishing and not.

The trail immediately led me to an uphill section, followed by another descent, and this pattern repeated as I continued my journey. The next aid station, Red Star Ridge, was located 16.3 miles into the race. From there, I faced another daunting descent, this time descending another 1,700 vertical feet to reach Duncan Canyon station at 24.4 miles. Robinsons Flat was my next milestone, six miles further along the trail. This leg of the race involved a steep 1,700-foot vertical climb, which left both me and my fellow athletes resorting to a power walk at best.

Upon reaching Millers Defeat at 34.4 miles into the race, I had successfully ticked off a third of the total distance to Auburn. The descent leading to this aid station had exacerbated the growing discomfort I was experiencing inside my shoes. Relentless friction, made worse by wet socks from small river crossings and earlier encounters with melting snow, had taken a toll on my feet.

As I rolled into the aid station, I wasted no time and grabbed a handful of potato chips along with a couple of energy gels. Then, I signalled to the aid station captain that my feet were in trouble. They quickly ushered me over to a chair set up at the medical table. A volunteer helped me remove my backpack and asked for instructions regarding refilling my hydration bladder.

"Just water, please", I instructed as I smiled back in appreciation."

"So, what's up, buddy, asked the medical attendant as he carefully slipped off my trail shoes.

"The heels of both feet are very sore, and my right forefoot."

He settled on the ground and surveyed one foot and then the other. His concerned look said it all.

"Well, you have a large blister on each heel and one large one emerging on your forefoot. I would recommend that I repair the two main ones." He spoke.

"Ok, whatever you think, doc."

As he took a few items from the table and turned me sideways so he could access my rear heel, he said, "This won't hurt, but it might smart a little, ok."

I nodded in agreement as I observed him using a surgical scalpel to create a small incision in the skin. Fluid began to pour out as he gently pressed down on the skin.

"Right, just a little sting now."

He was correct; the super glue he applied inside the incision stung. He then tore a small strip of duct tape and carefully sealed the entire area. Wow, I thought, only a third of the way into the race and my blisters were already being superglued. At that moment, I regretted not paying more attention to proper foot care. He completed the second incision procedure and helped me put my socks back on.

"Thanks, Doc." I smiled, slipped my trail runners back on, and I was away, hobbling as I adjusted to the soreness.

The day was heating up, and I knew that the next few canyons would likely take the temperature above 100 degrees Fahrenheit. So, I continued to focus on my hydration, a critical element of ultra-running that I had never been able to perfect. There is an exceptionally fine line when it comes to consuming electrolytes – too much, too quickly, and it will sit in your stomach, causing severe nausea. I could already feel this happening and could hear the liquids starting to slosh in my stomach. The issue now was that as the miles and the consequences of massive elevation change began to take their toll, there was no shortage of things to worry about. For the next ten minutes, these issues consumed my mind until I blocked them out and concentrated on running downhill.

It would be easy to think that running this far downhill would be a benefit, but it is the opposite. The impact on your quadriceps is brutal, and this accumulates over the course of the race until it becomes harder to go downhill than it is to go uphill. From Robinson's Flat to the bottom of the canyon was around 15 miles, descending 4,000 feet in vertical elevation, although the descent during that distance was a great deal more as there were sharp ascents along the way. The impact is further exacerbated by the constant directional change from switchbacks, often taking the form of weathered, stone-lined gullies. Switchbacks are created on mountain trails to lessen the gradient, and in this stretch, there were 45 of them.

Finally, a short stretch of bitumen road emerged into civilisation at the town of Forrest Hill. With just over 12 hours of running in the remote wilderness, covering almost two-thirds of the course, Forrest Hill, with its thousands of spectators, was just the adrenaline shot that I needed. Cheering spectators lined the streets, some hosing down the overheated athletes as they ran past, others handing bottles of water or shouting encouragement. Forrest Hill was where I hoped to find David, who I had managed to contact online in California to be my support runner for the last third of the race, most of which would be run in the pitch-black mountains. I was really looking forward to finding him, and he was exactly where he said he would be, all ready to go. He had managed to meet up with Jen and Cal, whom I was about to see for the first time since the race started. I had estimated my arrival time to the various aid stations, but I was running much faster than I had planned and had managed to well and truly beat them through every single aid station.

We exchanged a hug as I refilled my hydration pack, grabbed some fruit, and refreshed myself by splashing cold water on my head multiple times. I also embraced Cal and shared how I was feeling. After a brief pause, we resumed our run, vanishing into a steep trail section. Forrest Hill had provided an adrenaline boost, but its effects wore off within a few minutes, and the harsh reality of having to complete the equivalent of one and a half marathons through the mountain terrain sank in. Taking a 5-minute break in a chair hadn't been beneficial for my body or my mental state. In the early part of this downhill stretch, the combined strain of continuous descent and overall fatigue caused my quadriceps to seize up in intense pain. I resorted to running sideways on the steeper slopes, occasionally sliding on the loose rocks. Descending fourteen hundred feet in elevation nearly took everything out of me by the time we reached the Dardanelles aid station. There, I once again stopped for medical attention. While descending, the agony in my toes, as they pressed against the front of my running shoes, became unbearable. I sat down for a few minutes as the medical team examined my feet. I was afraid to look.

"It looks like you have displaced several of your toenails, which is not unusual at all. Four of them look like they will die and could completely tear off with the remaining distance and terrain that you still have ahead," declared the female doctor.

"Shit, really?" I responded.

"It's quite likely. The decision is yours; we can attempt to fix them or remove some if you prefer," she stated.

As she examined my toenails, they shifted, causing a sharp pain, though not as intense as the agony of running downhill with them. I decided to go with what I believed was the safest option at that moment, acknowledging that they would likely fall off after the race.

"Tape them up, doc and let's get out of here."

"Ok," she replied and set about quickly taping each individual toe.

Standing up from the comfort of the chair was becoming increasingly challenging, and I wasn't sure that if I sat down again, I would ever get up. It's a common mistake among ultra runners that everyone wants to avoid, if possible, but as the hours pile up during a race, even the best intentions can go out the window. David jogged alongside me at the pace I aimed to set, offering words of encouragement to keep me going. During the run, we exchanged stories about our lives. The taping on my toes had provided some relief from the pain, so I continued running as best as I could, fully aware that the situation could change at any moment. Over the next four miles, we mostly ran uphill to Peachstone, reaching 70.2 miles into the race. My primary goal was to cover as much ground as possible while it was still daylight because things would become a whole lot tougher after dark.

Dusk was descending upon the day. Running through the night on mountain trails with only a headlamp to illuminate your path and pink ribbons marking the route every 400 meters was a perilous endeavour, one I had no prior experience with. The risks of getting lost, injured, or straying off the trail were very real, particularly as exhaustion set in. There's a peculiar phenomenon known as night blindness that can affect runners, leading them to become disoriented and confused, sometimes even curling up to sleep dangerously off the trail, ultimately risking their lives. Having a support runner was going to be invaluable, although they are not allowed to support you in any other way than encouragement and assistance with navigation. From this point forward, it was all about survival, self-preservation, and calculating how to finish within 24 hours to earn that coveted handcrafted silver belt buckle. I would continuously crunch the numbers in my head to determine what I had left in the tank to achieve this goal.

We descended another 1,400 feet vertically, aiming to reach Rucky Chucky Crossing before darkness fell. However, our pace had slowed, and I found myself facing the prospect of crossing the American River in the dark at the 78-mile mark. Depending on the conditions, the river's flow could be controlled upstream to ensure it was manageable downstream. I entered the swiftly flowing river, which quickly turned into a category six rapid. I clung to the rope for dear life as my exhausted legs and feet struggled to find purchase on the slippery rocks beneath the water's surface. I waded in up to my chest, then gradually fought my way onto the opposite bank without requiring assistance from the volunteers stationed in the water, ready to help or rescue as needed.

Once on the other side, we took a couple of minutes for me to hydrate and refuel while changing into another pair of trail runners from my third special needs bag, thoughtfully provided by the race organisers for this purpose. Soon after, we began ascending another 800 feet vertically to the next peak, which was two miles away. This climb was so steep that, at times, it felt like we were on all fours, crawling up the mountain.

The sun had set around 8:20 pm, marking nearly fifteen and a half hours of continuous running. We pressed on through the dark forest, navigating the natural maze of trails and trying to stay on the correct path. There were moments when I stumbled repeatedly on tree roots and rocks as my feet struggled to negotiate the unpredictable terrain. After passing the Auburn Lakes aid station at the 85-mile mark, we descended for another five miles towards Quarry Road. Along this trail, we encountered sections with sheer drop-offs, raising the stakes of the race. At times, we had to scramble on hands and knees over rocky terrain.

By now, my body was in excruciating pain, coming from every fibre of my body, and I couldn't decide which source of discomfort to focus on; everything hurt like hell. The only thought that kept me going was the knowledge that I had just a half marathon's distance left to possibly achieve one of my greatest accomplishments, and I had time up my sleeve.

We reached the Quarry Road aid station at the 90-mile mark, leaving only 10 miles to go until the finish line in Auburn. At this stage, I was so physically trashed that I couldn't force myself to eat or drink anything. It was the first time during the race that I allowed myself to imagine crossing the finish line. Another daunting 1,000-foot vertical climb awaited us as we ascended to the Pointed Rocks aid station before beginning our final descent. I remember feeling like I was on the homestretch when we reached No Hands Bridge with just 3.5 miles remaining, most of which involved a 1,000-foot vertical climb. At this point, I didn't mind the uphill because I wasn't sure if I could run anymore. Shortly before this, I had calculated that a brisk walk would still enable me to finish within the 24-hour time limit. As we approached Auburn, the trail continued to rise, becoming steeper and steeper. I asked David if the climbing would ever end, to which he chuckled and replied.

"You are there, buddy. You are only a couple of miles from getting this done. You are a f**kin' champion", he declared proudly.

We finally reached the summit about a mile from the stadium in Auburn, entering the well-lit streets of the town. I was overwhelmed, ecstatic. I was so close, almost there, almost time to rest. I wanted to run. I tried to run, but my legs had completely seized up by now, my blisters had torn open again, and I was certain that some of my toenails had been completely torn away. Even as I entered the stadium, I attempted to run for the last 300 meters, but my body couldn't comply. So, I walked to glory, savouring the atmosphere as other brave individuals cheered me on.

At 4:38 am, 23 hours and thirty-eight minutes after starting in Squaw Valley, I crossed the finish line. Within moments, I had collapsed onto the grass inside the athletics track, unable to go any further.

After resting for a while, I expressed my profound gratitude to David and shared the moment with my family before we headed to our temporary overnight accommodations in Auburn. Despite my body's protests, it was already morning. Covered in dirt, spit, various food residues, sticky gels, and blood from my toes, I had no choice but to find a way to climb into a huge bathtub. A while later, I managed to drag myself out and collapsed on the bed, where I slept for a few hours.

By the next morning, I felt as if I had been in a washing machine for the past 24 hours. I could barely walk, and I had to wear thongs due to the state of my blisters and my now-missing toenails. This truly embodied the concept of "leaving it all on the table" because there was absolutely nothing left on that table.

We went for a celebratory brunch and later headed down to the Auburn running track in the afternoon to soak up the sun and participate in the awards ceremony. I caught up with Dave Eadie, who had finished ahead of me and was the top-placed Aussie with a formidable run. I also chatted with the other Australian runners, who had made history by having the highest participation of a single nation outside of US citizens. In the 40-year history of the race, only six Australians had earned the coveted silver buckle.

The outdoor ceremony was attended by hundreds of people, with only half of them fitting under the massive open-sided marquee. Medals were presented to the podium finishers of both the women's and men's races, followed by the announcement and presentation of the silver buckle winners. When it was my turn, I walked proudly to the stage and received my handcrafted Western States Silver Buckle, which has since become my most prized possession in the world.

Round and around and around – The Tan Ultra

Among all the ultra-distances I raced, the 100-kilometre version became the most common distance at which I challenged myself against the clock and other competitors to secure a spot on the Australian Elite team at the World Championships. My first attempt on the Gold Coast resulted in a time of 9 hours and 8 minutes, which I needed to improve by an additional 1 hour and 8 minutes to achieve an A qualifying time. After successfully earning a Silver Belt Buckle at the Western States 100 in 2007, my pursuit of a 100-kilometre qualification began in 2008. This journey involved gaining experience and accumulating miles to reach the point where I might be fast enough to meet the qualification standards.

I set my sights on a new race scheduled for August, which revolved around The Tan, located in the heart of Melbourne. While it wasn't the most repetitive race I'd ever entered (that distinction belongs to the 12-hour or 100-kilometre races on a 400-metre athletics track), it did involve running more than 26 laps around the same 3.827-kilometre Tan Track. The name "The Tan" came from its tan-coloured surface and was surrounded by the

Royal Botanical Gardens. The track, mainly composed of loose gravel, featured undulating terrain, including a steep climb up Anderson Hill, followed by a gradual and almost imperceptible downhill stretch leading to the finish of each lap.

Training began in earnest in November 2007, following a period of recovery after the WS 100. Around this time, I had also changed jobs, and my new workplace was primarily located in Sydney's CBD. This allowed me to run to and from work daily, which improved time efficiency. However, it also introduced new challenges. Since I lived relatively close to the office, I had to run past my building, away from the office, and then return to get sufficient miles each day. I had to run with a backpack most of the time, which, while not as heavy as an army pack, still added weight and altered my body's dynamics. This adjustment presented some physical challenges until I fully adapted. Nevertheless, it made each kilometre more demanding, adding an extra 5% to my body weight.

My training routine remained largely consistent, quickly building up to 150 kilometres per week and then increasing to 200 kilometres per week for about six months leading up to February. An interesting observation during this time was that despite my weight being only 65 kilograms, I consistently lost between 1.5 and 2 kilograms every night while sleeping.

Throughout this rigorous training period, I experienced the usual physical discomforts that come with high-volume training. However, I was fortunate to avoid injury, largely due to regular deep tissue massages. Maintaining flexibility is a crucial aspect for athletes to minimise the risk of injury, and it's essential for long-term physical wellbeing, a principle that applies to everyone.

Maintaining flexibility is the most important aspect for athletes to minimise the risk of injury, and it's essential for everyone to ensure long-term physical wellbeing. Additionally, the choice of shoes is of paramount importance. Ironically, many people tend to overlook the significance of both flexibility and proper shoe selection in maintaining their overall health and fitness.

Engaging in two daily runs and accumulating a high volume of kilometres sharpens your awareness of your body's condition on any given day, as well as the state of your running shoes. Throughout my training, I could easily gauge the approximate number of kilometres I had already run in a pair of shoes within the first few minutes of wearing them. As a result, I maintained a routine of purchasing and replacing my shoes approximately every four to five weeks. It might seem unusual to some, but there was an extraordinary thrill in lacing up a fresh pair of responsive running shoes. Such is the life of a dedicated runner.

Upon arriving in Melbourne a few days before the race, my first order of business was to familiarise myself with the Tan track, as I had never been around it before. It proved to be a popular circuit, and I anticipated potential challenges on race day as it would remain open to the public for their usual activities, including dog walking. This 100-kilometre course was atypical in its profile, as it featured constant changes in elevation. Unlike the traditional flat terrain of most 100-kilometre courses, this one promised to provide some variety, which I hoped would keep things interesting. I had meticulously planned my race strategy, aiming to maintain a pace that I believed I could sustain on this more demanding course compared to the Gold Coast 100.

Right from the start, I kicked off the race with a burst of speed to the 200-metre turnaround. This turnaround had been added to the course to ensure that the 26 laps we were slated to complete would add up to exactly 100 kilometres. I reached the 200-metre point ahead of the rest of the field and aimed to maintain that position throughout the day. My primary objective was to win the race and test my pacing strategy.

The initial ascents of Anderson Hill felt relatively comfortable as I worked on building a small lead over my friend Michael Lovric, who stayed determined and pushed me relentlessly. As the morning progressed, the temperature rose, and more people came out for their Sunday morning activities. The track soon became crowded with people walking their dogs, forcing me to weave in and out of pedestrian and canine traffic. At the halfway point, I was still leading the race with a time of 3 hours and 53 minutes, slightly ahead of my planned pace. However, I knew that maintaining this faster pace would take its toll, but the motivation to stay in the lead helped balance the growing fatigue in my legs.

As the laps continued to accumulate, the ascent up Anderson Hill began to take its toll. Gradually, the climbs became more challenging, and I had to muster all my strength just to complete them without walking. My usual dip in energy and overall wellbeing occurred, as it often does, between the 60th and 70th kilometres. During this stretch, my mind grappled with the distance covered versus the distance remaining, all while my legs were feeling the strain. At each loop around the starting line, I gathered updates on Michael's position, which fluctuated slightly with each completed lap. My pace had significantly slowed, and my primary focus now was simply to finish the race in first place, regardless of the time.

As I approached the point where I had just one lap remaining, it became evident that unless a disastrous turn of events occurred, I was on track to secure a first-place finish in the race. Exhausted but determined, I set out on that final lap. There's something cathartic about pushing through the pain and fatigue when you can envision the finish line and feel the sense of accomplishment waiting for you. The victory was mine as I entered the long finishing straight, with Callum waiting for me at the finish line.

"And the winner is Jason Dunn, in a time of eight hours and fifty-one minutes. Congratulations, Jason!" declared the race director as I crossed the finishing line. I couldn't help but beam with delight, realising that I had achieved my first outright victory in an ultramarathon."

My finishing time at the Tan Ultra was seventeen minutes faster than my first attempt at running 100 kilometres, but it was still fifty-one minutes slower than the A qualifying time for the World Championships, albeit the Tan Ultra had a much tougher course than the Gold Coast 100.

To work towards my World Championships goal and shake things up a little, I lined up a couple of races for 2009. The first race on my list was the Caboolture 24-hour race, which had a 24-hour cutoff and involved running around a 500-metre undulating dirt circuit around the Caboolture Historical Village, with the winner being the runner who covered the furthest distance in those 24 hours. I didn't intend to run for the full 24 hours and had arranged with the organisers to record my time at 100 kilometres before withdrawing. This race would be incredibly repetitive, with 200 consecutive laps to complete, testing my mental strength.

Jen couldn't attend this race in Queensland, so I persuaded my wonderful in-laws, Bob and Helen, to come up and support me for some of the race, which they kindly agreed to do. I stayed at their place in Brisbane for a couple of nights before driving up to Caboolture very early on race day.

I set up my aid table within the inner circle of the track, loaded it with snacks, hydration replacements, and energy gels, and then went for a few slow warm-up laps to familiarise myself with the track. To my surprise and great delight, my friend Michael, who had pushed me to victory at the Tan Ultra, was there crewing for one of his friends. We chatted for a while before the race director called the start of the race.

The temperature was already 24 degrees Celsius at 7 am, and it was forecasted to rise into the early thirties during the day with 90% humidity. It was going to be a hot one, and staying hydrated would be crucial. We started the race within two minutes, and my lap countdown began. Counting the laps grew increasingly tedious, and so one of the main distractions was checking the rankings and timing on the live board at the end of each lap. This kept my spirits up and gave a boost to my ego as I had been in the first place from the first lap, although it was a bit skewed because others were running for either twelve or twenty-four hours.

Bob and Helen arrived at 10 am, which boosted my morale significantly. They set up their chairs at the table and basically handed me food, drinks, and words of encouragement on almost every 500-metre lap until the end of my run. Most of the race went according to plan until around the 55-kilometre mark when I started feeling extremely nauseous. My stomach had reached its limit in processing liquid carbohydrates. I had perhaps been a bit too eager to stay hydrated and had consumed too much carbohydrate-loaded fluid. For the next ten kilometres, I slowed down due to the persistent nausea. This condition also led me to stop drinking and eating, which wasn't a good sign, with 45 kilometres left to go on a stinking, sweltering day.

At the 65-kilometre mark, I couldn't stand the sloshing liquid in my stomach any longer. It was not only a discomfort but also something I could audibly hear and feel. I decided to stop on the side of the track and knelt down, deliberately triggering my gag reflex until I vomited the contents of my stomach. A few minutes later, I resumed running, feeling better with the relief that vomiting had brought. However, I had also expelled all the vital calories and hydration I had gone without for the past 90 minutes or so.

Soon after, I noticed Michael handing his friend drinks as they passed, and I quickly communicated my condition to him. On the next lap, he handed me a small pop-top bottle of sparkling mineral water and advised me to sip it as I ran. This was not the last time that Michael provided me with carbonated water, and his quick thinking likely saved my race from a Did Not Finish (DNF) status that day.

For the rest of the 100 kilometres, I couldn't consume any more calories, whether in the form of food or drink. Consequently, I ran on empty until I finished in 8 hours and thirty-nine minutes. Despite my failure to execute my race nutrition plan, I had achieved my fastest 100-kilometre time yet, but I still fell short of the qualification time by 39 minutes.

My next race was a return to the Tan Ultra 100-kilometre race at the end of August, which I had won the previous year. Returning to a race always brings a sense of being better equipped and more confident, and that was certainly the case as August approached. My training underwent some changes, incorporating at least one tempo session per week with 90 percent effort sprints interspersed into training sessions, followed by short stretches of recovery jogging. I needed to build some speed into my legs to improve my 100-kilometre time.

As I have mentioned in an earlier chapter, a few months before this race, a small lump began to appear in my left groin. I initially ignored it, hoping it would go away, but it continued to grow. Eventually, I decided to see my doctor, who diagnosed it as a hernia and referred me to a specialist. I saw the specialist just two weeks before the race, and the surgeon confirmed the diagnosis.

"Yes, I can see that your hernia has broken through and is grow-ing quite quickly. My recommendation would be to schedule surgery as soon as possible." explained the surgeon.

During the consultation, we discussed the procedure and recovery in more detail before I posed a question, "I have an especially important running race in 2 weeks that I've been training a long time for. Could I delay the surgery and come in a week or so after the race?"

The surgeon paused and asked, "How long is the race?"

"It's a 100-kilometre race," I responded, and he fell silent for a moment, his expression conveying a mix of disbelief and concern. "That's a long way to run for anyone, especially with a hernia."

I pressed on, "I'm more concerned about it suddenly becoming a severe health issue if I choose to run. I don't mind the discom-fort it's going to cause."

He replied, "It's unlikely to suddenly burst open if that's what you're asking."

After our discussion, we decided that I would proceed with the race as planned, and he would perform the surgery a couple of weeks afterwards. The plan was set.

Once again, we journeyed to Melbourne, with my hernia still protruding, perhaps slightly further than when I saw the surgeon. By now, I had decided that just to be on the safe side, I would duct tape the lump for the race itself. As always, I kept a close eye on the weather to be as prepared as possible, but the forecast for Sunday's race in Melbourne wasn't looking good at all. Gale-force winds and rain were predicted for the entire day. While monitoring the weather as a race draws near is helpful for planning, it can also be mentally challenging if the conditions are expected to be extreme. I reminded myself that what will be, will be. This marked the first time I had returned to a race as the defending champion, which earned me some remarkably kind treatment and media coverage—a rare and novel experience for me.

The night before the race was predictably sleepless as the wind picked up and drove a neighbouring tree into the wooden fence only a few feet from our window. At some point during the night, in a half-asleep state, I heard the rain beginning to fall. When I woke up at four am, I really didn't want to get out of bed. I reminded myself that the longer I stayed in bed, the harder it would be to get up, and within five seconds, I forced myself out of bed and started preparing. It was toward the end of winter in Melbourne, and the morning temperature was a chilly six degrees Celsius. The daily high was expected to be only eight degrees higher, making for a frigid range of temperatures. Personally, I preferred 34 degrees over 14. Adding to the challenge, the day was forecasted to bring rain and gale-force winds. Things were not looking good.

We drove toward the Botanical Gardens, and the weather was absolutely dreadful. Jen and Cal stayed in the 4WD hire car while I checked in and set up my table. My table blew over twice due to the strong winds, but I managed to properly weigh it down. The start of the race couldn't come soon enough.

From the start, my plan was to lead from the gun. The wind was already gusting at 60 kmph and was forecasted to reach up to 80 kmph as the morning progressed. On top of that, it was raining. The first lap set the tone for the rest of the day. The sharp climb up Anderson Hill was aided by a gusting tailwind, which was a welcome change. However, there was a long, open, exposed stretch on the way back that would smash and challenge all competitors for about 1.5 kilometres of every lap. Despite the challenging conditions, which continued to deteriorate, I was running as well as I ever had and extending my lead in the race.

By the 50-kilometre halfway mark, I had completed it in three hours and forty-eight minutes, which was roughly where I had hoped to be. I was banking on my improved fitness to carry me through better than the previous year. From this point on, the wind intensified significantly and, at times, literally stopped me in my tracks. During those moments, trying to force my way through and expending valuable energy seemed pointless, so I backed off my pace slightly until the wind eased a bit. Nevertheless, on the way out of each lap, I still had to face the taxing climb up Anderson Hill, followed by a gale-force headwind for 1.5 kilometres on the return leg. At kilometre 65, I was feeling miserable and cold. I asked Jen if she could get me a strong cup of coffee in a takeaway container as I rounded the top end of the course. Upon my return, she handed me exactly what I had asked for, and I drank it as I continued to run.

At this point, I realised that I would likely finish the last thirty kilometres at a similar pace, but I wouldn't meet the qualification time. Nevertheless, I was on track to achieve my personal best time unless something disastrous happened. The remainder of the race threw up the usual mental and physical challenges, coupled with the extreme weather conditions. I cannot adequately convey how relieved I was to cross the finish line in first place, but more importantly, to just get the thing finished and get out of those conditions.

In the end, I finished in 8 hours and 25 minutes, beating my previous best time by fourteen minutes. This placed me 47th on the list of the fastest times ever run by an Australian. It was also the 6th fastest time overall in Oceania that year, at any age group, and the top time in my age group in Oceania for that year. Overall, I ranked 280th in the world.

In 2010, I took a brief break from ultra racing, except for a couple of 50-kilometre races. However, in 2011, I set my sights on the Gold Coast 100 and the National Championships as an opportunity to qualify for the World Championship. My training was in full swing in mid-April 2011, with a focus on the 100-kilometre Athletics Australia National Championships on the Gold Coast in Queensland. This wasn't my first time competing in these championships. A few years earlier, in 2006, I made my first attempt at running 100 kilometres nonstop on the Gold Coast, finishing in 9 hours and 8 minutes and securing 6th place in the Australian Championships.

Now, with more experience and several major ultramarathons, including the Western States 100 and a couple of victories at the Tan Ultra 100 kilometres in Melbourne, I had refined my training plans and improved my understanding of pacing, which had always been my singular most significant challenge in long-distance events, whether running or in Ironman triathlons. Nevertheless, I remained dedicated to serious training for 8 to 9 months each year, always with a significant race or challenge in mind.

June 2011 arrived, and everything in our world seemed to be going well. This marked my second participation in the Gold Coast 100 super marathon, five years after my first attempt. However, there was no significant experience advantage this time around, as the course had undergone a complete change. Instead of a ten-lap, multi-loop course inland from the coast, it had transformed into a 50-kilometre, two-lap course that tracked along the Gold Coast shoreline.

For this race, my goal was to secure a spot on the podium at the National Championships and finally achieve the World Championship qualification I had been chasing. The burning questions in my mind were: Could I run fast enough this time? Was I truly prepared for this challenge? I had already checked the entry list of athletes competing in the Gold Coast race and was pleased to see that my friend, "The Running Man" Dave Eadie, was also running once again. Although I didn't believe I could beat him, it was wonderful to catch up with Dave at the briefing, and he looked to be in fantastic shape. Dave mentioned his goal of achieving a World Championship qualifying time, and he certainly looked capable of doing just that.

Race day arrived with sunny skies as predicted and the promise of mid-twenties temperatures.

While these conditions might not have been ideal for achieving top speed, I personally enjoyed running in the sunshine. There was a buzz in the air as racers prepared to run the new course along the beautiful coastline of the Gold Coast. The Gold Coast, being a popular destination, meant that the race course would be flooded with many people enjoying their day along the beach. Even as we set out from Broadbeach at 6:30 am, there were many people taking early walks or going for a swim.

Dave Eadie took an early lead at a pace I couldn't sustain for the entire race. So, I settled in with a bunch of runners near the front. My time at the first turnaround point, 25 kilometres into the race, was 1 hour and 57 minutes, and I was on track for a sub-8-hour finish. However, it was evident that maintaining that pace for another 75 kilometres would be challenging. As the temperature continued to rise, I regularly replenished my hydration pack with fluids and grabbed ice from aid stations on my way back to the start.

By the time I reached the 50-kilometre turnaround point, I had moved up to fourth place. If I could maintain this position, it would be my best finish yet and possibly my fastest time ever. The route was bustling with activity on this beautiful day, making navigation tricky in certain stretches as I had to weave through crowds of people on the footpaths.

Around midday, the temperature had significantly risen, and on a course with little shade, I decided to cool down my rising core temperature. I grabbed a cap full of ice without stopping and used it to help regulate my body heat. At the 65-kilometre mark,

I felt extremely fatigued until I approached the last turnaround point. Heading back towards the finish, no matter how far away it still seemed, always brings a sense of inspiration, especially when the race is going well. I turned in what I believed was the third position, but there was no precise way of knowing for sure. However, the thought of potentially finishing on the podium at a National Championships gave me the motivation I needed to keep pushing through the remainder of the race. Entering the final kilometres, I began to feel confident that I would finish with at least a bronze medal, as I estimated the next competitor to be at least four kilometres behind at the last turn.

The last five kilometres of the race consisted mainly of long, straight, flat stretches. I felt completely exhausted during this final homestretch, but nothing was going to stop me on this day. Despite losing some time in the final hour, I crossed the finish line in 8 hours and 33 minutes, my second-fastest time for a 100-kilometre race.

Uncertain if I had finished in either the silver or bronze place, we headed to the presentation breakfast at the local surf club the next morning. Breakfast always tastes amazing the morning after an ultra race when you haven't eaten real food for the past twenty-four hours. The presentation ceremony began with the announcement of the new men's Australian Champion, David Eadie, who had scorched the field to claim his first national title.

"And the silver medallist is Jason Dunn from Sydney," announced the race director, Ian Cornelius.

Wow, what an extraordinary moment it turned out to be, and a fantastic conclusion to a special race. It ended up being the fifth fastest time in Oceania for the year, ranking 275th in the world, and once again, the fastest in my age group within Oceania.

My focus on achieving that elusive 8-hour mark and qualifying for the World Championships remained unwavering. Therefore, I set my next target on the Gold Coast race in June 2012. The course had changed once again, starting mid-way through the course of the previous year and heading South for 12.5 kilometres, then home again, with four of these laps making up the race. Since I had covered this section four times in the previous year, I was quite familiar with it. Much of the course was flat, except for a hill shortly after the start that we had to ascend 8 times and another short, steep hill with a long flight of steps on the other side, adding four more sets of hills and steps to the challenge.

I found myself racing once again against my friend David Eadie, though I didn't spot him until we were warming up at the new starting location near the beach in Burleigh Heads. The rain had persisted throughout the night, keeping me awake, and it showed no signs of letting up during the day. It was shaping up to be an awfully long and wet race day. When the starter's horn sounded, we began our race, immediately facing the first significant hill just a few hundred metres in. It's curious how you can feel invincible when tackling a hill so early in a race. However, six or seven hours later, that same hill can feel like an insurmountable challenge. The Kiwi runner, Martin Lukes, took the lead, closely followed by Dave Eadie, while I focused on finding my rhythm and settling into around 5th place. I was trying to conserve as much energy as possible for the first lap.

By the time I reached the first turnaround at 12.5 kilometres, I was completely soaked. It was clear that I would spend over 8 hours that day running in wet clothes, with my shoes squelching at every step of the 120,000 I would take. My determination and physical endurance were put to the test multiple times as I slowly moved into third place overall and second place in the National Championships, considering Martin was a Kiwi. At the halfway mark, I began to experience chafing in all the uncomfortable places, which added to my discomfort. The usual tough stretch between 55 and 70 kilometres challenged my mental strength to its limits, with a convincing inner voice suggesting, "It's dry and warm at home. This is too difficult. Let's just call it a day." David Eadie finished in second place, securing his second consecutive National Championship title. I hung in there and finished in third place, only seconds faster than my time from the previous year at 8.33. I had missed my goal time by about half an hour, but I earned another silver medal at the Australian Championships at the age of 47.

After reading many accounts of the benefits of building foot strength along with the merits of a higher cadence, I began to run barefoot at my local park.

I would ride my bike to the cricket oval, then run barefoot on the soft grass, gradually increasing the distance until I could run nonstop for 30 kilometres.

In 2014, I had a significant year in terms of running, participating in three entirely different races over the course of three months. The first race took place in June on the Gold Coast at the Australian 100-kilometre road championships. Unlike my recent attempts at this race, where my focus was on competitiveness and qualifying for the Elite World Championships, this time, it was meant to be a good practice run and preparation for La Ultra, The High, in August. Given the extreme volume of training I had undergone to prepare for the multi-day run in the Himalayas, my body was pushed to its limits, resulting in some minor injuries and significant muscle fatigue.

Waking up to the sound of rain on race day is probably one of the worst scenarios when preparing to run a significant distance. It brings forth a host of challenges, both physical and psychological. From the physical perspective, dealing with wet clothes causing chafing and the discomfort of soggy socks and shoes, among other issues, is already demanding. However, the psychological impact is equally daunting. Imagine how you feel on a rainy, cool, and windy day compared to a clear, warm, and sunny one. Now, amplify that feeling when you're running 100 kilometres, unable to seek shelter and warmth indoors.

On this particular race day, the conditions were far from ideal, and I couldn't help but feel miserable. Huddled beneath the awning at the surf club with fellow racers as the rain poured down, my motivation was at an all-time low. However, I knew I had to push through and complete the race, viewing it as one of the toughest training sessions I'd ever undertaken. The race consisted of four 25-kilometre laps, taking us south along the Gold Coast shoreline with some detours to navigate areas where paths were missing along the oceanfront.

The rain fell constantly all day, and there were plenty of times when I could have easily quit, especially considering the race held no particular significance, but I ground it out and completed the race. I crossed the finish line in a respectable time of 9 hours and six minutes, turning it into a challenging but worthwhile day of training.

How high can you go?

Following this race, only a few weeks later, I faced an extreme endurance event that boasted not only being the highest altitude ultramarathon globally but also the most challenging single-stage ultra to finish within the designated time limit. Often, race organisers exaggerate the toughness of their events for marketing reasons, aiming to appeal to and attract extreme athletes. However, in this instance, my research suggested that the claims were justified.

La Ultra is an ultramarathon and running event situated in the Ladakh region of Indian Administered Kashmir. This marathon exposes participants to extreme climates, distances of up to 555 kilometres, and altitudes of up to 18,300 feet, earning its reputation as one of the toughest runs in the world. It is unquestionably the highest ultramarathon and is renowned for being the most challenging continuous race globally to complete within the time limit. The race features multiple categories, ranging from a welcoming 111-kilometre run to a forbidding 555-kilometre ordeal. All races begin at high altitudes and involve steep ascents and descents, making the event exceptionally demanding. However, what truly distinguishes this race is the extreme altitude. The 111-kilometre ultramarathon concludes at an altitude of 5,359 metres (17,582 feet), while the 222-kilometre ultramarathon takes runners to the world's highest motorable pass at an altitude of 5,602 metres (18,379 feet). Due to the race's harsh conditions, La Ultra is only open to seasoned ultra runners who have successfully completed other arduous races and have received medical clearance. Runners must also undergo acclimatisation training to prepare for the high altitudes. Back when I competed, the 333 Kilometre version was the longest on offer, so that was the one that I was racing.

The La Ultramarathon was established in 2010 by Dr. Rajat Chauhan, a sports physician and ultra runner. Now in its twelfth year, the race has earned a renowned status as one of the most demanding and prestigious ultramarathons globally. With a limited number of participants each year and a gruelling course, this race serves as a genuine trial of endurance and resilience.

In addition to its reputation as a challenging race, the La Ultra marathon also plays a role in promoting sustainable tourism in the Ladakh region of India. This area is renowned for its breathtaking natural beauty and rich cultural heritage. The organisers of the La Ultra marathon collaborate with local communities to ensure that the race has a positive impact on the region and its inhabitants. The La Ultra marathon stands as an incredible test of endurance, drawing participants from all corners of the globe to push their boundaries in the breathtaking yet demanding terrain of the Indian Himalayas. While it is not a race for the faint of heart, it offers a unique chance to immerse oneself in the beauty of the region and push personal limits. Fortunately, I was accepted into the race based on my experience and past achievements in ultramarathons.

To give greater purpose to my extreme undertaking, I made the decision to set an ambitious fundraising target for the Salvation Army Youth Homeless Program, an organisation I had previously been involved with in a coaching capacity. Homelessness has always been a heart-wrenching issue, and my understanding of the struggles faced by countless individuals deepened when I participated in the St. Vincent's CEO Sleepout. This event involved spending a night under the stars during the Australian winter with only cardboard for insulation above and below me. Recognising the immense challenge of running La Ultra, my employer generously agreed to match any donations I aimed to raise for the Salvation Army. My objective was to collect $25,000 in funds.

The adjustment to my training program marked the most significant change in my training routine since I began 15 years earlier. The primary concerns were spending ample time on my feet and preparing my body for the extreme conditions of high altitude and sleep deprivation over three consecutive days. I sat down and crafted a new training plan, aiming for a weekly running mileage ranging from 250 to 300 kilometres.

My goal was to build up to a marathon into each workday, with a 70-kilometre-long run every Sunday. Additionally, every three weeks, I challenged myself to complete a 100-kilometre overnight run, starting at 7 pm and ending at 6 am the following day. These nighttime training sessions proved to be particularly intriguing due to the reactions and curious looks I received while running during the wee hours. I encountered a few unusual sights during those nighttime adventures.

Balancing the logistics and demands of training with work, nutrition, family life, and recovery was a challenge, to say the least. Another significant addition to my weekly routine was a three-hour treadmill session in an altitude chamber simulating conditions at 9,000 feet above sea level, which was only half the altitude I would face in the race. During these sessions, I would focus solely on a monitor mounted on the chamber wall, which also tracked my blood oxygen saturation levels through a sensor attached to my finger. It might sound mundane, but it's not often you experience and watch your oxygen saturation levels drop from 99% to 70% while running on a treadmill.

It was a brutal and demanding regimen, and life essentially boiled down to a constant battle for survival. There were numerous days when, leaving work in the winter darkness at 6:30 pm, the very last thing I wanted to do was embark on another two-hour run with a backpack, especially when I had already completed my initial two-hour run by 7:30 am. And the same routine awaited me the following day and the day after that. During those moments of exhaustion and reluctance, I would remind myself of a mantra: "To be truly succssfull, you must first do what you don't want to do when you don't want to do it – until you do."

Writing this and looking back, it's surprising I managed to endure it all. However, there was never an instance where I chose to skip a planned training session. It was a daily, non-negotiable commitment to never opt for the easier path. The physical toll this regimen exacted pushed me to the brink. Old physical niggles and injuries resurfaced, and I did my best to manage them with ice treatments and regular massages.

Jen drove me to Sydney International Airport at 5 am on the 2nd of August, and I found myself standing outside the terminal. To reach Leh in the Himalayas within the mandatory two weeks before the race, I had to follow a specific travel route. First, I flew into Delhi, then had to change airports to the domestic one on the other side of town. After booking into a less-than-ideal (read: dodgy & rancid) hotel at an ungodly hour, I tried to get a few hours of rest before heading to the domestic terminal for my flight to Leh.

The flight to Leh would land at the military-controlled Leh Airport, situated in the Ladakh region high in the mountains. I was nervous enough about things going well, given all that I had sacrificed and the importance of arriving on time to start my minimal acclimatisation period between 11,500 and 18,500 feet above sea level. So, the last thing I needed was the unsettling response I received from the lady checking me in for the flight.

"Thank you, Sir," the lady at the check-in counter said as she lifted my passport from the countertop. With a perplexed expression, she examined its pages and then addressed me.

"Sir, do you have a visa to travel to India?"

"A what?" I exclaimed.

"Yes, a visa. You will need one to enter India."

"Fu…………..!!!!!!!!" screamed the voice in my head.

My heart sank, and my stomach churned with anxiety. At that very moment, I faced the daunting reality of needing to depart today to meet the mandatory timeframe, yet I lacked the necessary visa for my trip to India. My flights had become invalid for a destination that had proven to be one of the most challenging I had ever coordinated flights for, and this dilemma had arisen months ago. I hastily left the airport, hailed a taxi, and headed home, where I immediately began researching the visa application process for India, exploring any potential ways to expedite it. Due to the early hours, making phone calls was not an option, so I focused on finding alternative flights, assuming I could arrange everything within a day or two. Following this, I hurried to the Indian embassy passport office, aiming to secure a spot at the front of the line before they opened their doors. After an hour-long wait, I poured out my unfortunate situation and implored for assistance. The lady at the embassy was remarkably helpful and informed me that, under emergency circumstances, it might be possible to resolve my visa issue by the end of the day, albeit for a fee of $450. "That's fine," I responded, "just please guide me on what steps I need to take."

So, I spent half of the day completing all the necessary tasks, including getting new passport photos. Then, I headed home to wait a few anxious hours to see if my visa application had been processed. At 3.30 pm, I received notification that my visa had been approved, and I rushed back to pick up the paperwork. After that, I headed home to try to rebook the exact same flights and accommodation for the next day. Fortunately, there was one seat left on each flight. I was emotionally exhausted but nervously back on track.

I think I hardly slept that night, but I was so relieved that every-thing went smoothly the next day, and I was on my way, finally. Once I had landed in New Delhi, I hopped on a rickety bus to cross town, despite being accosted multiple times while walking to the bus stop. As we pulled away, I just hoped I had picked the right bus, which I had. I disembarked at 11 pm to check into the short-term dump I had booked, which hadn't been apparent when I initially made the reservation. After only a few hours of broken sleep, I was up, into a taxi, and off to the domestic airport. There, I had to show my passport and flight documentation to a heavily armed soldier before even entering the terminal.

Shortly thereafter, one of the most incredible experiences of my life unfolded, and it was certainly the most amazing among the many hundreds of flights I had taken. As I gazed out of the window while we approached the Himalayas, I was spellbound by the sight of huge mountain peaks puncturing through the thick layer of clouds. It was a truly breathtaking sight, and I remained utterly captivated until the clouds dissipated, revealing an even more remarkable spectacle.

I have travelled extensively in my life, but never before had I felt so small and insignificant in the world as I did when I absorbed the endless Himalayan mountains and glaciers below. It was a feeling I have never experienced since. In no time at all, our 747 aircraft was tilting from side to side as it skilfully navigated its way through the mountains during its descent into Leh. That was the only instance I have ever witnessed such agility from such a large plane.

The airport was under complete military control, which mirrored the situation in the region and one of the major mountains we would need to traverse during the race. Thus, clearing customs was quite an interesting experience. The assistant Race Director, Chetan Segal, was there to greet me upon arrival and kindly drove me to my nearby accommodation.

Even as I arrived, I was already grappling with a terrible, almost debilitating headache caused by the effects of the high altitude. Leh, where I had just landed, was situated at 11,562 feet above sea level, where the oxygen saturation is only 63% of that at sea level. In a few days, I would be ascending to over 18,000 feet, reaching the highest race altitude, where the oxygen level would be merely 50% of that at sea level, and equivalent to being above Everest base camp.

I settled in and spent the next couple of days focused on alleviating the persistent headache while adapting to sleeping difficulties due to the reduced oxygen levels and subsequent breathing issues. I also had the opportunity to meet the race organisers, connect with my support crew, get acquainted with fellow competitors (there were only 11 participants from around the world), and attempt to get my body and mind to function somewhere near normal. The acclimatisation process involved a couple of short runs at altitudes above 12,000 feet, which nearly killed me. I couldn't help but wonder how on earth I was going to manage to run 333 kilometres non-stop at much higher altitudes, within temperature ranges fluctuating from minus 5 degrees to nearly 40 degrees Celsius within a 12-hour period on the first day of the race. And this would hardly allow me to stop or rest for more than 30 minutes or so, and only a couple of times, to finish within the 72-hour cutoff.

Leh and its surrounding areas offered me the adventure of a lifetime, and I constantly had to remind myself of that. There were some really unique characters among the participants, but none larger than John Sharpe from the USA, who kept us entertained and laughing throughout.

Most of the racers were staying at the same hotel, so we went out together for coffee and food. More importantly, we rented a couple of vehicles and gradually travelled to high altitudes to train on Khardung La, the highest driveable mountain pass in the world along the main trade route through India linking Pakistan and China. Khardung La is also rated as one of the five most dangerous roads in the world, and it's closed for six months each year, with temperatures dropping as low as minus 37 degrees Celsius. I had read a story about how, not many years ago, 234 vehicles became completely stranded on the upper slopes, and all occupants had to be rescued by the army, leaving their vehicles behind.

The first trip we made was in a small minivan driven by a local taxi driver. We ascended to 15,000 feet above sea level, reaching the gates of the local Indian Army control point, where we had to submit our passports and apply for permission to go further up to the summit. This approval process took two days, so, in the meantime, we alighted and explored the area. I went for a run at 15,000 feet in altitude, which proved incredibly challenging, and then walked back up. The difficulty in breathing reminded me of the first minute after a maximum-effort 400-metre sprint. This race was going to be extremely tough, and it was clear why it was described as the toughest single-stage endurance race to even finish within the cutoff time.

A couple of days later, we received approval from the military to proceed, and the day after, we hired two small vans to take all eleven runners to the top of Khardung La. What I hadn't realised was that once past the security point, the winding road deteriorated into a perilous dirt and rock track. The journey up was treacherous, with the vans teetering on the edge of sheer 1,000-foot drops, trying to pass large trucks travelling in both directions between Pakistan and China. At times, we had to get out of the vans and watch as the drivers and co-drivers guided each other around and past other vehicles. Occasionally, a traffic jam would occur. While standing on the dirt road, I dared to look over the edge and immediately regretted it. At that point alone, there were two wrecked vehicles below that had fallen over the edge once upon a time. This felt, and was, nuts. I began to question what the heck I was doing. We all breathed a sigh of relief when we finally reached the top of the pass at 18,383 feet.

As we prepared to climb out, a couple of tourists stepped down from their small taxi van, and a lady collapsed face down within a few steps of walking. *Christ!* I thought. Soldiers quickly lifted her onto a stretcher and carried her into their makeshift station for treatment. We stayed at the top for about half an hour, taking photos and savouring magi noodles that one of the locals constantly cooked up for visitors. The pass itself was a barren, inhospitable place, with the only burst of colour coming from the lines of prayer flags strewn from a few primitive buildings and flagpoles. It was not the kind of place where you could linger for too long without dire consequences. This trip certainly gave me a lot to think about. We took one other long trip to explore the desert stretches we would need to run and the second of the three major mountain peaks we would need to summit during the race.

Gradually, we all acclimated to the high altitude, but I still had headaches and running at 12,000 felt like hell. The day before the race, we left in the morning to head to our Himalayan desert camp, where we would start the race the next day at 9 pm. The reason for this early departure was to complete as much of the Khardung La pass as possible before the endless parade of trucks started rolling through in the early morning. We had seen the last of our designated crew until the first point of contact, which would be around midnight the following night, a few hours into the race.

Once we arrived at the desert camp, we occupied ourselves as best we could in the middle of nowhere to pass the time until lights out. Our tents were sturdy and reasonably comfortable, given our location, but that night, I didn't sleep much at all. I attempted to rest the next day, but I was too nervous.

At 8.55 pm the following day, we gathered on the start line in the middle of nowhere, with temperatures hovering around five degrees Celsius. We knew it would soon plummet below zero. Then, the race began, and we set off with our headlamps piercing the darkness, venturing into the unknown. Our first challenge was to ascend the mountain, which peaked at around the 75-kilometre mark. As always, I had to restrain myself from pushing too hard, but John Sharpe and I quickly established ourselves at the front of the pack. As I ran, I couldn't help but be mesmerised by the endless stars that illuminated the night sky more brilliantly than I could have ever imagined.

Soon, I found myself alone, slowly ascending the first major peak. The altitude was taking its toll on my body, and I could feel the heavy strain on my lungs. It was a surreal experience, and for the first time in my life, I felt truly isolated on this planet. Then, at 1 am in the morning, the sky before me burst into a mesmerising meteor shower, a once-in-a-decade event. Without a doubt, it was the most extraordinary sight I had ever witnessed, and it remains etched in my memory as a once-in-a-lifetime experience.

I could see John ahead, about a kilometre or so in front of me, as I approached the next aid station, hoping my crew would be there waiting for me. When I arrived, John was still there, eating noodles and sipping on an electrolyte drink. A volunteer handed me the same, and I stood beside him, refuelling as John bid me farewell and disappeared into the darkness ahead.

As the hours rolled on, the altitude continued to rise, and I found myself slowing to a fast walk. My breathing became increasingly laboured, and I was almost breathless, needing to pause every few kilometres, hunched over with my hands on my knees to catch my breath and stabilise myself. The temperature also plummeted, and I encountered more patches of ice on the dirt road, making certain sections treacherous. Approaching the summit of the first peak, I struggled to maintain any sustainable pace, eventually coming to a complete stop. I felt disoriented and was considering taking a rest when, suddenly, the sun began to rise over the other side of the mountain.

The first rays of dawn revealed the jagged peaks of the surrounding mountains, their regal splendour rivalling the intensity of their rugged contours. These natural formations had been sculpted over millions of years, creating some of the most breathtaking landscapes I had ever witnessed.

In a state of awe, I continued to move forward as the mountain's majestic peaks were unveiled before me. The surge of adrenaline temporarily alleviated my extreme fatigue. Fifteen minutes later, I turned the last bend and found myself at the summit, surrounded by prayer flags fluttering in the morning breeze. Almost instantly, my support crew, Samiksha and Arpit, were around me, attending to me and fussing over my nutritional needs. In reality, I was feeling utterly exhausted and struggling to think clearly. However, I reassured them, made a few requests, and then quickly set off to descend from that inhospitable peak and the debilitating altitude. As I gradually made my way downhill, my awareness of my physical condition grew, and my initial assessment was not good.

Was I suffering from extreme altitude sickness? Had I pushed myself too hard for the conditions, opting to race rather than focus on survival? I suspected both were true. The pre-race advice was to descend from the peaks as quickly as possible so I didn't linger. Now, running downhill, I tried to convince myself that I would be descending for a while, that the altitude would slowly decrease, and the pressure would ease.

For about ten minutes, I found comfort and encouragement in this thought. However, I soon began to feel increasingly unwell, and

I struggled to run in a straight line. I attributed this to the uneven, dirt, and rock-pitted surface of the road. But my condition didn't improve, and my staggering gait became more pronounced as if I were intoxicated. I continued to push forward, but after another 15 kilometres, I could go no further. I stumbled over to the official race vehicle.

Rajat, the race founder and director, spotted me as he approached in the official race vehicle. He came over to check on my condition and measure my oxygen saturation, which was not looking good. He inquired about how I was feeling.

"I am shattered," I declared, admitting defeat. This decision was now the most painful one I had ever made. I knew that pushing on would risk a severe health issue, as Rajat had suggested I was bordering on severe altitude sickness, which could take one of a few dangerous or even fatal turns. My mind was clouded with confusion, and I sat in the truck in silence for a few minutes amidst the mental fog. Eventually, I mustered the words: "I'm done." And that was it. Nothing seemed to make sense as I grappled with the pain of failure versus the physical pain I was experiencing.

Later that day, now rested and beginning to recover, I joined a few crew members and fellow competitors who had also been withdrawn from the race after receiving treatment for altitude sickness at the local hospital. We set out in our rented van to drive to the second mountain and cheer on the only two remaining athletes. Interestingly, six people were withdrawn before reaching the first summit at 75 kilometres. Six of the original eleven partic-ipants required hospital treatment, and all six had been pulled out well before me. Only four people made it past my point, at which I was well ahead in second place. Ultimately, the race director's claim of being the toughest single-stage ultra race in the world to finish within the time limit was validated by the sole athlete, Kim Rasmussen, who made it to the finish with less than an hour to spare.

In the days following my withdrawal, I reflected extensively on my performance and where I had gone wrong. Without a doubt, I concluded that I had approached the race with a mindset to compete and race rather than to survive. The Himalayas had chewed me up and spat me out. I had not respected their challenges nearly enough and had paid the ultimate price of defeat.

Returning from La Ultra, I was in a low state, contemplating how I could salvage something from my perceived failure and leverage the extreme mileage I had accumulated in preparing for the race. The Western Sydney Marathon, which was likely the third-largest marathon in Australia at the time, following the Sydney and Melbourne marathons, was scheduled to take place three weeks after my return. Having never run a standalone marathon before, I thought it would be interesting to see how fast I could run one, considering I hadn't done any speed training for a long time and only possessed an exceptional endurance base.

With no additional training after returning from La Ultra, we headed off early on the morning of the race. It boasted about 800 entries, ranging from elite runners to various age groups. My sole plan for the day was to restrain myself, which went against all my instincts, and run the second half of the race faster than the first—a negative split. For once, I adhered strictly to my plan. This was a tough mental challenge as the race began, and many runners surged ahead into the distance. Ordinarily, I would have chased after them, but not today. Holding back required all my willpower, especially as we repeatedly encountered the race leaders on the four-loop course, passing each other along the way.

As the race progressed, it became apparent that my strategy was working. I grew stronger, gradually reeling in runners who had faded due to fatigue. The final lap proved to be a lung-busting effort as I pushed to increase my pace and aim for a sub-three-hour finish, if possible. When I finally crossed the finish line, I had secured third place overall with a time of 2 hours and 55 minutes, achieved at the age of 52. This accomplishment provided some redemption after my Himalayan setback.

That 12-hour itch

Every year, the International Union compiles results from sanctioned ultramarathon events in Australia and internationally to create annual and record rankings. While I've previously shared some of my race times and rankings, I've always been realistic about my chances of competing with younger athletes who had dedicated their lives to competing in ultramarathons. Nevertheless, I achieved silver medals in consecutive years at the Australian Elite 100k road championships when I was 46 and 47 years old. As my ability to compete at an elite level in longer races like the 100-kilometre events waned, I reset my goals to stay motivated and aspirational.

I turned my attention to time-limited races, such as the 6-hour, 12-hour, or 24-hour events that are popular worldwide. When I turned 55, my next significant goal was to break an all-time Australian age group record. I ultimately decided to focus on 12-hour races, aiming to surpass the Australian age group record for the 55 to 59 age category, which had been set at 118.5

kilometres many years ago. In 2019, at the age of 56, I embarked on two attempts to achieve this goal, starting with the "Narrabeen All Nighter" race on Sydney's Northern Beaches. I had previously used this event as a training session for a 100-kilometre race on a road surface many years ago.

Race records are typically established on fast, flat courses, neither of which described the undulating, out-and-back 5-kilometre trail course used for the All Nighter race. To complicate matters further, the event took place in the middle of Sydney's scorching summer, making it exceedingly hot and humid. As if these challenges weren't enough, the night of the race saw torrential rain that persisted for the 24 hours leading up to the event and continued throughout the race itself. Consequently, by the time we commenced the race at 7 pm, more than 40% of the trail was either submerged underwater or transformed into thick, clinging mud.

As we started the first lap, I quickly grasped the arduous nature of the course. An hour later, I found myself running in a downpour, slogging through mud, with only the beam of my headlamp piercing the darkness for company. The race proved to be a formidable challenge, and between the three-to-nine-hour marks, I had to summon every ounce of determination to resist the urge to quit and head home. Despite the conditions, I battled on throughout the night and ultimately secured second place overall, covering 111 kilometres. However, it's worth noting that this distance was recorded at 11 hours and 41 minutes.

At that point, I halted my run at the starting line because only complete laps of 5 kilometres would be counted, and there wasn't sufficient time to complete another lap. My estimation was that I could have likely covered an additional 3 to 4 kilometres in that time, bringing me close to 116 kilometres within the twelve-hour period. This bolstered my confidence, as I had not only toughed it out and endured the challenging race but was also on track to beat past the record.

In the interim, between this race and the one planned for later in the year, I made an investment in a high-end road bike and decided to incorporate occasional cycling into my routine for the short commute to my office, providing a break from my running regimen. Within a week of starting to ride again after so many years, I was travelling down a bicycle lane in the city at about 35 to 40 kmph when a heavy truck suddenly turned across the bike, leaving me nowhere to go and no way of stopping. The impact was sudden and violent as I collided into the side of the truck, splitting my helmet in two, tearing my face up and breaking my ribs in 10 separate places. My recovery was excruciating, and I had to adapt to sleeping in a completely unfamiliar position on my back, a practice I continue to this day.

The day after my hospital discharge, just five days after the accident, I hopped on a train and returned to work. There was an incredibly significant and important business transaction taking place that only I could engineer. The pain was so significant I could barely move, and the next five weeks were excruciating. Eight weeks later, my ribs had healed, but I was running again at five.

Later that same year, I made a return to the Caboolture Historical Village to attempt to break the record during the 12-hour Dusk till Dawn race. Queensland, true to form, delivered scorching temperatures, with the lowest being 27 degrees Celsius that night. It turned into another taxing test, and I encountered numerous stomach problems, as I had experienced during previous races. While my standing in the race fluctuated, I once more summoned the determination to gut it out. In the end, I secured a 2nd place finish overall, covering 112 kilometres.

Me and my son, Callum.

THE BEST OF YOUR LIFE STARTS TODAY

"You will either step forward into growth or you will step back into safety."

— Abraham Maslow

With the milestone age of 60 years, only months away, I feel deeply privileged to have lived the life that I have, and I am certain that there is so much more to come. While this book tells my own story, my sincere wish is that the 8 daily practices that have allowed me to surpass my wildest expectations can become a part of your life. My hope is that by adopting these practices, you can transform your life starting today.

I have unwavering confidence that even if you incorporate just one of these 8 daily practices into your routine, you will witness improvements in your life and overall happiness. Moreover, with each additional practice you embrace and consistently follow, you will move closer to becoming the best version of yourself and accomplishing more than you ever dared to dream.

The key is to take that initial step, continue making the right choices, and never give up on your journey. Envision the legacy you want to leave behind and take ownership of creating it every single day. It all begins with the desire to change because that initial spark of motivation will inspire you to make the crucial decision to opt for the path less travelled. Remember, the easier roads may offer temporary comfort, but they ultimately lead to stagnation, remorse, and a life of mundane mediocrity. Sooner or later, the comfort of the ordinary becomes unsettling.

However, if you genuinely seek contentment in the ordinary, then that's the right path for you, and I hope you find your happiness there. Alternatively, you may need to discover the inspiration that will guide you towards the extraordinary life you deserve.

If you're fortunate enough to discover your wellspring of inspiration, you'll set challenging and worthwhile goals for yourself. These goals should stretch your capabilities to the point where achieving them feels euphoric. Worthy and even seemingly impossible goals will inevitably come with obstacles, failures, challenges, and moments of doubt. Paradoxically, it's these very challenges that imbue your pursuits with true value. In fact, without them, your accomplishments may seem hollow. This is the irony: the more arduous your path, the more you must persevere, and consequently, the greater your satisfaction in the struggle for what you desire and who you aim to become.

Moreover, embracing this inherent irony can reshape your mindset to welcome adversity and challenges as catalysts for your success. You might even learn to relish these challenges and, critically, recognise their role in the present as facilitators of your future triumphs. It's akin to running uphill, where you acknowledge the difficulty but instantly grasp that the challenge is what's strengthening you in that very moment—prompting a smile of acknowledgment. Remember, to be truly successful, you must first do what you don't want to do when you don't want to do it.

True success isn't measursed by outperforming others; it's the sublime realisation that you've given your all in any meaningful pursuit. The ultimate judge of this achievement is you alone, and in those quiet moments of self-reflection, you hold the key to that knowledge—only you.

Speaking from experience, there have been times when I've managed to convince others that I've done my best, but deep down, I knew I hadn't, and that sense of knowing weighed heavily within. Eventually, I would harness that disquiet and use it as fuel to rise once more and be accountable to myself.

In times of significant challenges and adversity, I hope you can draw inspiration from this book or at least some of the most significant obstacles that I have faced. When you experience failure or daunting hurdles, remember that it's your mindset and resilience that will propel you forward in a positive direction. The next time you find yourself in the midst of a challenge, tell yourself that it's not as tough as it may seem. Reflect on the fact that you've overcome more formidable obstacles in the past and emerged stronger. Remind yourself of the goodness in life and maintain your perspective. Express gratitude for everything you have and for the gift of each day, and swiftly shift into problem-solving mode instead of dwelling on the issue. Your focus should be on achieving the desired outcome, and then you can work backward to reframe your path to that outcome—because, in those moments, the outcome you desire is paramount.

In recent years, I've shifted my focus from athletic endeavours to personal and business growth. Prior to the COVID-19 pandemic's global impact, I challenged myself to leverage my 35 years of financial services experience to create a platform and program that would empower financial advisers and leaders to develop exceptional people engagement skills and achieve high-performance growth. I meticulously planned my goals about nine months in advance, and the launch of GROW was scheduled for March 2020, precisely when COVID-19 started to profoundly affect the world. Despite Australia's implementation of some of the longest and most restrictive lockdown measures, I persevered, and GROW is now successfully facilitating outstanding results for participants.

In addition to developing and launching GROW, I've finally found the inspiration to write "UNLIMITED," an aspiration that had been lingering in the background for a decade until I finally added the goal to write and publish it.

Whatever it is that you dare to dream, remember that with the right choices, you can embark on a different pathway and become anything you set your mind to. If you take that first step today, you can begin a journey during which you will achieve things that may seem impossible from your current vantage point. Whether it's personal growth, family, career, community, charity, or business, take that first step today. As you grow in one significant area of your life, you'll position yourself to grow in other areas. So please, start today.

Daily Practice Action

As you've been reading through this book, you may have already started implementing at least one of the daily practice actions or perhaps even multiple actions. If you haven't, I encourage you to prioritise and start one important change today. Remember, you can't afford to put things off until tomorrow, as tomorrow never truly arrives.

DAILY PRACTICE ACTION
Prioritising and starting implementation

What I am going to start to change today	1. 2.
How I will prioritise imple-mentation and when	1. 2. 3. 4. 5. 6.